Hiker's Guide to the
Superstition Wilderness

*with History and Legends of
Arizona's Lost Dutchman Gold Mine*

BY

JACK CARLSON

ELIZABETH STEWART

First Edition

DEC   2008

Hiker's Guide to the Superstition Wilderness

with History and Legends of Arizona's Lost Dutchman Gold Mine

by Jack Carlson and Elizabeth Stewart

Published by:

Clear Creek Publishing
P.O. Box 24666
Tempe, Arizona 85285 U.S.A.

Copyright © 1995, 1996, 1999, 2002 by Jack Carlson and Elizabeth Stewart
First Printing January 1995
Printed and bound in the United States of America

Cover and book design by Neal Berg Design, Tempe, Arizona.
Cover photograph of Superstition Mountain by the authors.
Cover photograph inset of Elisha Reavis by H. Beuhman, circa 1890s. Courtesy Arizona Historical Foundation.
Photographs not otherwise credited were taken by the authors.

Publishers Cataloging-in-Publication Data
Carlson, Jack C.
Hiker's guide to the Superstition Wilderness, with history and legends of Arizona's Lost Dutchman Gold Mine/ by Jack Carlson and Elizabeth Stewart.
1st ed.
320 p. : ill., maps ; 22 cm.
Bibliography: p. 302-305
Includes index.
1. Hiking--Arizona--Superstition Wilderness--Guidebooks. 2. Superstition Wilderness (Ariz.)--Guidebooks. 3. Lost Dutchman Mine (Ariz.)--History.
I. Stewart, Elizabeth J. II. Title.

917.9175 dc20   94-94270
978-1-884224-05-8 (softcover) : $14.95

10 9 8

Two roads diverge in a wood, and I —
I took the one less traveled by,
And that has made all the difference.

Robert Frost
1874—1963

Acknowledgments

Many people contributed to this guidebook. We thank everyone. Some sent us in the right direction with a few remarks, and others labored over the details as we pulled all the information together. Over the years we have hiked the Superstition Wilderness with many friends, and we thank them for those enjoyable trips. We are indebted to the other authors who have documented their Superstition Mountain travels and experiences. We acknowledge their books, photographs and contributions throughout the *Hiker's Guide*. We give special thanks to those listed below for their advice and assistance.

Superstition Mountain Historical Society and Museum, especially Tom Kollenborn, Larry Hedrick, Greg Davis, Clay Worst, George Johnston, Bob Corbin, Ruthanne Montague and all the Guild Members.

Arizona Book Publishers Association, especially Alan Korwin, Richard Dillon, John Reinhardt, Robert Farrell, Ted Parod, Gwen Henson, Mary Westheimer, Bud Carey, Scott Combs and Elaine Waterstrat.

Arizona Authors Association, especially Gerry Benninger and the Eastside Critique Group.

U.S. Forest Service, Mesa Ranger Office, especially Greg Hansen, Russ Orr, Don Van Driel, Jack Conner and Connie Lane.

Bill Sewrey, veteran outdoorsman and owner of Desert Mountain Sports.

John Wilburn, author of *Dutchman's Lost Ledge of Gold.*

Ray Ruiz and Louis Ruiz, Bluebird Mine and Gift Shop.

Dave Hughes, spelunker, hiker, outdoorsman, author and superb editor.

Forest Supervisors Office, Tonto National Forest, especially Pete Weinel, Michael Sullivan, Scott Wood and Martin McAllister.

Superstition Area Land Trust, especially Rosemary Shearer, John Kevin, Anne Coe, Tom Kollenborn, George Johnston, Helena Magee, and Dr. Jack Pritchard.

Goldfield Ghost Town, especially Bob Schoose and Jay Zingler.

Lost Dutchman State Park, especially manager Bob Sherman.

Town of Tortilla Flat, especially Jerry Bryant, Mary Jo Bryant and Lois Potter Sanders.

Jane Cole, Garden Librarian for the Richter Library, Desert Botanical Garden.

Peter Busnack and Angelique Zelle, Reevis Mountain School.
Steve Krause, author of *Sedona Guide* and *Streamside Trails.*
Tom Kreuser, hiker, climber and outdoorsman.
Helen Corbin, author of *The Curse of the Dutchman's Gold* and *Senner's Gold.*
Brad Orr, U.S. Forest Service, Tonto Basin Ranger District.
Neal Berg, hiker, photographer and owner of Neal Berg Design.
Salt River Project History Services, especially Ileen Snoddy and Len Lopez.
Stew Herkenhoff, U.S. Forest Service, Globe Ranger District.
Milt Dahl, author and publisher of *Arizona Trails Monthly.*
Tempe Library, especially Clay Workman.
Arizona Historical Foundation, especially Jean Mahalov, Evelyn Cooper,
   Kimele Carter and Edward Oetting.
Apache Junction Chamber of Commerce, especially Carolyn Doty.
Jan Holdeman, hiker, climber and articulate outdoorsman.
David Elms, Jr., hiker, outdoorsman and professional photographer.
Bill Hall, hiker and outdoorsman.
Lowell Bailey, hiker and outdoorsman.
Nancy Kaplan, kayaker and owner of Studio Artworks.
Pat Ten Eyke, teacher, hiker and owner of Ten Eyke Artworks.
L.L. Lombardi, author of *Tortilla Flat, Then and Now.*
Bob and Kay Stewart, outdoor enthusiasts and Elizabeth's parents.
Kathy Winston, writer, researcher and editor.
Barbara Stewart, chiropractic physician and outdoor enthusiast.
Robert Stewart, hiker, nature photographer and outdoor enthusiast.
Bill and Gini McKenzie, teachers and Jack's sister and brother-in-law.
John Bell, U.S. Air Force major general, retired.
Cyndie Jensen, hiker, nature photographer and outdoor enthusiast.
Pete Kushibab, friend of the authors.
Anita O'Riordan, friend of the authors.
Kathy Menke, author, photographer and outdoor enthusiast.
Wendy Perkins, author of *Temporarily Yours.*
Betty Leavengood, author of *Tucson Hiking Guide.*
Richard and Sherry Mangum, authors of *Flagstaff Hikes* and *Sedona Hikes.*
Paul Daniels, Gorden Allen, Kaveh Parsi, circuit designers and outdoorsmen.
Arizona Department of Library, especially Ray Tevis.
Tempe Historical Society, especially Richard Bauer.
Arizona Historical Society, especially Deborah Shelton.
Mesa Library.
Pinal County Sheriffs Department.
Town of Apache Junction, especially the Engineering Department.

Warning and Disclaimer

Hiking, climbing, horseback riding and all outdoor activities are inherently dangerous. The information provided in this book is designed to entertain and inform. The final judgment and decision to pursue these outdoor activities is always your responsibility as the user of this book.

It is your responsibility to obtain the skills and abilities needed to pursue hiking, climbing, horseback riding, and other outdoor activities. You must be physically fit before attempting any activities described here. Trail and route conditions continually change due to flash floods, erosion, and other natural or man-made events. Although every effort has been made to check the accuracy of the information in this book, errors and omissions may still occur. You must decide whether the trail and weather conditions are safe and satisfactory for you to initiate or continue your trip. You must judge whether you possess the skills, abilities and fitness required to pursue a particular trip.

The authors, publisher and those associated with this publication, directly or indirectly, assume no responsibility for any accident, injury, damage or loss that may result from participating in any of the activities described in this book. This is a hiking guidebook only—you are on your own, and your decisions are totally your responsibility.

Table of Contents

Preface

"Don't include my favorite getaway in your hiking guide" was the response we received from many hikers after announcing our plans to write this guidebook. Many of our hiking companions and friends were not eager to see their exceptional hikes in print. We have tried to accommodate everyone's wishes and at the same time write an exciting and informative guidebook.

This dilemma of all guidebook writers brings up an ethical question. How many favorite and exceptional places and hikes should be included in the *Hiker's Guide* with the prospect that increasing the number of hikers results in loving the wilderness to destruction? One technique that sidesteps the issue is to give rather vague directions and general descriptions of exceptional areas, letting the hikers discover the beauty on their own. Popularity of the areas then spreads more slowly by word of mouth.

On the other hand, if the place descriptions are too vague, historical areas could be lost forever. This issue is of great concern to us. Somehow we need to balance the need to know and enjoy with the risk of loss due to vandalism. The Forest Service rangers also struggle with this same problem. Making prehistoric sites public often results in damage and vandalism beyond repair. Then the resource is lost forever. Every trip leader and individual hiker must be willing to exert peer pressure on those few who vandalize our prehistoric and historic sites.

The Superstition Wilderness is steeped in history starting with the early Indians, Mexican miners, American settlers and gold miners, cattle ranchers, U.S. military, and continuing with the contemporary Lost Dutchman gold mine aficionados. Many of the old publications describing events in the Superstition Mountains are out of print. Many of the place descriptions in the old publications are vague or distorted to conceal the "real" clues to the Lost Dutchman legend.

History is slowly being lost as the old timers pass on. So, it seems there is some merit in trying to preserve history. We are challenging our readers with the responsibility to abide by the Wilderness Code of Ethics—with greater knowledge comes greater responsibility. We hope you find our selection of hikes rewarding.

Introduction

The Hiker's Guide to the Superstition Wilderness is a unique book offering the hiker, horseback rider and history buff an informative trail guide annotated with history and legends. We describe trips for all levels of hiking ability. We have included many hikes where you can experience the surroundings of an historic event and see the sites or structures of former inhabitants.

We go beyond the traditional guidebook format. Rather than concentrate on walking from one place to another, we write about attractions frequently overlooked by the typical hiker. We have researched many books and articles for references to the Wilderness landmarks. The reference sources are identified for those who would like to read and investigate the subject in greater detail. With many differing opinions about the facts and legends, we do not attempt to take one side or the other. You will have to decide what is history and what is legend.

Even if you don't believe there was a Lost Dutchman Mine, the history of the treasure hunters and the relationship of the legends to the trails, passes, streams, mountains and canyons will give you a greater appreciation of the prominent landmarks in the Superstition Wilderness and surrounding areas. We feel this is a fascinating subject. As Walt Whitman said, "You must not know too much, or be too precise or scientific about birds and trees and flowers and water craft; a certain free margin, and even vagueness—perhaps ignorance, credulity—helps your enjoyment of these things." We think this also applies to the Lost Dutchman Story. It's a grand Wilderness—we should enjoy every aspect of it.

How To Use This Book

TRAILHEADS AND AREAS. *Trailhead* defines the point normally accessed by vehicle and *Area* defines a starting location accessed by walking or riding. Trips are organized in the Table of Contents according to the nearest Trailhead or Area. This arrangement will help you quickly find all the hikes available for each starting point. The Table of Contents shows the page number for the Trailhead or Area description and the location map. For a general orientation to the highways and trailheads see the following section, How To Get There.

ITINERARY. This section gives a brief explanation of the trip noting alternate routes and trails.

SPECIAL ATTRACTIONS. This section highlights points of interest, historical and legendary landmarks, and scenic places.

DIFFICULTY. The trips are rated *easy, moderate, difficult,* and *very difficult.* The ratings are established on the premise that a hiker can complete the hike in the time suggested under the Length and Time heading. The rating considers both physical and mental abilities needed to complete the hike. Hikes covering a short distance with a long hiking time indicate extremely rough terrain or a large elevation gain. The *hiker's boot* symbol is printed on the first page of each trip for a quick reference to the hike difficulty.

Difficulty Legend

Easy	👢
Moderate	👢 👢
Difficult	👢 👢 👢
Very Difficult	👢 👢 👢 👢

Bouldering is a term used in the text to describe a type of climbing familiar to most hikers who explore canyons blocked by large rocks. The highest point of this climbing is usually within jumping distance to the ground; therefore, this technique requires no climbing equipment. The hiker should be skilled in balance and have a knowledge of foot and hand hold techniques. Do not try any of the hikes requiring bouldering unless you have the necessary skills. Join a climbing club or take a class to learn how to *boulder.*

Hikers need not complete the entire trip to have an enjoyable outing. Beginning hikers may enjoy the first part of a more difficult trip by selecting a turnaround point such as a stream crossing, pass, ridge line, or a trail intersection as their destination. It is more important to have fun and walk at your own pace than to complete the entire trip.

EASY TRIP. An *easy* hike usually follows established trails with trip length less than 5 miles and a time less than 3 hours. A few easy trips follow the creek bed through a canyon. Some beginning hikers may find the elevation gain or length of the hike more strenuous than they expected.

MODERATE TRIP. A *moderate* hike usually involves some off-trail hiking and may require basic route-finding skills. The trip length is less than 10

miles and less than 6 hours hiking time. The abilities to follow rock cairns, use a compass, and read a map are necessary. These treks are for experienced hikers only.

DIFFICULT TRIP. A *difficult* hike requires extensive off-trail hiking over rough terrain. Trip length is less than 15 miles with hiking time less than 12 hours. Hikers will often need excellent route-finding skills and basic rock-bouldering techniques.

Elizabeth Stewart on the Reavis Gap Trail near Campaign Creek.

These treks are for experienced hikers only.

VERY DIFFICULT TRIP. A *very difficult* hike has all the characteristics of the *difficult* hike along with the distinct possibility that the hiker may not be able to complete the entire hike in one day. Trip length is less than 18 miles with hiking times less than 14 hours. On a *very difficult* trip hikers may find the challenge rewarding and inspiring upon completion of a successful hike. On the other hand, hikers may find themselves stranded overnight due to errors in route-finding or underestimation of hiking times. Hikers must be familiar with rock-bouldering skills. None of the hikes require technical rock climbing equipment. Hikers can extend the *very difficult* hikes to make enjoyable and leisurely overnight hikes. These treks are for experienced hikers only.

These ratings are subjective and are based on our own skill level—experienced hikers, well seasoned in outdoor skills. Consistency in the ratings may vary due to "good days" when we hiked better than normal, and to "lucky days" when our route finding was better than normal.

LENGTH and TIME. We show the round-trip length and time for all trips unless noted otherwise. Some loop hikes that have alternate return routes list only the one-way distance. The length of the hikes has been estimated from USGS maps and from U.S. Forest Service trail mileages wheeled in the early

1970s. We thank the Mesa District Forest Service, especially Ranger Russell Orr, for allowing us to review their excellent trail survey records. Use the distance for off-trail hikes as a guideline, since the mileage is approximate.

Hiking time is a more useful measurement for off-trail hiking. Our hiking times include short rest stops and time to enjoy the scenic highlights of the trip. Backpackers carrying heavier packs should expect to experience longer hiking times. Faster and slower hikers will need to adjust the times for their style of hiking.

The elevation change tells you how much uphill (indicated by a plus sign, +) and downhill (indicated by a minus sign, -) there is on each hike. For loop trips, the uphill and downhill elevation change is the same. On one-way trips, the uphill and downhill elevation change is usually different. Elevation change is not the same as the difference between the high and low points of the trip. For example, if you go up and down two hills, one 1500 feet high and another 2000 feet high, the total elevation change is "+3500" and "-3500", expressed in the book as ±3500 feet.

The shuttle distance (for a one-way hike) is the one-way road distance you need to drive to place a vehicle at the destination of your hike. You need two cars to arrange a shuttle trip or a good friend who is willing to wait for you at your destination. Another way to make a one-way hike is to arrange for two groups to start from opposite trailheads and hike to the other group's vehicle. Be sure both groups have keys to each vehicle. Don't try to exchange keys during the hike.

Map Legend

————	Main Road (both paved and dirt)
- - - - - - -	Main Trail
···············	Abandoned Trail or Off-Trail Route
SS	Point of Interest (letters from **A** to **ZZ**)
🚶	Trailhead or Area Starting Point
(102)	U.S. Forest Service Trail Number
FS78	U.S. Forest Road Number (usually a dirt road)
{88}	State Highway Route Number (mostly paved)
(60)	U.S. Highway Route Number (paved)

MAPS. Here we list the USGS 7.5 minute topographic (topo) maps used for each hike. The scale for the USGS maps is about 2.5 inches per mile. On several hikes, you may wish to make a composite copy of the four USGS map corners for a handy area-reference. If your local outdoor store does not carry the USGS maps, you can order them directly from the U.S. Geological Survey, Denver, Colorado 80225. On all hikes, we always carry the Superstition Wilderness, Tonto National Forest map issued by the Forest Service and available at Forest Service Offices and local outdoor stores. The scale of the Superstition Wilderness map is one inch per mile. Another useful map, although not listed for the hikes, is the *Superstition Wilderness, West, Recreation Map* by Earth Tracks in Phoenix, Arizona. This is a two inch per mile topo-map. Another map issued by the Forest Service is the Tonto National Forest map. It is good for viewing the big picture but is not very useful as a hiking guide. The scale is about 0.5 inch per mile.

Reproductions of the 7.5 minute USGS topographic maps in the Hiker's Guide show the trails and suggested route for each hike. When ordering maps from your dealer, specify the names shown in the index below. We show main trails with dashed lines, and off-trail routes and abandoned trails as dotted lines. Main roads open to vehicles are shown as solid lines, but roads behind locked gates are shown as trails, dashed lines.

Index of 7.5 minute USGS topographic maps for the Superstition Wilderness Area

Mormon Flat Dam	Horse Mesa Dam	Pinyon Mountain	Two Bar Mountain
Goldfield	Weavers Needle	Iron Mountain	Haunted Canyon

FINDING THE TRAIL. Getting started is sometimes the hardest part of a hike. This section helps the hiker get out of the parking lot and onto the correct trail. For hikes not starting from a parking lot, a narrative is provided describing the terrain and local landmarks near the beginning of the hike.

THE HIKE. This section describes the trip description, water availability, and other information necessary to complete the hike. A topographic map containing point of interest notations identifies the major landmarks. For example, **[4-E, 2.6, 4152]** indicates point of interest **E** on Map 4, 2.6 miles from

The First Arizona Territorial Officers, 1863. COURTESY ARIZONA HISTORICAL SOCIETY/TUCSON AND HELEN CORBIN, ARIZONA SHERIFF COLLECTION.

the beginning of the hike, at an elevation of 4152 feet. Mileage is rounded to the nearest tenth of a mile. For some points of interest, the mileage and/or elevation are not included. We indicate the U. S. Forest Service official trail numbers in parenthesis, for example, Dutchman's Trail (104).

Superscript numbers in the text are reference notes to the source of information. They are listed in the back of the book in the section titled Reference Notes.

HISTORY AND LEGENDS. This section describes the stories related to each hike. In most cases it is impossible to separate history from legend. Read and enjoy. We included reference notes for more in-depth reading. Many of the old manuscripts are available as a Reprint Series by the Superstition Mountain Historical Society and are on sale at the Superstition Mountain Museum.

How To Get There

The Superstition Wilderness is 40 miles east of Phoenix, Arizona, 100 miles north of Tucson, Arizona, and 18 miles west of Globe, Arizona. U.S. Route 60 bounds the southern portion of the Wilderness and State Route 88 encloses the western, northern and eastern regions of the Wilderness.

The closest town on the western side of the mountains is Apache Junction, Arizona. Apache Junction is located next to the southwest corner of the Wilderness where the prominent Superstition Mountains rise from the desert floor to 5057 feet.

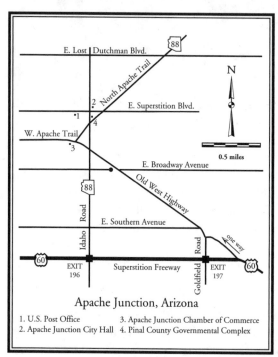

Apache Junction, Arizona

1. U.S. Post Office
2. Apache Junction City Hall
3. Apache Junction Chamber of Commerce
4. Pinal County Governmental Complex

Access to the trailheads is easily made from State Route 88 (the North Apache Trail) heading north out of Apache Junction and from U.S. Route 60 east of Apache Junction. Detailed information and maps for each trailhead and hike are provided.

The Superstition Freeway, U.S. Route 60, provides easy access to the Superstition Wilderness from the metropolitan areas of Phoenix, Tempe, Mesa and Apache Junction. At the eastern end of the Superstition Freeway, U.S. Route 60 continues east as a divided four lane highway. Stay on U.S. Route 60 for the turnoffs for the Hieroglyphic, Peralta, Woodbury, Rogers Trough, Miles Ranch, Upper Horrell, and Tule Trailheads.

For the trailheads on State Route 88 (Lost Dutchman State Park, Massacre Grounds, First Water, Canyon Overlook, Canyon Lake, Tortilla Flat, Peters Mesa, Tortilla, and Reavis Trailheads), exit the Superstition Freeway at Idaho Road (exit #196) and drive north on Idaho Road into Apache Junction to connect with North Apache Trail. State Route 88 north of Apache Junction is a winding two lane road. Allow extra driving time for slow traffic along this stretch of road. State Route 88 is unpaved from the Tortilla Trailhead junction to Roosevelt Dam.

If you approach the Superstition Wilderness from the towns of Globe, Miami, or Roosevelt several trailheads are close by. For the Miles Ranch Trailhead drive west on U.S. Route 60 from the towns of Globe and Miami. Go north from Globe and Miami on State Route 88 to Roosevelt, Arizona and the Roosevelt Lake area for the Tule, Upper Horrell (Campaign), Frazier, and Reavis Trailheads. Roosevelt Lake has very nice camping facilities

The routes to the popular Rogers Trough and Woodbury Trailheads begin on U.S. Route 60 several miles west of the town of Superior. Forest Service road FS172 to these trailheads offers spectacular views of rugged cliffs and the surrounding Sonoran Desert. Flat areas along FS172 provide easy car camping if you need to rest before your Wilderness trip.

Most of the trailheads described in this book are usually accessible by automobile although the graded dirt roads sometimes have the characteristic washboard surface. Some trailheads are directly next to the paved State Route 88. The trailhead description indicates when four-wheel drive or high-clearance vehicles are required. We recommended slow and cautious driving to avoid any road hazards and to reduce the inevitable road dust.

Superstition Mountain viewed from the end of Broadway Avenue, near Apache Junction, Arizona.

Superstition Wilderness

The Superstition Wilderness has evolved through several official classifications during this century. In 1908 the area was set aside as a Forest Reserve. It was established as the Superstition Primitive Area in February 1939 and later upgraded to a Wilderness classification in April 1940. Finally, it was designated as the Superstition Wilderness in the National Wilderness Preservation System by Congress on September 3, 1964.

The present size of the Wilderness is 158,345 acres. The north-south distance varies from 9 to 12 miles while the east-west length stretches across 24 miles. Most of the Wilderness is surrounded by the Tonto National Forest except for 13 sections along the southwest boundary. On the southern boundary, one section of land has been converted to private holdings which has restricted access to Hieroglyphic Canyon.

The State of Arizona Land Trust holds the other twelve sections. If this land is sold to private owners, we will lose access to the south side of Superstition Mountain, to Carney Springs Trailhead and the land east to Fraser Canyon. Cooperation between the U.S. Forest Service, State of Arizona, and the public can provide solutions to the access problems. Please support any endeavors to provide a transitional zone between the Superstition Wilderness and privately-held land.

The Superstition Wilderness is managed by the Tonto National Forest, U.S. Forest Service, Department of Agriculture. One of the management objectives for the Wilderness is to perpetuate a long-lasting system of high quality wilderness that represents a natural ecosystem. Other objectives are to provide public enjoyment of the resource, to allow for the development of indigenous plants and animals, and to maintain the primitive character of the Wilderness as a benchmark for ecological studies.

High use and human influence on our wilderness lands requires the Forest Service to manage the wilderness by providing wilderness-value education; by prohibiting permanent structures such as campgrounds, buildings, and antennas; by managing trail use and party size; and by allowing fires to burn only under preplanned conditions.

Hunting, fishing, and trapping in the Superstition Wilderness are managed under State and Federal laws. Outfitting and guide services are managed under special use permits with the Tonto National Forest. Livestock grazing is still permitted where it existed prior to designation of the area as a wilderness, but the number of animals is managed by the Forest Service.

The Wilderness Act prohibits motorized equipment and mechanical transport in the Superstition Wilderness. The prohibited equipment includes motorcycles, chain saws, generators, mountain bikes, and wagons. Hiking, camping and horseback riding permits are not required for individuals but group size is limited to 15 persons (contact the Forest Service for group-size exceptions), and the length of stay is limited to less than 14 days.

Two offices with current information and publications on the Superstition Wilderness are the Tonto National Forest Supervisor's Office in Phoenix, Arizona and the Mesa Ranger District in Mesa, Arizona. The Mesa Ranger District is the lead district under a consolidated management system with the Globe Ranger District and the Tonto Basin Ranger District. The Tonto National Forest map shows the boundaries for these three districts. Addresses and telephone numbers for these offices are listed in the back of this book under Useful Addresses.

Wilderness Ethics

Take Pictures And Memories—Leave Nothing is a motto every hiker and trip leader should adopt. *No trace* hiking and camping are not only the trend, but are necessary to preserve the Wilderness for future enjoyment. Please join us in preserving the natural and historical heritage of our beautiful Superstition Wilderness.

Large groups have a greater impact on the Wilderness than small groups of hikers. If you have a large group (more than five hikers), stay on the trails—avoid off-trail and cross-country route hiking. Riparian zones are the most fragile. Large groups should use previously-occupied campsites and avoid establishing new camps. It is nearly impossible for a large group of campers to restore a campsite to its natural condition. Small groups of campers should be able to return a camp to its natural state if they avoid digging holes, cutting vegetation, and building fires. Every attempt should be made to restore the ground cover so it will look visually appealing to the next group of campers.

Campfires are permitted, and enjoyable on occasion, but we found that the use of a lightweight backpacker stove is a convenient alternative to the pot-blackening campfires. There is almost no fuel wood in many areas so a stove is often a necessity. If you need to build a fire, use an existing fire site. Do not use a fire ring (a ring of rocks), do not try to burn the unburnable (foil, plastics, metal, etc.), and keep the fire away from cliffs and boulders to avoid coating them with black soot. If firewood is scarce, do not pick the ground clean. Put out campfires with water, not dirt, so they are cold to the touch of your hand.

Pack it in—Pack it out. Everything that you take into the Wilderness must be taken out. If you take food items that don't have a lot of waste and take only the amount you will consume on the trip, you will lighten your load and also reduce the amount of trash that needs to be packed out. Don't bury trash because animals will dig it up and scatter it. Remember that cigarette butts, orange peels, apple cores and candy wrappers are litter. Unpacking after a day hike or overnight trip is much easier if you store all of your trash in a plastic bag. When you get home, just toss the bag in the garbage. If you include a small plastic bag with your lunch it makes for easy disposal of orange peels, pits, wrappers, etc.

Never vandalize prehistoric sites. Adding graffiti to petroglyphs (prehistoric rock art) or creating your own contemporary petroglyphs may seem artistic at the moment. To the rest of us who enjoy viewing petroglyphs, the new graffiti is just what it looks like—graffiti. Trip leaders should suggest that potential graffiti addicts draw in the sand and then smooth it over before leaving. Digging or removing artifacts is not permitted and is prosecutable by law. Even taking pot shards that are exposed on the surface is not allowed. Enjoy them but leave them for the next person to admire.

Sometimes we can damage a prehistoric site by just being there. Loss of vegetation from overuse of an area can increase erosion and degradation. In Utah, careless campers built a fire on ground that was actually the roof of a kiva—the prehistoric ruin was severely degraded by that fire.

Horse travel in the Wilderness is common and still holds the romance and color of the Old West. The following suggestions will help minimize the effects of stock use and preserve the wilderness for your next trip. Don't tie horses directly to trees. Set up a picket line between two trees so the horses won't damage the tree roots and bark. When breaking camp, scatter manure piles to aid decomposition. Pack in your own feed because natural forage is very limited. Grazing horses is not allowed. Avoid using whole grain feeds which can grow if spilled and compete with the natural vegetation.

Human waste should be buried in a hole four to six inches deep (in soil, not sand) at least 300 feet away from water-sources and dry-washes. After use, fill the hole with soil. Do not burn or bury the toilet paper. Store the used toilet paper inside the cardboard tube or store it in a plastic bag for disposal when you return home. Preserve the water sources by keeping human waste at least 300 feet from streams, springs, pot holes, and dry washes. Do not contaminate the water with soap or any leftover food. Wash dishes and articles with soap away from the stream, not directly in it.

Personal items must not be stored in the Wilderness—it's illegal. Many former and some recent explorers and treasure hunters have stashed equipment and supplies in the Wilderness. Special Forest Order 12-59-R prohibits storing anything in the Wilderness for more than 14 days. Outfitters and the Forest Service rangers pack this equipment out to the trailheads for disposal outside the Wilderness. Let's give the rangers a break by packing out what we pack in.

Safety And Dangers

The most important rule to remember for your safety is that everything you do is your responsibility and that your safety is determined solely by your judgment, skill, condition and actions. Visiting the Superstition Wilderness carries the individual responsibility of knowing your own abilities and recognizing the potential dangers of outdoor activities. There are no warning signs, handrails or rangers pointing out the hazards. The hints and suggestions provided by the authors should complement your outdoor skills and not be considered a substitute for proper training and outdoor experience. Be a safe hiker, know your limits. **Never hike alone.** See Useful Addresses in the back of the book for a list of emergency telephone numbers.

The Superstition Wilderness is a desert mountain-range where extreme heat poses a very real threat in the summer when temperatures can reach more than 120 °F in the lower elevations. Always carry adequate water to avoid dehydration or heat exhaustion. See the section on Water that describes the amount of water we carry on hikes.

In the winter, at elevations above 4800 feet, snow is often encountered. Nighttime temperatures can dip down to -10 °F with daytime temperatures ranging from 20 to 55 °F. To avoid frostbite and hypothermia be prepared with warm and waterproof clothing.

All hikes listed in this book are physically and mentally challenging—even the "easy" hikes. You should ascertain your own abilities from previous experience. Knowing when to abort a hike or modify the original plan is essential and is the responsibility of each hiker.

Off-trail hiking, bouldering, and climbing are inherently more dangerous than hiking on a trail. Injuries due to falling are common. Loose or slippery rocks, on and off the trail, are the primary cause of falls. Bouldering, climbing and hiking near cliffs are hazardous and may result in injury or death.

As an individual hiker in a larger group, you must be aware of the inherent danger in this activity and must use your own judgment, based on your own skill level, when confronted with a difficult situation. The responsibility always lies with you as an individual and not with the group. Do not let peer pressure force you into a situation that may be dangerous.

While hiking in Canada on the Athabasca Glacier, noting the dangers of crevices and mill wells, we asked a local guide if there were any restrictions on hiking the glaciers in the Canadian National Parks. He said, "No. Every Canadian has the right to kill himself in a National Park." Along with the humor in that statement lingers the thought that our own decisions and plans may result in our death or the death of a fellow hiker. Be a safe hiker— know your abilities and the hazards of the area.

A special caution to inexperienced horse riders is in order. For your safety, we do not recommend riding off the established trails. Although some experienced riders successfully follow off-trail routes, we have heard that inexperienced riders have been injured in an attempt to emulate their heroes. There are no restrictions on where you may ride, but the Forest Service classifies several steep or rocky trails as "Not Recommended for Horses." The list includes Peralta Trail (102), Boulder Canyon Trail (103), Red Tanks Trail (107), Rogers Canyon Trail (110), Frog Tanks Trail (112), Fire Line Trail (118), Haunted Canyon Trail (203), and Bluff Spring Trail (235). Before you go, consult the Forest Service or your favorite outfitter for current trail conditions. Don't injure yourself or your animal by attempting a ride that is above your ability.

FALLING. Injuries due to falling can be a major problem when hiking, whether it be from slipping on an algae covered rock in a stream, stumbling on an obstacle in your path, or careening off a precipice. Falling has probably caused more injuries than rattlesnakes and scorpions. The chances of incurring an injury from a fall will increase as you get tired. Lack of attention and declining physical ability are sure signs of a hiker in danger of injury from a fall.

RATTLESNAKES. By letting rattlesnakes know you are in their territory you can avoid an unwanted encounter. We found that a snake-stick (any small wooden stick) is handy for beating the brush where you suspect snakes. When you hear that rattlesnake "buzz" there will be no question whether it is really a rattlesnake. Beating the brush is not a foolproof technique since rattlesnakes don't always "buzz," so look around when you're walking and check nearby vertical walls of stream banks and ravines. Never put your hands or feet where you can't see.

The snake stick is useful for probing overhead rock ledges before you climb up. Also, a small stone thrown in the bushes helps announce your presence. Forget about trying to shoot a rattlesnake. If you have time to pull out a gun and have a steady enough hand to shoot, you are probably not in

A December 1992 flash flood in La Barge Canyon near Marsh Valley.

danger of a snakebite. Don't kill rattlesnakes, just learn to avoid them. Many rattlesnakes are protected or endangered. Always carry a snake bite kit and know how to use it.

VENOMOUS CRITTERS. Along with rattlesnakes, hikers need to be aware of scorpions, centipedes, black widow spiders, brown recluse spiders, tarantulas, Gila Monsters, etc.

FLASH FLOODS. Flash floods are a real danger, especially during the rainy season. Most people don't realize the danger of a flash flood until they see the power and force of the water in action. Camp on high ground. Crossing a flooded stream with water over your knees is dangerous—water at waist level will result in an almost certain swim and possible drowning in the current.

HEAT AND COLD. Both heat exhaustion and hypothermia (a drop in body temperature) are potential hazards in the Superstition Wilderness. Extreme changes in weather during the same day and the extremes during the seasons require the hiker and camper to be prepared with the right equipment and provisions. The single most important provision is adequate water. Be sure to read the section in this book on Water. Because of the heat and lack of protection from the sun, heat exhaustion and dehydration are very real dangers. Extreme caution must be exercised from June to September and anytime the temperature exceeds 100 F.

FIREARMS. Discharging a firearm is not permitted in the Superstition Wilderness except for taking game with a valid hunting license. This means no target shooting. We suggest you leave your guns at home. There are more people hiking and riding in the mountains than you realize. You could put the life of another hiker or horseback rider in danger with a misdirected shot or the accidental discharge of your gun if you fall.

Jacob Waltz
The Dutchman And His Gold

How did Jacob Waltz discover his mine? We can't be sure, so we will just tell the tales and let you decide if this is history or legend. Two good sources for the longer versions of these stories are Swanson and Kollenborn, *Superstition Mountain, A Ride Through Time;*[1] and Robert Blair, *Tales of the Superstitions.*[2] Robert Blair makes a scholarly analysis of the Dutchman in his book, but Dutchman aficionados will be disappointed since Blair concludes the mine is not in the Superstitions. A good 1994 novel by Mark Squiers, *The Dutchman,* adds a bit of color and local lore to the legend.

Sometime in the late 1870s or early 1880s, Jacob "Jake" Waltz and his partner, Jacob Wiser, were prospecting in the Superstition Mountains when they heard the sound of clanking metal. Approaching the sound cautiously, they saw two men mining gold. Thinking the miners were Indians, they shot them from behind. Later they discovered they had just killed two Mexican miners. The Mexicans may have been men who escaped the Apache massacre of the Peralta expedition in the 1850s. Waltz and Wiser mined the gold and packed it out to either Florence or Phoenix.

Several stories recount the death of Jacob Wiser. Waltz left the mine for more supplies and upon returning he found the camp had been raided by Indians. Wiser was missing and Waltz assumed him dead. In one rendition of the tale, Wiser shows up at John D. Walker's ranch in the nearby Pima Indian Village. Wiser dies of wounds inflicted by the Apache. Other versions of the story credit Waltz with killing his partner. Waltz then makes up the story that Wiser was killed when the Apache Indians raided their camp.

Another variation on the same theme recounts a Good Samaritan story involving Waltz and Wiser while they were in Mexico. After they rescued a wealthy Mexican from a card-game fight, the Mexican (named Peralta) gave Waltz and Wiser a map to his gold mine in the Superstition Mountains. In

Author and historian Tom Kollenborn with his horse Crow and dog Duke.
COURTESY TOM KOLLENBORN.

one variation of the story, the wealthy Mexican sends a guide with Waltz and Wiser to show them the location of the mine.

Some say that Jacob Waltz never had a mine, but he high-graded the ore from the Vulture Mine near Wickenburg. (High-grading is a term used to describe the theft of ore when miners conceal it in their clothing.) Critics of this story say Waltz's gold did not look like Vulture Mine ore samples or any other gold ore mined in Arizona.

Many believe that a mine never existed. They think Jacob Waltz stumbled on a buried cache or found a cache of gold ore in a cave. They claim Waltz made up the story about the mine to elude those who were following him. Indians, Jesuits and Mexican miners are possible owners of the hidden caches of gold.

Of those who think Jacob Waltz had a mine, not all agree on the location or even general area of the mine. There have been dozens of prospectors searching the Superstition Mountains for the last century even though some geologists and authors continually state that the volcanic area is poorly mineralized and it would be unlikely to find gold here. Others do not agree with the poor mineralization conclusion. Robert Sikorsky, author, geologist and former Maria Jones employee, surveyed the Superstition Mountains and concluded that it was very possible that there could be metal deposits in the area.[3] Clay Worst, author, prospector and past president of the Superstition Mountain Historical Society, makes a case for mineralization in the

Superstitions. In a talk at the Superstition Mountain Historical Society 1994 annual meeting, Clay Worst stated that many of the richest mines in the world are associated with volcanic geology. Several examples of rich gold mines in volcanic regions are the mines in Goldfield, Nevada, the Capitol Mine in Cripple Creek, Colorado, the El Indio Mine in Chile, South America and the Hishikari Mine on Kyushu Island in Japan.[4]

Not everyone believes the Lost Dutchman Mine is located inside the Superstition Wilderness. John Wilburn, in his 1990 book, *Dutchman's Lost Ledge of Gold*, places the Dutchman's mine west of the Superstition Wilderness at the site of the Bull Dog mine near Goldfield.[5] Jay Fraser establishes the Dutchman's mine northeast of Carefree, Arizona in his 1988 book, *Lost Dutchman Mine Discoveries*.[6] And, Robert Blair in his 1975 book, *Tales of the Superstitions*, locates the one and only known Peralta Mine, originally owned by Miguel Peralta, at the Gloriana Mine (Valenciana Mine) west of Interstate Highway I-17 near the Bumble Bee exit.[7]

A true Lost Dutchman Mine aficionado does not let the plethora of information dull the desire to dream and search for the elusive treasure. Acquire your own set of clues and enjoy the never ending quest.

The Search for Gold

The search for the Lost Dutchman Gold Mine began after Jacob Waltz died in Phoenix, Arizona on October 25, 1891. Although labeled a Dutchman, Waltz was a German immigrant who started prospecting in Arizona about 1862.[8] Just before his death, Waltz told two close companions, Julia Thomas and Rhinehart Petrasch, the location of his gold mine. Julia Thomas, Rhinehart Petrasch and Rhinehart's brother Hermann, entered the Superstition Mountains, in 1892, via the First Water Trailhead and searched for the gold mine without success. Julia Thomas died in 1917.[9] Rhinehart Petrasch died in 1943. Sims Ely, author of The Lost Dutchman Mine, credits cattle rancher Jim Bark with naming the Lost Dutchman Mine in 1893.[10]

The cover of Helen Corbin's 1990 book, *The Curse of the Dutchman's Gold,* shows a picture of the gold ore and a matchbox reputed to have been made from the Dutchman's gold. Dick Holmes, Bob Corbin, and Tom Kollenborn are reported to have seen the actual gold that Waltz had in his possession.[11] The gold was taken from Waltz (from a box under his bed) the day he died. Richard J. "Dick" Holmes, Jr. said the Dutchman gave him the gold. The gold is now the property of an unnamed Phoenix businessman

Richard Holmes, Jr.
COURTESY SUPERSTITION
MOUNTAIN HISTORICAL
SOCIETY, CLAY WORST
COLLECTION.

who received it from George "Brownie" Holmes (son of Dick Holmes).[12]

Stories of Mexican mining around the 1850s in the area of the Superstition Mountains were told by the Apache Indians. The most famous story described the massacre of a large group of Mexican miners by Apache Indians in a running fight that lasted several days. Gold ore mined in the area, supposedly cut loose from the Mexicans' pack animals by the Apache Indians after the massacre, was found in 1912 by two prospectors, Carl A. Silverlocke and Carl Malm, on the north slopes of the Superstition Mountains—an area known as the Massacre Grounds.[13] See the Massacre Grounds Trailhead for more of the story.

There is no question that gold was found in the area, but many argue that the Superstition Wilderness lacks gold bearing rock formations and all the gold in the area is west of the Wilderness in Goldfield. Mining claims were filed on July 7, 1892 in the Goldfield area by prospectors who discovered the remnants of an old mining camp assumed to be of Spanish origin.[14] John Wilburn describes these events and the history of the rich gold discoveries to the west of the Superstition Mountains in his book, *Dutchman's Lost Ledge of Gold*. The Mammoth Mine in Goldfield became the largest gold producer in the area. No producing gold mining operations have been recorded within the Superstition Wilderness area. See the Lost Dutchman State Park Trailhead for more stories about the Goldfield area.

After a century, the first and second generation Lost Dutchman Mine seekers and many of the third generation followers have died. These prospectors, miners, ranchers and treasure hunters have become entwined in the Lost Dutchman legend. Their stories of discovery and adventure are as colorful and exciting as the legend of the Lost Dutchman Mine itself. Jim Bark and later Tex Barkley, cattle ranchers in the Superstitions, played host to the many gold and treasure seekers since their grazing allotment covered the two main gateways to the Superstition Mountains—Peralta Trailhead and First Water Trailhead. Jim Bark and partner Frank Criswell bought the Superstition Cattle Ranch in 1891. Bark sold his interest to Tex Barkley around 1907.[15]

Sims Ely, general manager of the Salt River User's Association, in his 1953 book, *The Lost Dutchman Mine*, with rancher Jim Bark, covered the early stories and interviews with Julia Thomas and Rhinehart Petrasch.[16] Early treasure seekers such as Dick Holmes, Brownie Holmes, and Herman

Petrasch spent most of their lives searching for the Dutchman's Mine without success.

After the death of rancher Tex Barkley in 1955, the Barkley Cattle Company began to decline. By 1968 it was divided into three ranches, Quarter Circle U, First Water and Three R's, then sold.[17] During those final years Tom Kollenborn, author and historian, worked for both Tex and Bill Barkley as a cowboy. Tex's son Bill Barkley died in 1967.[18] Kollenborn documented his experiences in the book, *Superstition Mountain, A Ride Through Time*, which he co-authored with James Swanson. Tom Kollenborn (aka James Colten) is the recognized expert on the legends and history of the Superstitions. He continues to write and lecture on the fascinating tales of the Superstition Mountains. We made extensive use of Tom Kollenborn's articles and books for reference to the place names and history of the Superstitions. Kollenborn's original works are well worth reading in their entirety.

We have only described a few of the many famous *Lost Dutchman* men and women. More stories and famous personalities are included in the

Tonto National Forest information sign for miners and treasure hunters, circa 1975.
PHOTOGRAPH BY RICHARD DILLON.

History and Legends section of each trip. The Lost Dutchman Gold Mine story continues; every year brings a new event of discovery or recollection of former episodes.

Mining And Treasure Hunting

The Wilderness Act of 1964 closed all Wilderness lands to new mineral claims effective January 1, 1984. In the Superstition Wilderness the Forest Service requires existing valid mining claims to show valuable and locatable minerals. These claims must operate with an approved Notice of Intent and/or Plan of Operations. The Forest Service has defined several categories of mineral-related activities to help clarify the regulations. Ask the Forest Service for a copy of the regulations.

Mining is the extraction of minerals and is subject to the Forest Service rules described above.

Prospecting is only allowed with an approved Plan of Operations. Extraction of a small grab sample is permitted. Anything more than what you can carry in your hands is considered mining.

Gold Panning is considered a type of mining if a mineral is extracted. If a mineral is not extracted, Gold Panning is allowed and is considered prospecting.

Treasure Trove Hunting is only allowed with a Permit from the Forest Service. A treasure trove is defined as money, gems, or precious worked metal of unknown ownership. You must prove you have treasure, gems, coins, etc. before the permit will be issued. If a permit is approved, it is issued for a specific number of days and the search site is subject to inspection.

Under the Archaeological Resources Protection Act, no artifacts may be removed which are over 100 years old. Archaeological sites may not be disturbed. Historic sites and artifacts are government property and your permit may exclude collection of these items.

Metal Detecting is allowed but may be considered Mining, Prospecting, or Treasure Trove Hunting depending on what you find.

Adventures In Route Finding

The off-trail routes in this book do not have obvious "trails" unless you know what to look for. Almost anyone can recognize and follow a trail such as the wide and well-worn Peralta Trail up to Fremont Saddle. In contrast, off-trail routes are often marked with rock cairns—three or more stones stacked in a pile. Rock cairns are also called *ducks* or *monuments*. Some outdoor purists disapprove of rock cairns but we feel they are appropriate since they are very useful to the average hiker and easily removed if desired.

Without the guiding path of a trail, you need to read the terrain if you want to be an off-trail hiker. Memorize the lay of the land from a high point and establish a route down and up the other side before descending into a ravine or canyon. Look for passes over a hill, breaks in a cliff and natural paths around large obstacles. Check the benches of washes above the high water line for trails. Following the natural contours of the land—dry washes, ridge lines, stream beds—makes off-trail hiking easier. Once you establish a route, keep a close lookout for cairns, game trails, footprints of other hikers and animals tracks that may make your path-finding easier.

It is a common practice for some hikers to put a row of rocks or a wood branch across the start of a seldom used trail. This helps them identify the main trail for their group of hikers. We often use these seldom traveled trails in our hikes, so every time you see a trail blocked by rocks, consider these rocks as a form of rock cairn (dismantled rock cairn) denoting a trail intersection. Sometimes trail-maintenance workers adjust and direct the flow of hiker traffic by blocking a section of trail for restoration with rocks and brush. Off-trail hikers must be able to distinguish between a seldom used trail and these restoration areas. Don't bushwhack through restoration areas.

Sometimes it is not appropriate to take short-cuts off the beaten path. Taking short-cuts across switchbacks on the main trails (Forest Development Trails) is prohibited by Special Forest Order 12-59-R and is punishable by a $500 fine and/or imprisonment of six months. Short-cutting switchbacks erodes the trails and makes a real mess of the landscape. If your off-trail hiking will have a deleterious effect on the landscape, don't do it. Otherwise, explore the Wilderness and enjoy the grandness of it all.

Water

For day hikes, it is usually more convenient to carry all the water you need than to try to purify water found in the creeks. In hot weather it is useful to carry some empty containers that can be filled with untreated water—from pot holes, springs, and creeks. You can use this water for keeping a bandanna or shirt wet which will act as your personal evaporative cooler and reduce the amount of water you need to drink. On hot days and in the summer, we freeze plastic bottles of water so we have something cool to drink. On day hikes we carry one to four liters of water per person depending on the season and weather. In the summer, four liters per person is a minimum requirement for a day-long hike. Summer heat can make the water so hot it is not very pleasant to drink.

If you are looking for water, check the map for springs and streams. Plan ahead by checking with other hikers and the Forest Service rangers for the current conditions of the springs and water sources. Many springs are seasonal which means they are dry for long periods of time (months or even years). In the field, observe the color and type of surrounding vegetation. Cottonwood and sycamore trees sometimes indicate water. Green areas may have water or just catch more runoff than nearby areas. Pot holes in ravines and intermittent streams are often good sources of water. Purify all water to be certain it is safe for drinking. Some people have contracted Giardia from drinking untreated water. Boil water for at least five minutes or use a filter designed to remove Giardia. Always take your water from sources that are impacted by the least human and animal traffic. Although many of the springs developed by the ranchers and cattlemen are in disrepair, you can usually (but not always) obtain water by following the old pipes back to the spring.

Some of the more reliable springs are Charlebois, La Barge, Bluff and Hackberry. For the latest information on water conditions, check with the rangers at the Mesa Ranger District in Mesa, Arizona. Their address and phone number are listed in the back of this book under Useful Addresses.

Equipment And Clothing

Although equipment and clothing needs will vary from trip to trip, we can offer some general guidelines that will cover the typical hiker's needs. In our day packs, we each always carry a small homemade emergency first-aid kit, flashlight, compass, toilet paper, knife, map, pencil, extra bandanna, sunglasses, snacks and water. We usually wear hiking shorts, cotton shirt, bandanna and some kind of wide brim hat or baseball hat. Some hikers may prefer to wear loose fitting long cotton pants to protect their legs from cuts and scratches. In the winter and in periods of changing weather, we always add a breathable waterproof jacket with hood and a wool hat. If the weather is cool or really looks nasty, we take polypropylene long underwear tops and bottoms that can be worn under our shirt and shorts. If we expect rain or snow, we take rain pants and a poncho. We alternate between low top hiking shoes and light weight hiking boots with wool socks. If we will be hiking off-trail, we wear short gaiters to keep the stickers and foxtails out of our socks.

All our first-aid items are stored in a mesh bag that is six inches tall and four inches in diameter. The emergency first-aid kit contains:

- ❑ first-aid antibiotic ointment
- ❑ moleskin
- ❑ gauze pads
- ❑ adhesive tape
- ❑ bandaids
- ❑ alcohol swab pads
- ❑ aspirin
- ❑ lip balm
- ❑ snake and insect bite extractor kit
- ❑ sun screen
- ❑ Swiss army knife with scissors and tweezers
- ❑ lighter
- ❑ nail file
- ❑ thread and needles
- ❑ extra flashlight bulb
- ❑ money ($20 or more in small bills and 2 quarters)

For overnight camping trips you should consult one of the many instructional books on backpacking and develop your own list of equipment.

Trailheads and Areas

In addition to these brief descriptions, we suggest you read the Trailhead descriptions in the hike section of the book. Paved road mileage is rounded to the nearest mile. Roads are okay for passenger cars except as noted.

PERALTA TRAILHEAD. Eight miles east of Apache Junction on U.S. Route 60, between mileposts 204 and 205, turn north onto Peralta Road, FS77, and go 7.2 miles to end of road.

CARNEY SPRINGS TRAILHEAD. Eight miles east of Apache Junction on U.S. Route 60, between mileposts 204 and 205, turn north onto Peralta Road, FS77, and go six miles, turn west and go six-tenths mile to end of road.

HIEROGLYPHIC CANYON AREA. Six miles east of Apache Junction on U.S. Route 60, between mileposts 202 and 203, turn north on Kings Ranch Road and go 2.8 miles to cattle guard. See the Hieroglyphic Canyon Area for trailhead map and additional street directions.

LOST DUTCHMAN STATE PARK TRAILHEAD. Five miles north of Apache Junction on State Route 88, between mileposts 201 and 202, turn east into the Lost Dutchman State Park.

MASSACRE GROUNDS TRAILHEAD. Five miles north of Apache Junction on State Route 88, between mileposts 201 and 202, turn east on FS78 (First Water Road) for one mile, turn south and drive seven-tenths mile to end of road.

FIRST WATER TRAILHEAD. Five miles north of Apache Junction on State Route 88, between mileposts 201 and 202, turn east on FS78 (First Water Road) and go 2.6 miles to end of road.

CANYON OVERLOOK TRAILHEAD. Twelve miles north of Apache Junction on State Route 88, park at vehicle pull-outs between mileposts 207 and 208.

CANYON LAKE TRAILHEAD. Fifteen miles north of Apache Junction on State Route 88, between mileposts 211 and 212, park at Canyon Lake Marina.

TORTILLA FLAT TRAILHEAD. Seventeen miles north of Apache Junction on State Route 88, between mileposts 213 and 214, park at Tortilla Flat or on vehicle pull-outs down the road. Tortilla Flat is private property. Obtain permission from the store manager before parking at Tortilla Flat.

TORTILLA TRAILHEAD. Twenty-four miles north of Apache Junction on State Route 88, between mileposts 221 and 222, turn right and park in the parking area at the start of FS213, or take 4WD road FS213 to the Old Tortilla Headquarters area. FS213 may be upgraded, from four-wheel drive, to a high-clearance road, so check with the Mesa Ranger District for current road conditions.

REAVIS TRAILHEAD. Thirty miles north of Apache Junction on State Route 88, between mileposts 227 and 228, turn south on FS212 and drive 2.8 miles to end of road. High-clearance vehicle is required.

TULE TRAILHEAD. From Apache Junction, on U.S. Route 60 drive east forty-nine miles to State Route 88, just east of Globe. Turn north on State Route 88 for 21 miles to FS449 (Cross-P Ranch Road) between mileposts 252 and 251. Drive west on FS449 for two miles to junction with FS449A. Stay right on FS449 for 1.2 miles to end of road.

UPPER HORRELL TRAILHEAD. Follow directions to Tule Trailhead and take FS449A to left for 5.1 miles to Reevis Mountain School (Upper Horrell Place). Reevis Mountain School is private property. A new trail (Spring of 1994) around the west side of Reevis Mountain School provides access across USFS land. Deep sand and seasonal water make FS449A a 4WD road.

MILES RANCH TRAILHEAD. From Apache Junction, on U.S. Route 60 drive 32 miles to Superior. Continue on U.S. Route 60 for 12 miles to FS287 (Pinto Valley Mine Road) between mileposts 239 and 240. The FS287 junction is one mile east of the Pinto Creek highway bridge. Drive north on FS287 for 7.2 miles to FS287A, turn left and drive 5.5 miles to end of road. A medium-clearance vehicle is required.

ROGERS TROUGH TRAILHEAD. Two miles east of Florence Junction on U.S. Route 60, between mileposts 214 and 215, turn north on Queen Creek road for 1.6 miles to FS357 (Hewitt Station Road), go right three miles to FS172, go left 10 miles on FS172 to junction with FS172A. Go right on FS172A for three miles to end of road. High-clearance vehicle is required on FS172. Steep and rocky sections of FS172A make this a 4WD road.

WOODBURY TRAILHEAD. Follow directions to Rogers Trough Trailhead to junction with FS172A. From FS172A junction go straight on FS172 for 1.2 miles to end of road. High-clearance vehicle is required on FS172.

JF RANCH TRAILHEAD. Relocated to Woodbury Trailhead.

Easy Hikes

We are often asked, "What is an easy hike that I can take in the Superstitions?" These 15 easy hikes will let you explore the Superstitions from all directions. If you turn around at our suggested location or when you get tired, these trips will make ideal easy hikes. The difficulty of each hike varies within the easy category, so you will have to make your choice using the round-trip distance in miles, round-trip time, elevation change, trip description, destination and trail condition. Some of the hikes listed here are portions of more difficult hikes, so you must read the trip description carefully to identify your turnaround point.

Trip	Miles	Hours	Elev.	Destination		Trail Condition
3	1.2	0.7	±280	Dons Trail	loop hike	poor trail
4	1.8	0.9	±360	Barkley Basin	[3-L, 0.9]	good trail
22	3.0	2.0	±560	Hieroglyphic Canyon	[8-E, 1.5]	good trail
23	3.2	2.5	±1030	Siphon Draw	[9-H, 1.6]	good trail
24	3.0	3.0	±980	Massacre Grounds	[9-W, 1.5]	poor trail
25	0.9	0.8	±180	First Water Creek	[10-0, 0.4]	good road
26	2.2	2.0	±274	Hackberry Spring	[10-J, 1.1]	creek bed
27	3.8	2.0	±300	Garden Valley	[10-G, 1.9]	good trail
28	4.6	2.5	±360	Parker Pass	[10-Z, 2.3]	good trail
32	0.8	0.8	±160	Creek Overlook	[12-B, 0.4]	poor trail
34	1.2	0.7	±140	Boulder Trail	[13-B, 0.6]	good trail
35	1.4	1.0	±340	La Barge Creek	[13-H, 0.7]	creek bed
36	2.2	2.5	±60	Tortilla Creek	[14-B, 1.1]	creek bed
40	1.0	1.5	±145	Fish Creek	[17-N, 0.5]	creek bed
42	1.4	1.5	±80	Tortilla Creek	[18-U, 0.7]	creek bed

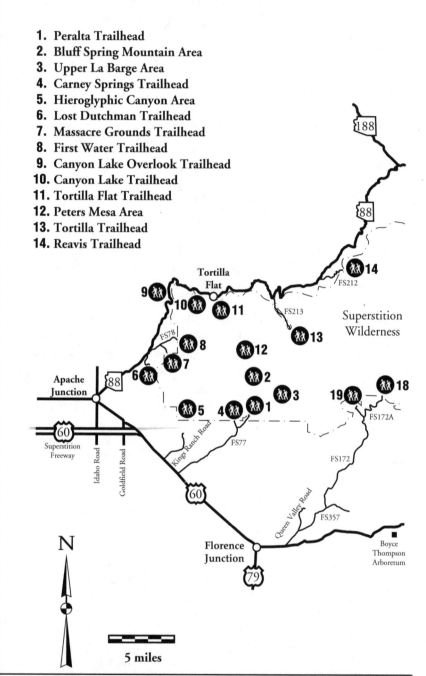

1. Peralta Trailhead
2. Bluff Spring Mountain Area
3. Upper La Barge Area
4. Carney Springs Trailhead
5. Hieroglyphic Canyon Area
6. Lost Dutchman Trailhead
7. Massacre Grounds Trailhead
8. First Water Trailhead
9. Canyon Lake Overlook Trailhead
10. Canyon Lake Trailhead
11. Tortilla Flat Trailhead
12. Peters Mesa Area
13. Tortilla Trailhead
14. Reavis Trailhead

Trailhead and Area Locator Map — Superstition Wilderness

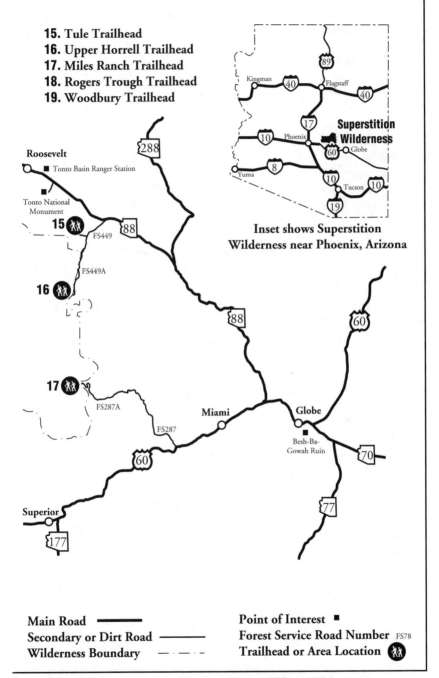

15. Tule Trailhead
16. Upper Horrell Trailhead
17. Miles Ranch Trailhead
18. Rogers Trough Trailhead
19. Woodbury Trailhead

Superstition Wilderness near Phoenix, Arizona

Kingman 40 Flagstaff 89
40
17
Phoenix 10 Superstition Wilderness
8 60 Globe
Yuma
10 Tucson 10
19

Inset shows Superstition Wilderness near Phoenix, Arizona

Roosevelt
■ Tonto Basin Ranger Station
288
Tonto National Monument
15 FS449 88
FS449A
16
17 FS287A
FS287 Miami
60 Globe
Besh-Ba-Gowah Ruin
70
Superior
177 77
88
60

Main Road ———
Secondary or Dirt Road ———
Wilderness Boundary — · — · —

Point of Interest ■
Forest Service Road Number FS78
Trailhead or Area Location 🚶

Trailhead and Area Locator Map — Superstition Wilderness

53 Siphon Draw Trail		**117** Reavis Gap Trail	
101 Hieroglyphic Trail		**118** Fire Line Trail	
102 Peralta Trail		**119** Two Bar Ridge Trail	
103 Boulder Canyon Trail		**122** Tule Canyon Trail	
104 Dutchman's Trail		**129** Bull Pass Trail	
105 Peters Trail		**195** Rock Creek Trail	
106 JF Trail		**203** Haunted Canyon Trail	
107 Red Tanks Trail		**212** West Pinto Trail	
108 Coffee Flat Trail		**213** Pinto Peak Trail	
109 Reavis Ranch Trail		**233** Cave Trail	
110 Rogers Canyon Trail		**234** Terrapin Trail	
111 Hoolie Bacon Trail		**235** Bluff Spring Trail	
112 Frog Tanks Trail		**236** Second Water Trail	

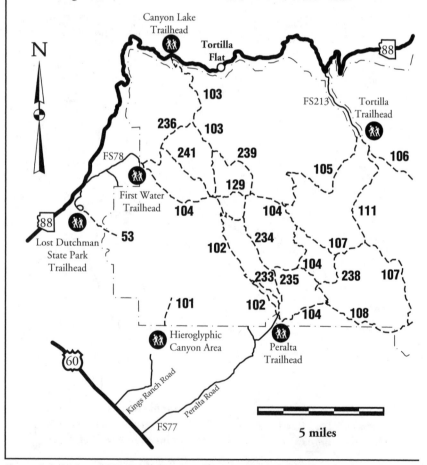

Forest Service Official Trails — Superstition Wilderness

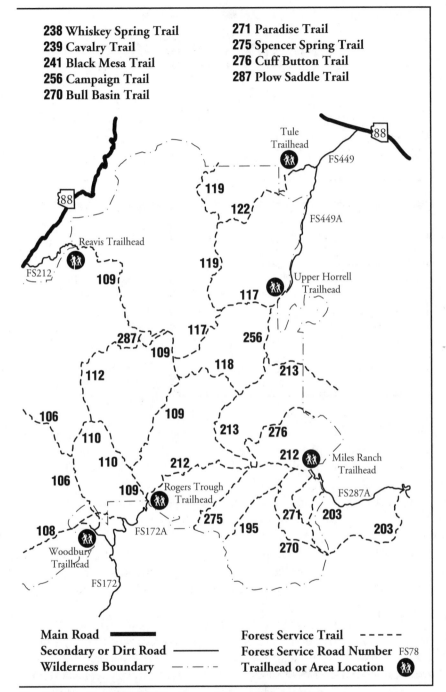

238 Whiskey Spring Trail
239 Cavalry Trail
241 Black Mesa Trail
256 Campaign Trail
270 Bull Basin Trail

271 Paradise Trail
275 Spencer Spring Trail
276 Cuff Button Trail
287 Plow Saddle Trail

Tule Trailhead
88
FS449
119
122
FS449A
Reavis Trailhead
119
FS212
109
117
Upper Horrell Trailhead
287
117
109
256
213
118
112
106
109
110
213
276
106
110
212
Miles Ranch Trailhead
109
212
FS287A
Rogers Trough Trailhead
275
271
203
108
FS172A
195
203
Woodbury Trailhead
270
FS172

Main Road ▬▬▬	**Forest Service Trail** - - - -
Secondary or Dirt Road ———	**Forest Service Road Number** FS78
Wilderness Boundary — · — · -	**Trailhead or Area Location** 🚶

Forest Service Official Trails — Superstition Wilderness

Peralta Trailhead

From Apache Junction go 8 miles east on U.S. Route 60. Turn left, north, between mileposts 204 and 205 onto Peralta Road, Forest Service road FS77. Peralta Trailhead is 7.2 miles at the end of FS77.

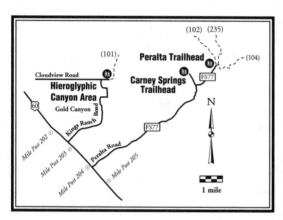

FINDING THE TRAILHEAD. While driving along FS77 take note of the turnoff for the Quarter Circle U Ranch, private property, on the right at mile 5.4. The Quarter Circle U Ranch was previously Jim Bark's Ranch from the late 1890s to 1907 and later Tex Barkley's Ranch from 1907 to 1955.

Carney Springs Trailhead is on the left at mile 6. Dons Club Base Camp is on the left at mile 6.7. Lost Goldmine Trail is on the left at mile 6.9. Horse trailer and overflow parking is on the left at mile 7.

There is a small trailhead parking lot at mile 7.2. If this lot is full you can drive back down the road about 0.2 mile and park in another area where the outfitters usually park horse trailers and saddle-up for their pack trips. Since January 1997 a $4 fee per vehicle per day is required for all parking.

FACILITIES. Handicap pit toilets are located at the main parking lot. No drinking water is available. **Be sure to bring your own water.** Seasonal water in Peralta Canyon creek, just north of the parking lot, is good for soaking your aching feet, but don't drink it.

In the prime hiking season, February and March, Forest Service rangers are here taking hiker-survey information, and they are available for any questions you have. They sometimes camp in a big white canvas wall-tent next to the parking lot. Due to vandalism, the Forest Service usually removes all the informational and trail signs when they leave for the season at the end of

March. They return again with the signs in January or February. Theft and vandalism are common at this trailhead so don't leave valuables in your vehicle. Thieves steal clothes, books, maps, camping gear, gasoline, tools, etc. Be sure everything is locked in the trunk or better yet, don't bring it to the trailhead.

THE TRAILS. Three trails start from the north end of the Peralta Trailhead parking lot. Peralta Trail, on the left, goes north up Peralta Canyon. This is the most popular and heavily traveled route in the area. If you haven't seen Weavers Needle, hike up Peralta Trail (102) to Fremont Saddle (Trip 1) to enjoy the spectacular view.

The Dutchman's Trail (104) begins at the northeast corner of the parking area and immediately crosses the Peralta Canyon creek bed. Fifty yards up the path Bluff Spring Trail (235) branches off to the left. The Bluff Spring Trail is the second most traveled trail in the area. It heads north up a rocky switchback taking you over to Bluff Spring and is very useful for connecting many of the loop hikes.

At the Bluff Spring Trail junction, the Dutchman's Trail heads right (east) and contours around some small hills before dropping down into Barkley Basin. The Dutchman's Trail winds its way through the legendary areas of the Superstition Wilderness, eventually ending at the First Water Trailhead, 18 miles later. The Dutchman's Trail, from the Peralta Trailhead, seems to have less traffic than others and offers some solitude once you pass over the first saddle on the trail.

Peralta Trailhead Parking Lot.

Fremont Saddle

For those who haven't seen Weavers Needle this is a required hike. Peralta Trail is wide and easy to follow. It takes you directly to Weavers Needle. Look for the "eye on the trail" window-rock on the eastern horizon as you hike to Fremont Saddle.

ITINERARY: From the Peralta Trailhead parking lot take the Peralta Trail (102), north, up Peralta Canyon to Fremont Saddle for a spectacular view of Weavers Needle. Return by the same route or by the more interesting, but less defined, Cave Trail (233) (Trip 2) which descends on the east ridge line of Peralta Canyon, connecting with the Bluff Spring Trail (235), ending near the Peralta Trailhead parking lot.

DIFFICULTY: Moderate. Trail walking on well-established trail. Not recommended for horses. Elevation change is ±1366 feet.

LENGTH and TIME: 4.5 miles, 2.5 hours round trip.

MAPS: Weavers Needle, Arizona USGS topo map.
Superstition Wilderness Tonto National Forest map.

FINDING THE TRAIL: Leave the north end of the Peralta Trailhead parking lot, go left, and follow the Peralta Trail up Peralta Canyon. The trail sign is usually missing (stolen).

THE HIKE: *Use Map 1.* This hike is very popular and as a consequence there will be many people both on the trail and on the cliffs above the trail. If you hike during the weekdays you will see fewer people here. Although Peralta Canyon is popular, it is a good choice for new hikers to the Superstitions. The view of Weavers Needle is spectacular, and the optional Cave Trail provides some experience in following rock cairns along a less defined trail. The hike is rated moderate, which means experienced hikers should be able to complete the trip without much difficulty. The 1366 foot elevation change is large so you may spend a few moments looking at the view back down canyon while you catch your second breath.

The hike starts at the north end of the Peralta Trailhead parking lot **[1-A, 0]**. Follow the sign to Fremont Saddle—this sign is often missing. The trail begins on the west side of Peralta Canyon and shortly thereafter crosses the small creek to the east side. It is normally easy to rock hop across the water as the trail crosses the seasonal creek several times. **Don't drink the water.** As you walk along the trail, let your imagination bring the spectacular rock formations on the ridge line to life in the form of animals, faces, and figures. Look for a window-rock **[1-B, 1.4]** on the east ridge near the top of the cliffs—*eye on the trail.*[19] Another window-rock **[1-C, 2.1]** is located next to the trail just before the trail reaches Fremont Saddle. This window-rock **[1-C]** has also been referred to as *eye on the trail*, but it doesn't have the distinctive eye features of the formation seen earlier on the hike.

At Fremont Saddle, **[1-D, 2.3]** you won't need directions to find Weavers Needle as it rises in the north, over 1200 feet from the bottom of East Boulder Canyon. Fremont Saddle is the turnaround point for this hike but Peralta Trail (102) continues north down the slope into East Boulder Canyon. For a closer view of Weavers Needle, follow the ridge line from Fremont Saddle north along a faint path for about a quarter mile to a lookout point where a lone piñon pine grows **[1-L]**.

The easiest return route is to retrace your hike down the Peralta Trail to the parking lot **[1-A, 4.5]**. The optional return for experienced hikers is via the Cave Trail (233) starting at Fremont Saddle following the Trip 2 (Cave Trail) description to the parking lot **[1-A, 5.0]**.

HISTORY AND LEGENDS. Peralta Canyon was named by the Dons Club in 1934. It was formerly known as Willow Canyon[20] and has also been called South Needle Canyon.[21] At one time Fremont Saddle was called Fremont Pass. Fremont Saddle is probably named after General John C. Fremont who led a military campaign in the mid 1800s for American control of California.

Weavers Needle was named for Pauline Weaver in 1853.[22] Pauline Weaver was born in Tennessee in 1797. His parents, an Anglo-American father and Cherokee mother, named him Powell Weaver. He called himself Paulin and Paulino in Spanish but became known as Pauline to the Anglos. He first ventured into Arizona in 1831 and became well known as a scout, trapper, mountain man and miner. Weaver was considered a friend by both Indian and pioneer for his fair judgment. He was a scout for Colonel Cooke when the Mormon Battalion made the trek from Santa Fe to southern California in 1846. In the late 1850s he prospected for gold and for a short time prospected with Henry Wickenberg. Pauline Weaver died in 1867

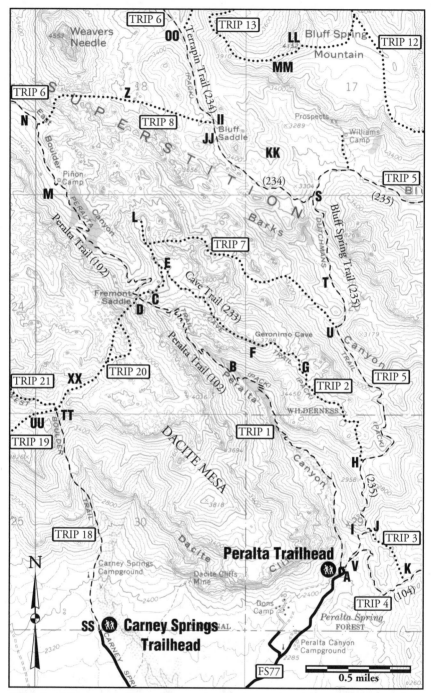

Map 1 - *Trips 1, 2, 18, 19, 20 and 21.*

Hiker's Guide to the Superstition Wilderness

Bob Corbin, Celeste Maria Jones and Louis Roussette at the Jones camp in East Boulder Canyon near Weavers Needle. FROM SUPERSTITION MOUNTAIN, A RIDE THROUGH TIME BY THOMAS KOLLENBORN. PHOTOGRAPH BY JACK KARIE.

while serving as a scout for the military at Camp Lincoln (near Camp Verde) and is buried in Prescott, Arizona.[23]

Experienced rock climbers ascend Weavers Needle starting from a gully on the west side. It is rated a 5.0 technical climb.[24] There are some flat camping places on top of Weavers Needle, elevation 4553 feet, and plenty of room for roaming around to view the surrounding Wilderness area. Some climbers make a day trip to the summit but others haul their camping gear up the cliffs and spend the night on top of the Needle.

Piñon Camp is just north of Fremont Saddle. The piñon pine trees are at the site of the 1949 Celeste Marie Jones camp, shown as Piñon Camp on the USGS topo map. She was the leader of a party of treasure hunters in the search for gold here in the late 1950s and early 1960s.[25] Deteriorating ladders and steel spikes on the face of the Needle are evidence of her early explorations. Her adversary, Ed Piper, had a camp farther down East Boulder Canyon.

See the History and Legends sections of Trips 6 and 8 for more information about the Weavers Needle region.

Cave Trail

*The Cave Trail is a fine choice for ridge line hikers who particularly
enjoy walking on weather worn rock—no dusty trail here. The route winds
its way along cliffs and boulders, passing Geronimo Cave (alcove), with
panoramic views into Peralta Canyon to the west and Barks Canyon
to the east.*

ITINERARY: This hike starts on the Peralta Trail (102) at Fremont Saddle. The
Cave Trail (233) descends to the south along the east ridge line of Peralta
Canyon, connecting with the Bluff Spring Trail (235) which leads to the
Peralta Trailhead parking lot.

DIFFICULTY: Moderate to difficult. Trail is obscure in most places and is
mainly marked by rock cairns. Not recommended for horses. Elevation
change is -1366 feet.

LENGTH and TIME: 2.7 miles, 1.75 hours one-way.

MAPS: Weavers Needle, Arizona USGS topo map.
Superstition Wilderness Tonto National Forest map.

FINDING THE TRAIL: The trail starts on the Peralta Trail (102) at Fremont
Saddle heading east along the top of the ridge. There are no signs or cairns
marking the start of the trail.

THE HIKE: *Use Map 1.* The Cave Trail (233) is more challenging than the
Peralta Trail. Inexperienced hikers may have a difficult time staying on the
trail since it is obscure where it crosses smooth rock surfaces. The trail is
marked by rock cairns, and the route may confuse the casual hiker when it
makes many seemingly unnecessary twists and sharp turns. The 1970 U.S.
Forest Service survey on this section of trail contained a note, "90 percent no
trail," and conditions haven't changed much since that report. The secret to
negotiating a trail like this is as follows. Realize the general direction is
southeast, down the Peralta Canyon ridge line. Look for obvious trail use by
other hikers or animals (footprints, tracks). Look for trail markers such as

rock cairns and in this case, paint on the rocks. We have seen paint on the rocks here for many years. Please do not paint any rocks in the Superstition Wilderness. Rock cairns can be three or more stacked rocks, with the smallest rock on top. With some experience you will be able to find the rock cairns just as easily as you notice the paint markings.

Start the hike by heading east from Fremont Saddle **[1-D, 0]** along the trail that leads out to the overlook for Weavers Needle. After walking 3 minutes, you will come to a junction in the trail marked by a small rock cairn **[1-E, 0.2]**. The cairn is usually disassembled and laid out across the start of the Cave Trail. While hiking the lesser traveled trails in the Superstitions, you will find many of them blocked by similar rocks—disassembled cairns. Many hikers mark the main trail to keep their group together. So, we travelers of the seldom traveled routes will have to accept this trait of our fellow hikers.

The left branch heads north to an overlook for Weavers Needle. The right branch is the Cave Trail (233) which goes east and then immediately turns south following the east ridge line of Peralta Canyon. After another 10 minutes, the trail makes a switchback and heads north for 100 yards, then doubles back and continues south.

Geronimo Trail (Cave Trail) sign in Peralta Canyon near Fremont Saddle, circa 1975.
PHOTOGRAPH BY RICHARD DILLON.

Farther down, the trail goes in front of Geronimo Cave **[1-F, 0.8]** on a wide cliff face. You must walk up a few feet to inspect the larger alcove. There is no actual cave here, only some shallow alcoves. A game trail goes around the backside of the cliff where you get a good view into Barks Canyon. You can see Bluff Spring Mountain and the diggings from the Williams Camp prospect. Bluff Spring Trail (235) is difficult to see from here unless someone is hiking on it.

About 20 minutes south of Geronimo Cave is a rock buttress that is named the Fortress **[1-G, 1.1]**. There are four technical climbs on this face rated between 5.5 and 5.7.

The Cave Trail continues to descend and at times it might seem as if you will never get to the intersection with the Bluff Spring Trail. If you persevere for another 25 minutes, and follow the cairns and most used trails, you will suddenly arrive at a relatively flat area at the Bluff Spring Trail intersection **[1-H, 2.0]**. The Cave Trail is often blocked here by a cactus skeleton, so look closely for the trail if you are starting from this end. There are no signs or rock cairns here so you will have to identify the Bluff Spring Trail by its well-traveled appearance. Take the Bluff Spring Trail right (west) and follow it down the hill for 20 minutes to the Peralta Trailhead parking lot **[1-A, 2.7]**. The parking lot is visible along several sections of the Bluff Spring Trail.

HISTORY AND LEGENDS. The Dons Club has been bringing people on the Cave Trail since they established the trail in the late 1930s. They call this "The Long Hike." The Superstition Mountain Journal shows photographs (in the 1930s or 1940s) of women in long dresses and men in ties making this trek on the Cave Trail.[26] In one photograph of the Dons Trek at Devils Slide **[near 1-G]** we counted 26 hikers. Some of the colorful names applied to sections of the hike are Cardiac Hill, Devils Slide, Geronimo Cave, and the Chimney. Of all these interesting names, Geronimo Cave is the only one printed on the USGS topo map. Geronimo Cave was named by the Dons Club. We haven't found any records indicating Apache Leader Geronimo was actually here. See Trip 3 for more stories about the Dons Club.

Dons Trail

If you drive all the way to the Peralta Trailhead just to take a look at the desert, you should at least hike the Dons Trail. It is a very easy walk that takes you around a small hill where we sometimes see mule deer. In the spring, you will find a varied selection of wildflowers along the trail.

ITINERARY: From the Peralta Trailhead parking lot follow the Bluff Spring Trail (235) to the Dons Trail. The Dons Trail goes southeast, connecting with the Dutchman's Trail (104) returning you to the parking lot.

DIFFICULTY: Easy. Not recommended for horses. Elevation change is ±280 feet.

LENGTH and TIME: 1.2 miles, 40 minutes round trip.

MAPS: Weavers Needle, Arizona USGS topo map.
Superstition Wilderness Tonto National Forest map.

FINDING THE TRAIL: Leave the northeast corner of the Peralta parking lot, go right (east), and cross the creek bed coming down from Peralta Canyon. Walk north about 50 yards up the path to a trail intersection and take the Bluff Spring Trail to the left (north).

THE HIKE: *Use Map 2.* This is an easy hike that gets you away from the parking lot **[2-A, 0]**, over a few hills into some scenic territory. Two minutes up the trail from the Bluff Spring/Dutchman's Trail intersection, an old, overgrown side trail goes straight **[2-I, 0.2]**. At one time this was a well-built trail with a supporting rock wall on the down slope. If you take this old side trail, another four minutes brings you to a 10 foot deep prospector's hole. Return to the main Bluff Spring Trail and continue up the steep grade to the first small saddle where you can see over the hill to the east **[2-J, 0.3]**. The Dons Trail starts at this saddle and is on the east side of the ridge. This is not a signed trail intersection. Follow the Dons Trail south, then east along the ridge line, continuing down and up to another saddle, from where you can see the Dutchman's Trail (104) cut across the hillside to the south. Barkley

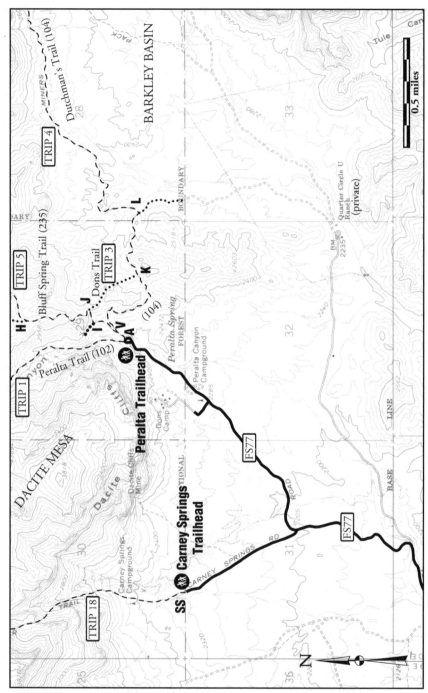

Map 2 - *Trips 3 and 20.*

Hiker's Guide to the Superstition Wilderness

U.S. Forest Service camp at the Peralta Trailhead in 1993.

Basin is the large flat area far to the east. From the saddle, drop down into the ravine and hike the short distance to the Dutchman's Trail **[2-K, 0.6]**. This intersection may be hard to see because a small tree is encroaching on the trail. From here it is less than 15 minutes back to the parking lot. This hike goes right (west) on the Dutchman's Trail back to the Peralta Trailhead parking lot **[2-A, 1.2]**, but if you have more time you can walk down the Dutchman's Trail to the east for a while and return the same way. See Trip 5 (Bluff Spring Loop) for information on the Dutchman's Trail (104).

HISTORY AND LEGENDS. Each year in March, the Dons Club holds a big event, called the Dons Trek, bringing hundreds of people to the Dons Club base camp to enjoy the legends and lore of the Lost Dutchman Mine and the scenic beauty of the Superstition Wilderness. Among others, the Dons Trail is used during the March event for short treks into the mountains.[27] It is quite a scene to see a Dons Club leader, dressed in red and black in the old Spanish tradition, leading a group of 20 city folks along the trail. Standing in the Peralta Trailhead parking lot, we watched an unending stream of these groups come over the hill from the Dons Camp, walk across the parking lot and then hike up the Bluff Spring Trail. The groups were spaced every 200 yards, which makes a spectacular show of humanity in the desert. There

Gregory Davis, Director of Research and Acquisitions for the Superstition Mountain Historical Society.
PHOTOGRAPH BY TOM KOLLENBORN. COURTESY SUPERSTITION MOUNTAIN HISTORICAL SOCIETY.

must have been several hundred people on that small section of trail. The first Dons Trek was held in 1934 and has continued ever since except for the war years 1943, 1944 and 1945.

Greg Davis, Director of Research for the Superstition Mountain Historical Society and member of the Dons Club, reported the history of the Dons Club in the 1982 *Superstition Mountain Journal.* The Dons Club began in 1930 when it was established as the Triangle Club within the Phoenix YMCA. The Triangle Club, in 1931, became an independent organization and changed its name to the Dons Club. Oren Arnold, author of the 1954 book, *Ghost Gold*, and past president of the Dons Club, is credited with selecting the new name. The Dons Club base camp, southeast of the Peralta Trailhead parking lot, has operated since 1955 under a Forest Service permit on Tonto National Forest land. Between 1935 and 1954 the base camp was located at the present site of the Peralta Trailhead parking lot.[28]

Bluff Spring Loop

This traditional loop hike takes you by Miners Needle and on to Bluff Spring where there is seasonal water and a large stand of sugar sumac, netleaf hackberry and oak shade-trees. You are rewarded with a superb view of Weavers Needle as you return past the site of Williams Camp. The alternate return trek adds a bit of off-trail adventure as it cuts across the base of Weavers Needle before connecting with the Peralta Trail.

ITINERARY: From Peralta Trailhead, the Dutchman's Trail (104) passes through Barkley Basin, climbs north past Miners Needle and descends Miners Summit to Bluff Spring Trail. The return trip goes west following Bluff Spring Trail (235) back to the Peralta Trailhead parking lot.

An alternate return trip uses Terrapin Trail (234), branches off on the route described in Trip 8 (Weavers Needle Crosscut) across the south side of Weavers Needle, follows Peralta Trail (102) south and goes up to Fremont Saddle. From Fremont Saddle continue south on Peralta Trail for the easiest return to the parking lot or follow the Cave Trail (233) south connecting with Bluff Spring Trail (235) and proceed south to the Peralta Trailhead parking lot.

DIFFICULTY: Moderate. The alternate return, Trip 8 (Weavers Needle Crosscut), requires route finding and some bouldering and is not recommended for horses. Elevation change is ±1400 feet.

LENGTH and TIME: 9.1 miles, 5 hours round trip. Add about 2.9 miles and 2 hours for the Weavers Needle alternate return.

MAPS: Weavers Needle, Arizona USGS topo map.
Superstition Wilderness Tonto National Forest map.

FINDING THE TRAIL: Leave the northeast corner of the Peralta Trailhead parking lot, go right, and cross the creek bed coming down from Peralta Canyon. Walk north about 50 yards up the path to a trail intersection and take the Dutchman's Trail to the right (east).

THE HIKE: *Use Maps 3 and 4.* This is a very popular loop hike but the hikers are spread out over a long length of trail and you will often be able to experience the quiet and solitude of the Wilderness. Hikers make this trip in either direction. We prefer to hike counterclockwise starting on the Dutchman's Trail (104) and returning on the Bluff Springs Trail (235). The Dutchman's Trail starts out more gradually and at once goes over a rise, quickly leaving the parking lot **[3-A, 0]** behind. On the Weavers Needle USGS topo map the Dutchman's Trail is named Miners Trail. Even more confusing, on the same map the Bluff Spring Trail is named the Dutchman's Trail. The Forest Service map shows the correct names, and we added the correct names to the topo maps shown in this book.

Follow the Dutchman's Trail (104) east, up and around the small hills. Keep a close lookout for mule deer on the left (north) side of the trail. We often see deer here. The trail continues down into Barkley Basin and meets an unmarked trail (old road) **[3-L, 0.9]** that leads south to the Quarter Circle U Ranch (private). This is the turnaround point for the easy hike. Near this junction is the grave site of a soldier who was shot in 1880.

Continue to follow the Dutchman's Trail across BarkLey Basin toward some rock pinnacles in the distance—Cathedral Rock **[3-M]**. You will see Miners Canyon to the north. The trail starts up some switchbacks **[3-N, 2.9]** and follows the east side of Miners Canyon up to the summit. Very early morning hikers might see some javelina on the trail. They move fast so you will be lucky to get more than a glimpse of their backsides bolting through the bushes. An old overgrown trail goes up the bottom of Miners Canyon and is sometimes used to explore the west side of the canyon.

At the Miners Summit **[3-O, 4.3]** there is a wooden sign showing Whiskey Spring Trail (Trip 15) heading east and Dutchman's Trail, which continues north, descending the slope to Bluff Spring Canyon. Continue down the Dutchman's Trail to the intersection with the Bluff Spring Trail **[3-P, 5.7]** which is on the north side of the wash. There is a wooden trail sign here.

On the old Weavers Needle USGS topo map Bluff Spring and Crystal Spring are interchanged, but on the newer map the springs are labeled correctly. This is confusing since the old and new maps bear the same date, 1966. Bluff Spring **[3-Q]** is located on the side of Bluff Spring Mountain. There is an old rectangular cement water-trough at Bluff Spring but the pipes leading to the trough have been broken. If you want water, you need to thrash through the vegetation in the small gully until you get back to the running water. On the flat area across from the spring are the remains of a corral that has been partially dismantled by the Forest Service.

Nearby is a horse trail up to the top of Bluff Spring Mountain which is thought to be the trail used by the Mexicans in the mid 1800s. The trail is located one minute (walking time) west of the wooden trail sign at the Dutchman's and Bluff Spring Trail intersection. If you have time, you could check this out for another trip. See the Trip 12 (Ely-Anderson Trail) for the exact trail location **[3-R, 5.8]**.

A large stand of sugar sumac trees provide shade in Bluff Spring Canyon where large groups of hikers often camp. When there is water in Bluff Spring Canyon this is a nice place to have a snack and get ready for the return trip. Bluff Spring Trail starts at the wooden trail sign and goes west up Bluff Spring Canyon, crossing the wash numerous times. Weavers Needle soon rises on the western horizon presenting an unforgettable image of the Needle in the background of Bluff Spring Canyon pass. This view of the Needle is another reason why we enjoy hiking the loop in this direction.

Williams Camp is to the north of the trail just as it tops out of Bluff Spring Canyon. Walk up the small knoll to check out the few remaining bits of trash from the mining camp—broken china, tin cans, some pieces of lumber, and other items. To the north by the cliff are the remains of the mine diggings.

After climbing out of Bluff Spring Canyon, the Bluff Spring Trail turns south and shortly intersects the Terrapin Trail **[3-S, 6.8]** which comes in from the right (west). At this point, you can continue with the traditional hike and follow the Bluff Spring Trail back to the trailhead or take the alternate return. The alternate return is described at the end of this section.

The easiest return follows the Bluff Spring Trail south down the hill into Barks Canyon. As the trail descends into the wash **[3-T, 7.2]**, it sometimes seems to disappear, but be assured it does continue. It is more difficult to follow in the opposite (northerly) direction. Many people have been lost here, and as a consequence there are several trails that abruptly end. If you find yourself on one of these phantom trails, backtrack and try again. Forest Service Trail (235) stays in the bottom of the wash in Barks Canyon a lot longer than most people expect.

The trail continues across Barks Canyon and climbs up the west side of the canyon **[3-U, 7.5]**. The unsigned Cave Trail (233) enters from the north **[3-H, 8.4]**. The Peralta Trailhead parking lot **[3-A, 9.1]** is another 20 minutes down the hill where the hike ends.

ALTERNATE RETURN TRIP. The alternate return takes the Terrapin Trail **[3-S, 6.8]** south to Bluff Saddle. This route is not suitable for horses. About 0.1 miles north of Bluff Saddle **[4-JJ, 7.6]**, you leave the trail **[4-II]** and head

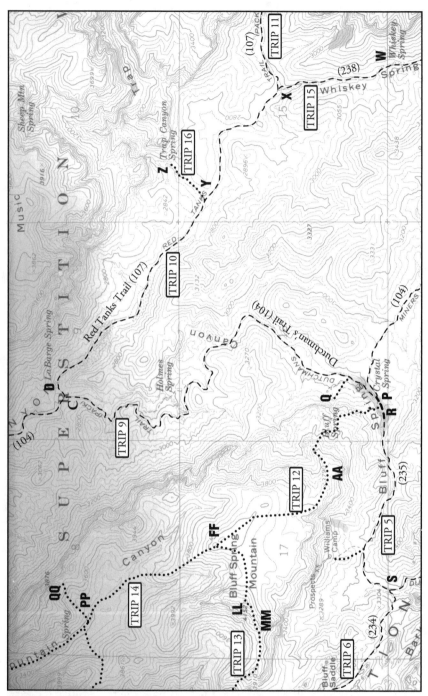

Map 3 - *Trips 4, 5, 9, 10, 11 and 15.*

Hiker's Guide to the Superstition Wilderness

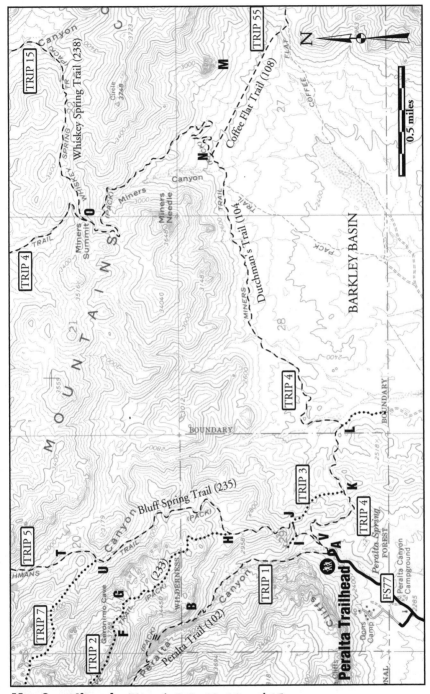

Map 3 continued - *Trips 4, 5, 9, 10, 11 and 15.*

west on a cross-country route south of Weavers Needle. See Trip 8 (Weavers Needle Crosscut) for a complete description. The route takes you to East Boulder Canyon **[4-N, 8.6]** where you hike south on the Peralta Trail up to Fremont Saddle **[4-D, 9.7]** and then down Peralta Canyon to the Peralta Trailhead parking lot **[4-A, 12.0]**. Refer to Trip 1 (Fremont Saddle) and Trip 5 (East Boulder–Needle Canyon Loop) for details.

HISTORY AND LEGENDS. In 1880 a young soldier was shot and killed near the Dutchman's Trail and Quarter Circle U Road intersection.[29] The grave is about a half mile north of the Jim Bark ranch house (now Quarter Circle U), but is not visible today. Sims Ely reports that the soldier and his companion found $700 of hand-sorted gold ore and were returning to their newly discovered mine from Pinal to set out the claim notices and monuments. Speculation in the camp of Pinal directed suspicion toward a saloon swamper as the murderer. When the citizens decided to run the suspected murderer out of camp, he took the stagecoach first to Florence, then Casa Grande, and out of Arizona. Joe Dearing allegedly found this same mine dump in 1881 but died in a mine accident before he could return to it.[30] In 1915 Ernest Albert Panknin arrived in Phoenix from Alaska with a map to a lost gold mine in the Superstitions. Later in1915, Sims Ely and Jim Bark

View of Weavers Needle looking west from the Bluff Spring Trail in Bluff Spring Canyon.

The ruins of Williams Camp (1938-1946) with Weavers Needle in the background.
COURTESY GREGORY DAVIS, SUPERSTITION MOUNTAIN HISTORICAL SOCIETY.

tied the story together when they learned the man from Alaska who drew the map for Panknin was the Pinal camp saloon swamper. Their key to the mystery was the fact that the man who drew the map had a twisted foot—the same as the saloon swamper. Panknin died in 1934 without finding the mine or revealing the memorized clues that accompanied the map.[31]

Sims Ely, in his 1953 *Lost Dutchman Mine* book, describes a two-foot rock wall that contained water from Bluff Spring. We have not been able to locate this well curbing. Above Bluff Spring in a recess in the cliff, rancher Jim Bark in the early 1900s discovered over a hundred Mexican sandals made of cactus fiber. We think this cave may be the one seen from the Ely-Anderson Trail (Trip 12). This physical evidence and the discovery of the nearby Spanish Trail up Bluff Spring Mountain led Ely to speculate that Bluff Spring might have been the area used by the Mexicans to stage their return expeditions to Mexico.[32]

Miners Needle is the prominent rock formation on the west side of Miners Canyon. It is a Class 4 scramble to the eye of the needle although some people prefer the security of a belayed climbing rope. The climbs to the top of the needle require technical equipment.

John Dahlmann described what we believe was Williams Camp in his 1979 book, *A Tiny Bit of God's Creation.* The camp was on a knoll just north of the trail near the head of Bluff Spring Canyon. There were six cabins that would accommodate 12 miners. The cabins, three on each side of the trail, were built of odd-shaped lumber remnants and roofed with galvanized sheet metal. Each cabin was about eight feet wide and twelve feet long.[33]

Bluff Spring Trail

The Bluff Spring Trail is the fastest way to reach Bluff Spring where you will find a pleasant cluster of shade trees and seasonal water. This hike description gets you quickly to Bluff Spring where you can end your trek or continue to the top of Bluff Spring Mountain or to Charlebois Spring in La Barge Canyon.

ITINERARY: The Bluff Spring Trail is the most direct trail to Bluff Spring. From the Peralta Trailhead, follow the Bluff Spring Trail (235) past the Cave Trail intersection, down into Barks Canyon, up the hill to the Terrapin Trail intersection. Continue on Bluff Spring Trail down Bluff Spring Canyon to Bluff Spring. Return the same way. An alternate return can be made over Miners Saddle via the Dutchman's Trail (104). A second alternate return uses Weavers Needle Crosscut Route off the Terrapin Trail (234) and returns over Fremont Saddle via the Peralta Trail (102) or Cave Trail (233). Be sure to read the Bluff Spring Loop description (Trip 4) which makes a similar trip in the counterclockwise direction.

DIFFICULTY: Moderate. Not recommended for horses. Elevation change is ±1320 feet.

LENGTH and TIME: 7 miles, 3.5 hours round trip.

MAPS: Weavers Needle, Arizona USGS topo map.
Superstition Wilderness Tonto National Forest map.

FINDING THE TRAIL: Leave the northeast corner of the Peralta parking lot, go right (east), and cross the Peralta Canyon creek bed. Walk north about 50 yards up the path to a trail intersection and take the Bluff Spring Trail to the left (north).

THE HIKE: *Use Map 3.* The Bluff Spring Trail is the most direct trail to Bluff Spring. On the Weavers Needle USGS topo map the Bluff Spring Trail is incorrectly named the Dutchman's Trail. Bluff Spring Trail is named correctly on the Superstition Wilderness map as Trail 235. We included this trail description for those wanting to get to Bluff Spring quickly. Use the Trip 4 (Bluff Spring Loop) description if you plan to make a loop hike.

The trail begins at the Peralta Trailhead parking lot **[3-A, 0]** by cutting through the side of a cliff as it goes up steeply to the first small saddle **[3-J, 0.3]**. This is the intersection with the Dons Trail which heads off to the east along the ridge. The Bluff Spring hike continues up the rocky trail passing several more saddles that provide good views to the west into Peralta Canyon. The unsigned Cave Trail (233) is on the left (north) **[3-H, 0.7]**. Continue on the Bluff Spring Trail across a flat area, up to a saddle, and down into Barks Canyon.

At the trail intersection with the bed of Barks Canyon **[3-U, 1.6]**, you can often find water. Hikers interested in a shorter hike can use this as a lunch and turnaround spot. Since this is a busy area, we do not recommend using the water for drinking. If it is hot, this is a good place for wetting a shirt or bandanna. Almost everyone gets lost around here where the trail goes up the bed of the wash. There is a trail to the north that goes up the side of a hill, but this is not Bluff Spring Trail, so don't follow it. There are some signs of a path where the trail crosses the bed of the creek. The trail tends to stay on the left side (north). After several hundred yards the trail turns north again and is well defined for a few more yards. Many trails in this area tend to lead you off into dead-end paths. The trail follows the creek bed again for several hundred yards **[3-T, 1.9]** and finally goes up the hill on a steep but well-defined horse trail. There's an unusual view of Weavers Needle along here. The spires and rock formations on the western horizon make good pictures. When the trail reaches the summit, the Terrapin Trail (234) **[3-S, 2.3]** comes in from the left (west). Continue on the Bluff Spring Trail north, then east as it crosses the saddle into Bluff Spring Canyon.

You can walk up the small knoll to the site of Williams Camp on the north side of the trail. There isn't much left of the mining camp here except a few remaining bits of trash—broken china, tin cans, some pieces of lumber, and other items. To the north by the cliff are the remains of the mine diggings.

Back on the Bluff Spring Trail, continue east down to the Bluff Spring and Dutchman's trail junction **[3-P, 3.5]** where this hike description ends. Return the same way. Be sure to read the Bluff Spring Loop (Trip 4) description for a narrative on the Bluff Spring area.

ALTERNATE RETURN ROUTE. See Trip 4 (Bluff Spring Loop) for the alternate-return description.

East Boulder—Needle Canyon Loop

This hike has more vistas of Weavers Needle than any other hike in the Wilderness. The trails are well defined, the views are great, and the trails are not crowded once you pass Fremont Saddle. Weavers Needle attracted many prospectors and the trail passes through their historic base camps. You may find seasonal water in East Boulder Canyon and Needle Canyon. An optional side trip takes you to Aylor's Arch and the Horse With Laid Back Ear rock formation.

ITINERARY: From the Peralta Trailhead, this loop hike follows the Peralta Trail (102), north, up Peralta Canyon to Fremont Saddle for a spectacular view of Weavers Needle. The hike continues north on the Peralta Trail, down East Boulder Canyon, east on the Dutchman's Trail (104), south on the Terrapin Trail (234), and returns to the Peralta Trailhead via the Bluff Spring Trail (235).

DIFFICULTY: Moderate. Trail walking on well-established trails. Elevation change is ±2646 feet.

LENGTH and TIME: 12.4 miles, 7.5 hours round trip.

MAPS: Goldfield, Arizona USGS topo map.
Weavers Needle, Arizona USGS topo map.
Superstition Wilderness Tonto National Forest map.

FINDING THE TRAIL: Leave the north end of the Peralta Trailhead parking lot, go left, and follow the trail up Peralta Canyon.

THE HIKE: *Use Map 4.* This is a popular loop hike that circles Weavers Needle. The hike can be extended or shortened according to your particular plans as described later. From the Peralta Trailhead **[4-A, 0]** follow Trip 1 directions north to Fremont Saddle **[4-D, 2.3]**.

From Fremont Saddle **[4-D, 2.3]** descend into East Boulder Canyon on the well-defined horse trail, Peralta Trail (102). Piñon Camp **[4-M, 3.3]** is the first landmark along the trail. This was the 1949 camp of treasure hunter

Celeste Maria Jones.[34] Piñon Camp has four piñon pine trees along with a nice sugar sumac tree that provide a shady place to rest near seasonal water—dry in the summer. Down the trail north of Piñon Camp, Jones had her 1959 camp **[4-N, 2.7]** across from Weavers Needle. Ed Piper had several camps in the area through the early 1950s. His last camp was located on a small flat area between the Peralta Trail and the bed of East Boulder Canyon **[4-O, 4.3]**. Piper Spring was also located here.

From Piper Camp **[4-O]**, it is possible to leave the main trail and cross the bed of East Boulder Canyon to the east side. This is where the old trail alignment is shown on the USGS map. Down the canyon a short way is a large flat area that would make a good off-trail campsite **[4-P]**. Farther down the canyon is a section of smooth and pot-holed bedrock in East Boulder near some Fremont cottonwood trees **[4-Q]**. When East Boulder has water, this is a nice place to relax or to use as a destination for a shorter trip.

North on the Peralta Trail, Hill 3113 is the prominent landmark on the horizon. The trail goes up over Granite Saddle **[4-R, 4.8]** and around the west side of Hill 3113 dropping through a pass that overlooks East Boulder Canyon. Near here are some flat areas along the trail that make good, but rather public, camping spots **[W]**. Looking east, you can see the Dutchman's Trail going across Upper Black Top Mesa Pass. Hiking along this ridge line provides fine views of Weavers Needle to the south, spires on the horizon to the southwest, with Yellow Peak and Black Mesa to the north. The old Quarter Circle U Trail (name removed from newer USGS maps) heads down into Little Boulder Canyon from this ridge line. We haven't taken the U Trail route, but we did check out part of the trail. Heading north on the Peralta Trail, before the trail turns east into a switchback **[4-X, 5.9]**, there is a faint trail running up to the ridge. If you want to take the U Trail to West Boulder Canyon, follow the faint trail west about 100 feet to the ridge, then go north along the ridge until the trail intersects a fairly good horse trail heading down the ravine. The trail drops into Boulder Basin connecting with the Dutchman's Trail in about one mile.

Continue down the Peralta Trail switchbacks. At a sharp left turn to the north **[4-Y, 6.1]** there is an old trail, blocked by rocks, heading south along the west bank of East Boulder—also marked on the USGS map. The trail is easy to follow at first, then becomes overgrown in spots, and finally disappears. We continued to bushwhack along the bench where the trail should have been and came out just below the smooth and potholed bedrock area in East Boulder **[4-Q]**. Near the bedrock area we found extensive stone trail-construction for about 20 feet. We don't recommend this abandoned trail unless you like to bushwhack through the "killer" vegetation.

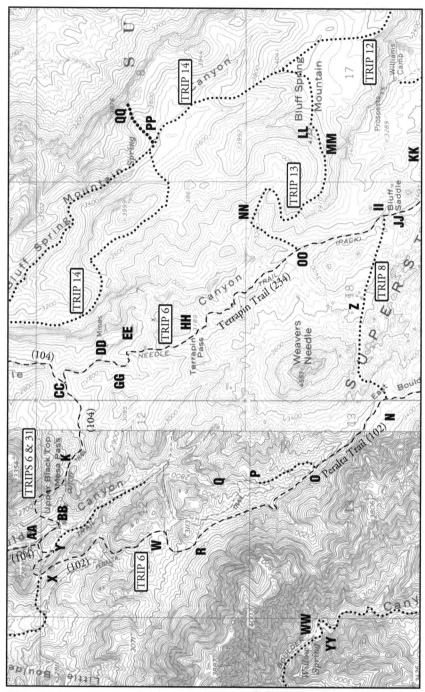

Map 4 - *Trips 4, 6, 7, 8, 19 and 21.*

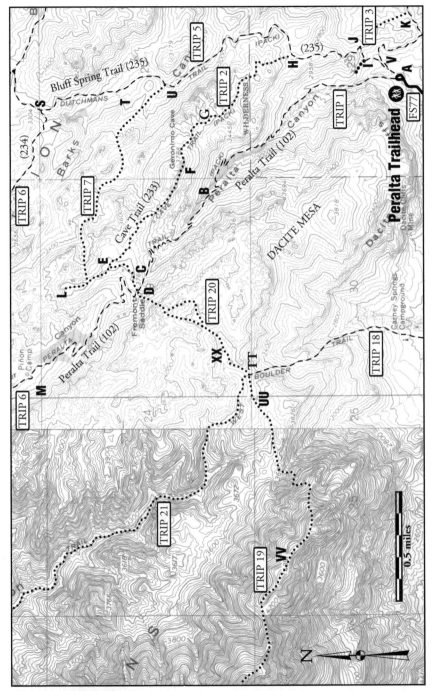

Map 4 continued - *Trips 4, 6, 7, 8, 19 and 21.*

Peralta Trail ends at the intersection with Dutchman's Trail (104) at a wooden trail sign **[4-AA, 6.2]**. As an optional hike down East Boulder Canyon, take the Dutchman's Trail north to see Aylor's Arch, Aylor's Camp area, and the *Horse With Laid Back Ear* formation. Allow an extra hour for the round trip. See Trip 30 for a description of the attractions.

At the Peralta and Dutchman's Trail junction, this hike continues right (south) and soon crosses the bed of East Boulder Canyon **[4-BB, 6.3]**. The trail heads up a long grade going across Upper Black Top Mesa Pass. On the east side of the pass, the Dutchman's Trail intersects the Terrapin Trail (234) at a wooden trail sign **[4-CC, 7.3]**. At the trail junction, go south on the Terrapin Trail. In three-tenths mile the Terrapin Trail crosses Needle Canyon, which usually has seasonal water **[4-DD, 7.6]**. The old Needle Trail goes up the west bank following the Needle Canyon drainage. One of Al Morrow's camps was located near here **[4-EE]**. At the creek crossing **[4-DD]**, this trip leaves the Needle Canyon creek bed. Take the right fork (west) and follow the well-defined horse trail along a small ravine.

Continue up the Terrapin Trail a few minutes. On the west side of the trail you will see a horseshoe-shaped stone wall surrounding the bed of the ravine **[4-GG, 7.7]**. It's about 1.5 feet thick, 3 feet high, 24 feet long, 36 feet wide and made of small stones. We don't know its purpose, but we're guessing it could have been a water-catch basin.

Terrapin Trail heads up and down hill as it crosses several saddles and goes over Terrapin Pass **[4-HH, 8.1]**. On the east side of the trail there are limited views into narrow Needle Canyon while the view to the west eventually opens up to a panoramic vista of Weavers Needle. The jumping off point **[4-II, 9.3]** for the Weavers Needle Crosscut (Trip 8) is about 0.1 mile north of Bluff Saddle **[4-JJ, 9.4]**. From the south side of Bluff Saddle there are some interesting rock formations on the eastern horizon. We named the one that is part of a window, *The Emperors Dog* **[4-KK, 9.5]**. The trail cuts through a scenic area of relatively flat basins circled by low rocky hills.

The intersection with the Bluff Spring Trail is less than 30 minutes ahead. At the Bluff Spring Trail junction **[4-S, 10.1]** turn right (south) and follow the Bluff Spring Trail back to the Peralta Trailhead parking lot **[4-A, 12.4]**. See Trip 5 (Bluff Spring Trail) for a description and any side trips you might want to take from the Bluff Spring Trail junction. From the Bluff Spring and Terrapin Trail junction, allow about one hour and fifteen minutes for the hike back to the parking lot.

HISTORY AND LEGENDS. The two canyons surrounding Weavers Needle, East Boulder Canyon and Needle Canyon are rich in tales of the search for the

Weavers Needle viewed from Piñon Camp in East Boulder Canyon.

Lost Dutchman Mine. A few of the more famous searchers were Maria Jones, Ed Piper, Chuck Aylor, Al Morrow, Barry Storm, Glenn Magill, and Sims Ely. The names of these treasure hunters are memorialized on government maps and in the journals of historians.

In upper East Boulder Canyon, treasure hunter Celeste Maria Jones established her 1949 base camp in the trees at Piñon Camp.[35] Jones was looking for a hidden treasure in Weavers Needle—the Lost Jesuit Gold.[36] Down the trail about a mile north of Piñon Camp, Ed Piper, in the early 1950s, located his mining camp on a small flat area between the Peralta Trail and the bed of East Boulder Canyon. At his camp on the west side of the canyon, he used his skills as a rancher and farmer to grow vegetables, roses and fruit trees.[37]

Bill Sewrey, veteran rockclimber and owner of Desert Mountain Sports, remembers two big army tents at Piper's camp and a trash can in the bed of the creek to catch water—Piper Spring. In 1970 there was a Forest Service sign here—Piper Spring—and everyone considered it a permanent spring.[38] On our recent hikes, we have never found a spring here when the bed of East Boulder was dry.

John Dahlmann recounted his meetings with Ed Piper in the book *A Tiny Bit of God's Creation*. He describes an eight by sixteen foot hut that Piper constructed with four-foot high earthen walls (others recall a low wall) and a tarp roof. There was a drift tunnel at the rear of the hut that ran a few feet into the mountain.[39] *Hunting Lost Mines by Helicopter* by Erle Stanley Gardner shows a picture of this drift, but we haven't seen the drift on our recent hikes to Piper's Camp.[40]

Feuding between the Jones and Piper camps became violent between 1959 and 1962.[41] Robert Sikorsky, in *Quest for the Dutchman's Gold*, wrote

Ed Piper. COURTESY GREGORY DAVIS, SUPERSTITION MOUNTAIN HISTORICAL SOCIETY, *APACHE SENTINEL (1961).*

of his experiences during the early feuding. The Jones camp was situated close to the Piper camp in 1959, about 0.4 mile north of her 1949 location at Piñon Camp. Employed as a geologist by Jones, Sikorsky would occasionally visit with Piper and get water from Piper's Spring. Ed Piper seemed to like him and offered him a job with his crew but Sikorsky did not accept.[42] In the summer of 1959, after the Jones camp received rifle fire from the cliffs above, Sikorsky decided to leave the Jones crew.[43] It was getting dangerous. Later that year, in November, Ed Piper shot and killed Robert St. Marie of the Jones camp, in East Boulder Canyon. Ed Piper testified at the trial that Robert St. Marie pulled a gun from under a coat he was carrying and then he shot St. Marie. Jones testified in court that Piper and his men had them pinned down with rifle fire until dark while they shot-up her camp from the boulders above. Inconsistencies in her story led the jury to uphold Ed Piper's claim of self defense. The feud continued in 1962 when Piper was accused of stealing rifles from the Jones camp while Piper claimed Jones was stealing vegetables from his garden plot. On June 24, rock hunters found Piper incapacitated near his camp and had him helicoptered to Florence where he died of an ulcer on August 12, 1962, at the age of 68.[44] Maria Jones left the Superstitions a few years later without finding the lost treasure.

Although many prospectors welcomed visitors to their camps and often offered coffee or a bite to eat, recollections of shootings and unexplained deaths created an atmosphere of uneasiness. With everyone carrying at least a side arm, the wild west was still alive. The secretive nature of prospecting led some miners to block public access to their claim areas and since there was so much violence in the region, everyone took the warnings seriously. For example, near the start of the Terrapin Trail, author Harry Black, in his book *The Lost Dutchman Mine*, tells of finding a barbed wire fence along the trail in 1972 posted with *Apex Mining Company, Danger, Keep Out*. Harry Black contacted the Forest Service about this closure, and the rangers were successful in having these "improvements" removed.[45]

Many Lost Dutchman Mine researchers have tried to trace the 1875 route of two soldiers who found gold ore on a cross-country trek through the Superstitions from Fort McDowell to the Silver King Mine near the town of Pinal. Barry Storm believes the two soldiers crossed Upper Black Top Mesa Pass and found a partly exposed vein of ore half way up a black-topped hill. That hill could be Black Top Mesa. Barry Storm often refers to Black Top Mesa as the Peralta Mapped Mountain.[46] See Trip 4 for a related soldier incident near the Quarter Circle U Ranch.

Needle Canyon boasted at least six prospector camps established by well-known treasure hunters such as Al Morrow, Barry Storm, and Sims Ely.[47] The Glenn Magill camp was high above, to the east, on Bluff Spring Mountain. Albert Morrow had several camps in Needle Canyon while he prospected and lived in the Superstitions from 1950 until his death in a 1970 mine cave-in. Morrow was one prospector who never carried a gun.[48]

Ed Piper at his camp in East Boulder Canyon near Weavers Needle. Hill 3113 is in the background.
COURTESY GREGORY DAVIS, SUPERSTITION MOUNTAIN HISTORICAL SOCIETY. APACHE SENTINEL, 1961. DORIS J. MATHEWS, EDITOR.

Louis Ruiz, of the Bluebird Mine and Gift Shop, recalls Al Morrow cooking pancakes at his camp for the local Boy Scouts. Morrow would place some dynamite labels near the cooking area and tell the youngsters that a little dynamite added to the batter helped the flavor. Then, as the kids left camp with stomachs full of pancakes, he warned them not to be jumping off any rocks![49] In his 1957 book, *Famous Lost Gold Mines of Arizona's Superstition Mountains,* Albert Morrow expresses his feelings for the Superstition Mountains, "I have found it a place of wonder and solitude where I could think clearly, enjoy the wonders of nature and occupy myself in a pursuit that is interesting as well as healthful."[50]

Upper Barks Canyon

This is a challenging hike where you scramble among the boulders on the west side of Barks Canyon. Your hike through difficult terrain will be rewarded with solitude among the towering rock formations.

ITINERARY: This is an experts-only loop hike starting at Peralta Trailhead on the Bluff Spring Trail (235), leaving the trail at Barks Canyon and following a very rugged route, north up Barks Canyon to the summit near Fremont Saddle. From Fremont Saddle, descend south on Peralta Trail (102) for the easiest return to the parking lot or follow the Cave Trail (233) south connecting with Bluff Spring Trail and proceed south to the Peralta Trailhead parking lot.

DIFFICULTY: Very difficult. Experts only. Must use map and compass. Requires basic rock bouldering skills and strong, positive mental attitude. Not recommended for horses. Elevation change ±1560 feet.

LENGTH and TIME: 5.5 miles, 6 hours round trip.

MAPS: Weavers Needle, Arizona USGS topo map.
Superstition Wilderness Tonto National Forest map.

FINDING THE TRAIL: Leave the northeast corner of the Peralta Trailhead parking lot, go right (east), and cross the Peralta Canyon creek bed. Walk north about 50 yards up the path to a trail intersection and take the Bluff Spring Trail to the left (north).

THE HIKE: *Use Map 4.* This is a hike for experts only. The most difficult part of the hike is near the summit, before you top out at Fremont Saddle. Some of the rock bouldering requires you to commit yourself to climbing up the cliffs without the choice of returning the way you came. No technical rock climbing or special equipment is required, but you must be skilled in rock bouldering and Class 3 climbing. This means you must be comfortable with pulling yourself up short stretches of steep rock. If you don't understand these terms, don't attempt this hike.

There is no water available on this route so be sure to carry enough. From Peralta Trailhead **[4-A, 0]**, hike northeast on the Bluff Spring Trail until it crosses Bark Canyon (see Trip 5). At Bark Canyon **[4-U, 1.6]** there is a trail on your left (west) that skirts the side of a small hill. Many people mistake this for the Bluff Spring Trail so it is not hard to find. This is the point where Bluff Spring Trail follows the creek bed. Take the trail west and follow it, for about 0.1 mile, until it disappears and turns into meandering game trails. From here you are on your own.

We have suggested one route on the map, but there are other possibilities. If you hike like we do, each trip through here will be slightly different. Don't feel that you have to follow the line we have marked on the map. The brush on some of the hills is thick, and the ravines are full of impassable vegetation. Pick your route by line of sight heading in a northwesterly direction up toward the boulders and cliffs. When you are among house-sized boulders, the walking will become easier, and you will start to experience the presence of the huge monoliths around you. From here to the top is the best part of the hike and also the most challenging. On some sections of the route, you will be required to pull yourself up and over ledges and steep stretches of rock. We find it impossible to retrace the route backward, down these rocks. A word of caution—do not climb up and find there is no exit. Your ability to make the correct route-selection decisions is essential. Don't try this hike unless you are an expert hiker.

Bill Sewrey on the first ascent of The Glory Road route, Barks Canyon Wall, April 1966. PHOTOGRAPH BY DAVE OLSON. COURTESY BILL SEWREY, DESERT MOUNTAIN SPORTS.

The contours of the terrain will keep you headed in a northwesterly direction. Near the top you may see some large cairns or claim markers that tend to direct you to an intersection with the Weavers Needle overlook trail. You may have to look around here a bit to find a break in the cliff to get up to the trail. Once on top of the cliffs, take the Weavers Needle overlook trail south to Fremont Saddle **[4-D, 3.2]**. Return to Peralta Trailhead via Trip 1 on the Peralta Trail **[4-A, 5.5]** or Trip 2 on the Cave Trail **[4-A, 5.9]**.

Weavers Needle Crosscut

This seldom used trek takes you around the south side of Weavers Needle. A game trail through a narrow ravine allows the hiker to connect the Terrapin Trail to East Boulder Canyon. This trek provides the experienced hiker with another option for loop hikes near Weavers Needle.

ITINERARY: This route connects the Terrapin Trail (234) near Bluff Saddle with the Peralta Canyon Trail (102) in East Boulder Canyon via a route along the south side of Weavers Needle.

DIFFICULTY: Moderate. Requires route finding ability and some bouldering. Not suitable for horses. Elevation change is +280 and -500 feet.

LENGTH and TIME: 1.0 mile, 0.75 hours one-way.

MAPS: Weavers Needle, Arizona USGS topo map.
Superstition Wilderness Tonto National Forest map.

FINDING THE TRAIL: The route starts on the Terrapin Trail in Needle Canyon just north of Bluff Saddle.

THE HIKE: *Use Map 4.* This is a very useful route (no trail) for creating loop hikes in the Weavers Needle area. We normally hike this route in the east-west direction. The contour of the terrain makes the route finding considerably more difficult when traversed in the west-east direction.

About 0.1 mile north of Bluff Saddle on the Terrapin Trail (234), leave the Terrapin Trail and head in a westerly direction **[4-II, 0]**. Head up the first hill to the left, south, of a large solid rectangular-boulder pile on the horizon. Then select the easiest route by line of sight through the rocky terrain. From a high point, look down into the small basin southeast of Weavers Needle **[4-Z, 0.4]**. From this basin the route goes up a small ravine on the south side of Weavers Needle. There are several small game trails here. We usually start on the right, north, side of the ravine and then pick the path with the least vegetation. The ravine reaches a saddle and then descends into the East Boulder Canyon drainage. As you are going down, look to the left (south) for a slab of rock that has broken from the wall creating a large passageway. We always leave the ravine at this point and walk through this passageway which comes out on the slopes above East Boulder Canyon. As an alternate, you can continue down the ravine, but we believe that is more difficult. On the slopes above East Boulder Canyon, you need to exercise some caution since there are some steep cliff areas here. At this point you need to select a line of sight route down through the boulders and slabs to the bed of East Boulder Canyon and then west a few yards up to the Peralta Trail. You will need to do some bouldering and scrambling on loose rocks, but the descent requires no technical rock climbing equipment. Be careful and take your time. This route ends on the Peralta Trail (102) near the site of the 1959 Celeste Maria Jones camp[51] in East Boulder Canyon **[4-N, 1.0]**.

HISTORY AND LEGENDS. Bill Sewrey is a well-known outdoorsmen in the Arizona rock-climbing and hiking community. He has hiked and climbed in the Superstitions since the early 1960s and still finds time for a relaxing trip

Maria Jones posted this sign on the southeast side of Weavers Needle. Photograph by Bill Sewrey, December 1966. Courtesy Desert Mountain Sports, Phoenix, Arizona.

to the Wilderness. Sewrey has been the owner of the Desert Mountain Sports store in Phoenix since 1970 and is known for his friendly advice and fair opinions. He was exploring the Superstitions when well-known prospectors such as Jones, Piper, and Magill were scratching the earth for that elusive Lost Dutchman treasure in the 1960s. He recalls many encounters with these colorful characters. Sewrey gained his technical rock-climbing expertise in the days before all the high-tech hardware. Between 1964 and 1969, Sewrey is credited with at least seven first-ascents on the crags near Lost Dutchman State Park, Barks Canyon, and Miners Needle.[52]

During her quest for the Lost Jesuit Gold, treasure hunter Maria Jones concentrated her searches on the well-known spire, Weavers Needle. Bill

Sewrey had occasion to meet Maria Jones and her men near Weavers Needle in the early 1960s. Sewrey and friends were interested in technical rock-climbing on the Needle and one day asked Jones if she would let them climb the spire. She said okay, but she wanted them to call her Phoenix residence before their attempt. Sewrey called several times and Jones always refused permission. Finally they decided to go anyway—permission or not. Wasn't this public land? From the base of Weavers Needle in East Boulder Canyon they hiked up the west slope into the gully of the Needle. A Jones henchman approached the climbers as they prepared to ascend the Needle. He was armed with a knife and revolver—a grubby sort of fellow and not pleasant. He told them to leave the area, but after much disagreeable discussion the climbers proceeded, ignoring the threats. A little while later rocks came raining down on them. Apparently the Jones men climbed the Needle by the east face route and got above the climbers so they could tumble rocks off the cliff. After the rocks stopped, the climbers continued up the west gully, around the chock stone, and up to the top of Weavers Needle where they met the Jones men again and eventually found something in common to talk about. The Jones men wanted to know more about their rock climbing techniques. Sewrey and the other climbers were happy to show them everything they knew. From that point on, there were no more confrontations with the Jones camp.[53]

Bill Sewrey remembers every time they walked by the Jones camp, Maria would give them a look that seemed to say, "There they go again, what can you do?" Sewrey recalls that Jones eventually found a use for them and asked him and some others to come over to her house on Van Buren Street in Phoenix. He knocked on the door and one of her armed men answered. With arms folded, wearing a revolver and knife, just like in the Superstitions, he nodded them inside with a gesture of his head. They were motioned into the kitchen where they sat down at a table with a human skull. A candle was mounted inside the skull to light the room. It all seemed a bit melodramatic. Jones sat on one side of the table and explained her plan. She wanted Sewrey and the others to climb Weavers Needle and rappel off the north face to check out a notch in the rock. The treasure was supposed to be located there. A mining engineer employed by Jones was also to rappel with them. Sewrey said they needed to give the mining engineer some lessons in rappelling or he would be useless out on the cliff and would probably kill himself. The expedition never came off but rock climbers Doug Black and Bill Forrest, at a later date, made an agreement to do the work for Jones. They never got paid. Jones seemed to have a reputation for not paying the climbers.[54]

Charlebois Spring – Loop 1

This hike takes you through the heart of the Wilderness to Charlebois Spring where many prospectors, ranchers and explorers have established their camps. The "Master Map" petroglyphs are located nearby. Many short excursions are possible from this area including Peters Mesa, Music Canyon and La Barge Canyon.

ITINERARY: This is the most direct hike to Charlebois Spring. Take the Bluff Spring Trail (235) to Bluff Spring, then connect with the Dutchman's Trail (104) and follow it into La Barge Canyon down to Charlebois Spring. Return the same way or through Needle Canyon on the Terrapin Trail (234) or through East Boulder Canyon on the Peralta Trail (102).

DIFFICULTY: Difficult day hike due to length. Moderate overnight. All trail hiking. Elevation change is +1160 and -960 feet.

LENGTH and TIME: 7.0 miles, 3.25 hours to Charlebois Spring one-way.

MAPS: Weavers Needle, Arizona USGS topo map.
Goldfield, Arizona USGS topo map.
Superstition Wilderness Tonto National Forest map.

FINDING THE TRAIL: Leave the northeast corner of the Peralta Trailhead parking lot, go right (east), and cross the Peralta Canyon creek bed. Walk north about 50 yards up the path to a trail intersection and take the Bluff Spring Trail to the left (north).

THE HIKE: *Use Maps 3 and 5.* This is the most direct way to get to Charlebois Spring from Peralta Trailhead **[3-A, 0]**. Start the hike by following Trip 5 (Bluff Spring Trail) to Bluff Spring Canyon **[3-P, 3.4]**. There may be water at Bluff Spring but you have to push your way through the brush to get back to the spring area. The pipes from the spring into the cement water basin have been broken for many years.

From Bluff Spring follow the Dutchman's Trail (104) north through Bluff Spring Canyon. The trail leaves the drainage and contours along the

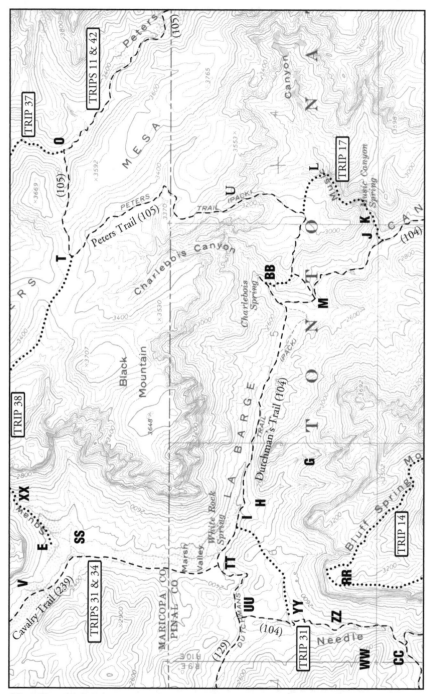

Map 5 - *Trips 9, 10, 11, 12, 13, 14 and 17.*

Hiker's Guide to the Superstition Wilderness

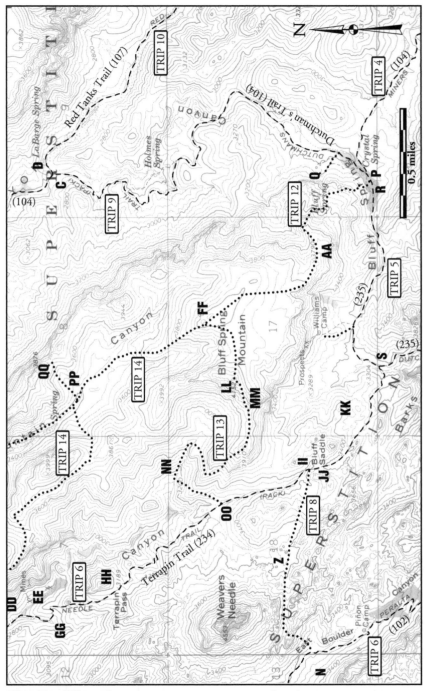

Map 5 continued - *Trips 9, 10, 11, 12, 13, 14 and 17.*

Author and treasure hunter Barry Storm set up a camp in La Barge Canyon near Charlebois Spring in 1938. Courtesy Superstition Mountain Historical Society, John Burbridge Collection.

western hillside. At La Barge Canyon **[5-C, 5.6]** it is normally possible to obtain water at La Barge Spring **[5-D]** since it is one of the more reliable springs. The spring is about 200 yards northeast of the trail intersection with the Red Tanks Trail (107). The spring is on the east bank in a large grove of trees. The hike continues down La Barge Canyon, passing Music Canyon and the seasonal Music Canyon Spring. Peters Trail (105) enters from the northeast **[5-M, 6.6]**. Continue on the Dutchman's Trail as it turns north into Charlebois Canyon. Charlebois Spring is a short distance north of the Dutchman's Trail in Charlebois Canyon **[5-BB, 7.0]**. Return the same way to Peralta Trailhead **[3-A, 14.0]**.

OPTIONS FOR RETURN TRIP. The alternate return leaves Charlebois Spring **[5-BB, 7.0]** on the Dutchman's Trail (104) heading west, down La Barge Canyon. The trail passes the Cavalry Trail (239) intersection **[5-TT, 8.6]** and then turns south into Needle Canyon to the junction **[5-UU, 8.9]** with the Bull Pass Trail (129). Continue west on the Dutchman's Trail to the junction **[5-CC, 9.8]** with the Terrapin Trail (234) where you have a choice to return via the Terrapin Trail or to continue on the Dutchman's Trail over to East Boulder Canyon and then head South in East Boulder Canyon on the Peralta Trail (102). In both cases you should read the descriptions for Trip 6 (East Boulder–Needle Canyon Loop) and Trip 31 (Marsh Valley Loop). The return distance, from Charlebois Spring, for the Terrapin Trail trek is 7.9 miles and the return distance using East Boulder Canyon on the Peralta Trail is 10 miles.

HISTORY AND LEGENDS. Since Charlebois Spring (locally pronounced "shar-le-boy") is a fairly reliable spring, it has been a natural destination and base camp for prospectors, ranchers and outfitters. Tom Kollenborn reported the history of the area in a 1992 *Superstition Mountain Journal* article titled "Superstition Mountain Place Names." The spring was originally named Black Mountain Spring and later renamed for cattleman Martin Charlebois who lived in a cabin here. The French name is often anglicized to *Charlie Boy.* After Charlebois' cabin burned in the early 1920s, rancher Tex Barkley rebuilt it, and then in 1948 it was moved to Bluff Spring where it remained until 1962.[55]

La Barge Canyon and Spring are probably named after Phil La Barge who was Charlebois' partner. The cement water trough at La Barge spring is inscribed with the date 7-1-39.

South of Charlebois Spring are the petroglyphs that many believe to be the Spanish (Peralta) Master Map detailing the location of 18 gold mines.[56] Others believe they are Indian petroglyphs. They are on a south-facing cliff at ground level next to La Barge Creek. They are not difficult to find and there is a Forest Service sign marking the location. If you stop to look at them, don't deface them or even touch them. Take pictures only.

While at Charlebois Spring you should review Trip 31 (Marsh Valley Loop), Trip 37 (Peters Canyon Loop), and the Peters Mesa Area trips for things to do in these nearby locations.

Some believe these petroglyphs in La Barge Canyon are the Spanish (Peralta) Master Map.

Charlebois Spring — Loop 2

Like Charlebois Spring–Loop 1, this hike takes you through the heart of the Wilderness to Charlebois Spring on a wider trek than described in Trip 9 (Loop 1). We like this itinerary because it takes you past Miners Needle and down Whiskey Spring Canyon. A short side trip to Trap Canyon is worthwhile when there is seasonal water at the spring.

ITINERARY: This hike follows the Dutchman's Trail (104) from Peralta Trailhead, to Miners Summit, down Whiskey Spring Trail (238), and into La Barge Canyon. Follow the Red Tanks Trail (107) northwest to La Barge Spring, connect with the Dutchman's Trail (104) and hike northwest to Charlebois Spring. Return on the Bluff Springs Trail (235), or through Needle Canyon on the Terrapin Trail (234) or through East Boulder Canyon on the Peralta Trail (102).

Difficulty: Difficult day hike due to length. Moderate overnight. All trail hiking. Elevation change is +1280 and -1080 feet.

LENGTH and TIME: 9.9 mile, 5 hours to Charlebois Spring one-way.

MAPS: Weavers Needle, Arizona USGS topo map.
Goldfield, Arizona USGS topo map.
Superstition Wilderness Tonto National Forest map.

FINDING THE TRAIL: Leave the northeast corner of the Peralta Trailhead parking lot, go right (east), and cross the Peralta Canyon creek bed. Walk north about 50 yards up the path to a trail intersection and take the Dutchman's Trail to the right (east).

THE HIKE: *Use Maps 3 and 5.* We think this is a more interesting route, compared to Trip 9 (Charlebois Spring Hike–Loop 1) and it still allows you to return on the Bluff Spring Trail. Start the hike from Peralta Trailhead **[3-A, 0]** by following Trip 4 (Bluff Spring Loop) to Miners Summit **[3-O, 4.3]**. From Miners Summit follow the Whiskey Spring Trail (238) along the ridge line east and then down into Whiskey Canyon. Trip 15 (Whiskey Spring Trail) describes the features of this area. Whiskey Spring **[3-W, 5.6]** has had water the times we hiked there, but others said it can dry up. Check with the Forest Service about the water conditions before you go.

Not far down canyon from the spring, Whiskey Spring Canyon intersects La Barge Canyon **[3-X, 6.3]**. When leaving Whiskey Spring Canyon, the best trail takes you a few hundred yards upstream into La Barge and then a faint trail crosses the creek bed, goes up on the north bench and heads westerly. This hike goes northwest following La Barge Canyon downstream on the Red Tanks Trail (107). The trail system here is not well defined so just look for the easiest walking.

Hermann Petrash had one of his camps here on the north side of La Barge Canyon below the mountain named after him—Herman Mountain. La Barge Canyon has seasonal water. If the sandy bed of La Barge is dry, there may be some water in the pot holes upstream in the narrow canyon area known as the Upper Box. Trip 11 (Charlebois Spring Hike–Loop 3) goes through the Upper Box.

This hike continues down La Barge Canyon a short distance where it crosses a small wash from the north **[3-Y, 7.2]**. This is Trap Canyon which is a pleasant side trip if there is water in the spring and canyon. See Trip 16 (Trap Canyon) for a description. There are several trails here, on either side of the wash, that lead into Trap Canyon. After the trail ends you can continue along the bed of the wash in Trap Canyon.

Further down La Barge Canyon is La Barge Spring which is usually a reliable water source **[5-D 8.4]**. Look for the spring and cement trough on the east bank in a thick grove of trees. Another 200 yards brings you to the end of the Red Tanks Trail (107) **[5-C, 8.5]** where it connects with the well-defined Dutchman's Trail (104) on the northwest corner of the junction with Bluff Spring Canyon. The hike now follows the Dutchman's Trail northeast, down La Barge Canyon, passing Music Canyon and the seasonal Music Canyon Spring. The Dutchman's Trail passes the Peters Trail (105) intersection **[5-M, 9.5]** and continues to Charlebois Spring **[5-BB, 9.9]**. Charlebois Spring is a short distance north of the Dutchman's Trail in Charlebois Canyon.

See Trip 9 (Charlebois Spring Hike–Loop 1) for a description and history of the Charlebois Spring area as well as the options for the return trek.

Charlebois Spring – Loop 3

This hike takes you on a wide loop to Charlebois Spring over trails that are lightly traveled. Seasonal water in La Barge and Peters canyons provides ideal camping, along the trail, where you can enjoy a good degree of solitude.

ITINERARY: This hike follows the Dutchman's Trail (104) from Peralta Trailhead, to Miners Summit. From here Whiskey Spring Trail (238) connects to the Red Tanks Trail (107) taking you east through Upper La Barge Box. The Hoolie Bacon Trail (111) heads north toward a pass into Peters Canyon connecting with Peters Trail (105) via a cross-country trek. Peters Trail takes you up to Peters Mesa and down Charlebois Canyon to the Dutchman's Trail (104). Charlebois Spring is a short distance to the north on the Dutchman's Trail. Return on the Bluff Springs Trail (235), or through Needle Canyon on the Terrapin Trail (234), or through East Boulder Canyon on the Peralta Trail (102).

DIFFICULTY: Moderate overnight. Almost all trail hiking. Much too long to do in one day. Not recommended for horses. Elevation change is +2800 and -2600 feet.

LENGTH and TIME: 15.2 miles, 7.75 hours to Charlebois Spring one-way.

MAPS: Weavers Needle, Arizona USGS topo map.
Goldfield, Arizona USGS topo map.
Superstition Wilderness Tonto National Forest map.

FINDING THE TRAIL: Leave the northeast corner of the Peralta Trailhead parking lot, go right (east), and cross the Peralta Canyon creek bed. Walk north about 50 yards up the path to a trail intersection and take the Dutchman's Trail to the right (east).

THE HIKE: *Use Maps 3, 5, and 6.* This hike is too long for a day trip but makes an enjoyable two or three day overnight hike that takes you through some lesser traveled regions of the Wilderness. From the Peralta Trailhead

[3-A, 0], start the hike by following Bluff Spring Loop (Trip 4) to Miners Summit **[3-0, 4.3]**. From Miners Summit follow the Whiskey Spring Trail (238) along the ridge line east and then down into Whiskey Canyon. Trip 15 (Whiskey Spring Trail) describes the features of this area. Whiskey Spring **[3-W, 5.6]** normally has water but it can dry up. Check with the Forest Service about the water conditions before you go.

Not far down canyon from Whiskey Spring, Whiskey Spring Canyon intersects La Barge Canyon **[6-X, 6.3]**. This hike turns right (east) following the Red Tanks Trail (107) into La Barge Canyon and through the narrow section named the Upper Box. Some pot holes in the bedrock here have seasonal water. The Hoolie Bacon Trail (111) enters **[6-B, 7.8]** the Red Tanks Trail from the north at the east end of Upper La Barge Box. Turn left (north) on the Hoolie Bacon Trail and follow it past Trap Canyon **[6-E, 8.9]** until the trail starts heading north **[6-N, 9.2]** in Horse Camp Basin. Starting at a wash which enters from the east **[6-N]**, the hike takes a cross-country route on a unmaintained trail, goes over the pass **[6-00, 10.1]** west of Horse Camp Basin, and drops down into Peters Canyon **[6-QQ, 10.5]**. Allow extra time along this route for getting lost and for exploring the Horse Camp Basin area. Although Kane Spring **[6-KK]** is not on the hike itinerary, it may be worth checking if you need water. Kane Spring is about a mile to the north

Prospector Hermann Petrash. Herman Mountain is named for him. PHOTOGRAPH BY CARL BODERICK, COURTESY SUPERSTITION MOUNTAIN HISTORICAL SOCIETY.

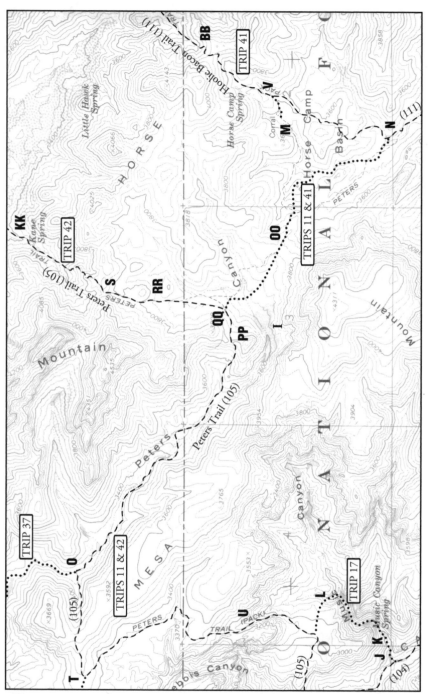

Map 6 - *Trips 11 and 16.*

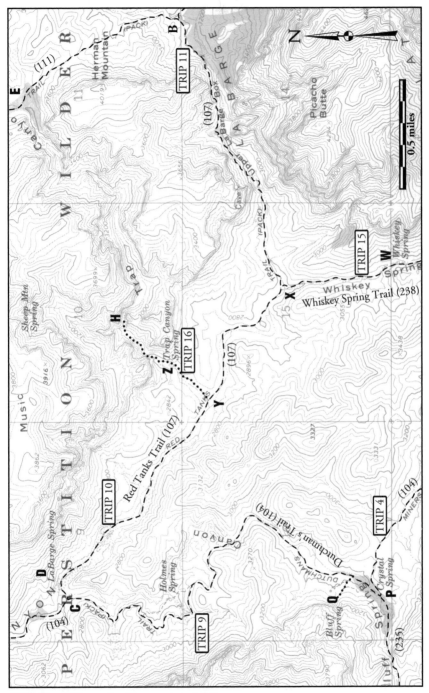

Map 6 continued - *Trips 11 and 16.*

on the other side of the hill. Ask the Forest Service about the water conditions before you go.

Once you are in Peters Canyon **[6-QQ]**, look for Peters Trail (105) on the north side of the drainage. The trail continues over a low pass **[6-PP, 10.6]** to the north of the knob on the horizon, and goes down canyon, crossing the wash several times, to a point **[6-O, 12.3]** where the trail heads left (west) up a ravine to Peters Mesa **[5-T, 12.8]**. See Trip 37 (Peters Canyon Loop) for a description of lower Peters Canyon.

The trail is faint in some places on top of Peters Mesa so it is best to locate the trail before proceeding south from Peters Mesa. See Trips 38 and 39 (Peters Mesa Area) for the history of this region. After losing the trail and then spotting some water in the Charlebois drainage, one of the authors decided to go straight down Charlebois Canyon. That was a big mistake. Charlebois Canyon is filled with house-sized boulders and vegetation for about a quarter mile.

As the trail descends into La Barge drainage, you will see a rock wall **[6-U]** built across the ravine. Tom Kollenborn suggested that the rock wall is a drift fence used to control cattle. Peters Trail ends **[5-M, 14.8]** in La Barge Canyon when it intersects with the Dutchman's Trail (104). Go right (west) on the Dutchman's Trail as it turns into Charlebois Canyon. The spring is a short distance north of the Dutchman's Trail in Charlebois Canyon **[5-BB, 15.2]**.

See Trip 9 (Charlebois Spring–Loop 1) for a description and history of the Charlebois Spring area. The return routes are also described in Trip 9.

HISTORY AND LEGENDS. For Sims Ely's stories about the Mexican camps, cut mine timber, and the Spanish Trails, see Trip 43.

Bluff Spring Mountain Area

From Peralta Trailhead take the 7.0 mile Bluff Spring Trail (235) to Bluff Spring Canyon. The trail description for the Bluff Spring Mountain Area starts near the intersection of the Bluff Spring Trail (235) and the Dutchman's Trail (104) in Bluff Spring Canyon.

FINDING THE TRAILHEAD. *Use Map 5.* The south end of the Bluff Spring Mountain Area is easily reached from the Peralta Trailhead via the Bluff Spring Trail (Trip 5). The Bluff Spring Mountain Area directions start from the junction of the Bluff Spring Trail and Dutchman's Trail in Bluff Canyon on the north side of the wash at the wooden trail sign **[5-P]**.

THE TRAILS. The old horse trail, Ely-Anderson Trail (Trip 12), is the best approach to the top of Bluff Spring Mountain. Other hiker routes off the top of the mountain are possible after you become familiar with the area. Hiking on Bluff Spring Mountain is for experienced hikers only. Unmaintained trails, loose and moving rock and exposed cliffs are true hazards here.

HISTORY AND LEGENDS. Bluff Spring Mountain became a topic of interest when Jimmy Anderson made the discovery of a trail in 1911. He reported the discovery to Sims Ely, general manager of the Salt River User's Association, who had collected information from other sources about a legend of an unnamed mountain where Mexicans grazed horses and mules while tending to their mining activities. Sims Ely connected the legend to the rediscovered trail and along with rancher Jim Bark and cowhand Jimmy Anderson explored the area. They concluded that Bluff Spring Mountain could be the site of Mexican activity in the 1800s.[57]

Walter Gassler was exploring the Bluff Spring Mountain area in 1936 but he did not report any important discoveries.[58] It wasn't until May 5, 1966, when private investigator, Glenn Magill, and his partners filed *The Dutchman* claim on the northwest side of Bluff Spring Mountain that national interest was aroused in another attempt at locating the Lost

Dutchman Mine.[59] Glenn Magill's adventures are described in Curt Gentry's book *Killer Mountains*. Tucson KCUB radio announcer George Scott made

View of Weavers Needle from the top of the Ely-Anderson Trail on Bluff Spring Mountain.

an on-site broadcast from *The Dutchman* claim and prominent Dutchman aficionados were interviewed about the discovery.[60] One photograph in Helen Corbin's book, *The Curse of the Dutchman's Gold*, shows Bob Corbin being interviewed by Scott at the mine.[60] Bob Corbin, former Arizona Attorney General, has been a prominent figure in the search for the Lost Dutchman Mine since 1957. Corbin has written the foreword for many of the books published on the subject. He is still an active speaker and aficionado of the legends and history of the region.

Glenn Magill used Adolph Ruth's famous maps to locate *The Dutchman* mine. Ruth's son, Erwin, supplied Magill with copies of the original Ruth-Gonzales maps. See the "First Water Trailhead" description for the story of Adolph Ruth. Magill's men set up a camp that looked into Needle Canyon from an overhanging ledge near a large flat area on the north end of Bluff Springs Mountain.[62] The pit that Magill's partners uncovered had walls of blackish stone while the fill material was a reddish sandstone. The fill-material rocks were laid out in rows and a cement-like seal was found farther down. Under a second seal at a depth of 25 feet, the fill material changed to mine tailings and timbers in the pit, all of which led Magill to speculate that this was one of the mines covered over by the Apache in the mid 1800s. After more work they found the pit to be void of gold. The vein was played out. Shortly after the pit was uncovered, someone set off Magill's store of dynamite which filled the pit with rubble.[63] The Forest Service has more recently performed restoration work to fill in the diggings.

John Dahlmann in his 1979 book, *A Tiny Bit of God's Creation*, describes his many trail rides across Bluff Spring Mountain starting up the Ely-Anderson Trail (Old Spanish Trail) on the south and descending a steep route to the north into Marsh Valley. We haven't taken Dahlmann's route off the north side but we understand it is now badly eroded and is not suitable for horses. Dahlmann never located the site of Magill's diggings while searching on Bluff Spring Mountain between 1966 and 1977. Dahlmann accompanied artist Ted De Grazia on trail rides here on Bluff Spring Mountain as well as throughout the Superstition Wilderness. Dahlmann's book will be of special interest to horse riders for fascinating tales of his Superstition Wilderness trail rides.

Tom Kollenborn's map shows the location of prospector Al Reser's camp (February 18, 1984) just south of the spring in Bluff Spring Mountain Canyon.[64] The Wilderness was closed to new mining claims just two months before—December 31, 1983.

Ely-Anderson Trail

This is a historic hike on a trail discovered in 1911 by cowhand Jimmy Anderson. Many people call it the Mexican or Spanish Trail. The cliffs of Bluff Spring Mountain surround a long open valley often referred to as Hidden Valley. There are good views into Hidden Valley from the summit and a feeling of openness surrounds you as you look across the landscape.

ITINERARY: This hike starts at the south end of Bluff Spring Mountain on an old horse trail that leads to a viewpoint summit overlooking Bluff Spring Mountain Canyon (Hidden Valley). After exploring the top of Bluff Spring Mountain, return by the same trail or take the Southwest Route (Trip 13) into Needle Canyon (Trip 6).

DIFFICULTY: Moderate. Requires route finding ability. Not recommended for horses. Elevation change is +1041 feet.

LENGTH and TIME: 1.2 miles, 1.5 hours one-way.

MAPS: Weavers Needle, Arizona USGS topo map.
Superstition Wilderness Tonto National Forest map.

FINDING THE TRAIL: *Use Map 5.* The hike starts in Bluff Spring Canyon. From the wooden sign **[5-P]** at the intersection of the Bluff Spring Trail and Dutchman's Trail, walk west for one minute on the Bluff Spring Trail **[5-R]**. This distance is less than 80 yards. There are no signs, rock cairns or evidence of a trail intersection at the beginning of the Ely-Anderson Trail. The Ely-Anderson Trail starts about 30 feet before the Bluff Spring Trail crosses the Bluff Spring Canyon wash **[5-R]**. Turn right (north) and walk up the slope, about 100 feet, along the eroding bank of the Bluff Spring Canyon wash. In this area you should start to see some rock cairns and evidence of a trail. The trail heads north up the slope.

Near the start of the trail **[5-R]**, there is a juniper tree on the south side of Bluff Springs Trail and two tall, skinny, Fremont cottonwood trees in the wash. Also, two saguaro cacti can be used as landmarks on the north side of Bluff Springs Trail. The first is a tall, single pole saguaro without arms. It is about 100 feet east of the start of the Ely-Anderson Trail. The second is a standing saguaro skeleton up on the slope about 100 feet west of the Ely-Anderson Trail. These landmarks will of course change with time, but they should be of some help in the short term.

THE HIKE: *Use Map 5.* From the Bluff Spring Trail **[5-R, 0, 3020]**, the hike goes up the slope of Bluff Spring Mountain heading directly north and then slowly turns west as it follows the natural contours of the terrain. The trail becomes easier to follow as it ascends. The buff-colored rock is worn through to the underlying white base when the trail crosses stretches of smooth rock. Remember that this is an old horse trail so the grade is not very steep for hikers, and no rock climbing is necessary. Several authors have written tales of experienced horse riders having problems on this trail due to the steepness and exposed cliffs.

Near the top, a small cave in the ravine to the north can be seen from the trail when the trail turns southwest. At the top of the cliffs the trail passes through a short section of stone wall **[5-AA, 0.7, 3760]**. Some hikers may have difficulty finding the top of the trail on the return trip, so you should take a look at the surrounding landmarks before you leave the rock wall. Look for Miners Needle to the south. There's a good view of the window in the needle along several sections of this trail. Weavers Needle is to the west.

From the stone wall, the trail continues north and quickly becomes faint with overgrown grass. Within a quarter mile, the trail disappears and the route continues across the grassy rolling hills. The horizon is broken only by the towering stalks of the century plant and sotol. If you continue north toward a high point on the mesa **[5-FF, 1.2, 4041]** you will be rewarded with a fine view of Bluff Spring Mountain Canyon also know as Hidden Valley. The open views down into the valley and beyond the ramparts of Bluff Spring Mountain will please everyone. The hike description ends here but you can continue to explore the area before returning on the same trail or by the Southwest Route (Trip 13).

HISTORY AND LEGENDS. This hike follows a trail that is believed to be the trail used by the Mexican miners in the mid 1800s. Horses and mules may have been driven to the top of Bluff Spring Mountain along this route. It has been suggested that this ideal grazing area on top of the mountain could be protected from Apache raids with as few as six men with rifles. The trail was rediscovered by Jimmy Anderson, one of Jim Barks' cowhands, in 1911.[65] The worn rock along the trail is evidence of heavy use in the past, although not necessarily heavy use by Mexican miners as Sims Ely suggests.

The tall stalks of the sotol (spoon plant) make a showy display on the desert vistas.

Sims Ely in his 1953 book, *The Lost Dutchman Mine*, tells the story of the rediscovered trail in detail.[66] Sims Ely searched for the Lost Dutchman Mine in the early 1900s with rancher Jim Bark. Ely is pronounced "ee-lee."

Some authors refer to the Ely-Anderson Trail as the Mexican or Spanish Trail. Glenn Magill referred to it as the Ely-Anderson Trail on one of his maps and we think that is a more appropriate name since these were the men who discovered the trail and made it famous.[67]

At the top of the Ely-Anderson Trail there is a stone wall running across the hillside. The wall, when viewed from the top of the mountain, is very low to the ground due to the steepness of the slope. This wall might have been used as a drift fence in the 1900s to keep cattle off the mountain, rather than as a fortification for defense or an enclosure to keep Mexican mules on top of the mountain in the 1800s.

Southwest Route

From the top of Bluff Spring Mountain there are several hiker routes that connect to the Forest Service trail system. This hike connects with the Terrapin Trail in Needle Canyon and provides spectacular views of Weavers Needle and the surrounding countryside. Off-trail hikers will enjoy this trek.

ITINERARY: The hike starts on top of Bluff Spring Mountain at the summit of the Ely-Anderson horse trail (Trip 12). A hiker route leads off the southwest side of the mountain into Needle Canyon connecting with the Terrapin Trail (234) where the hike description ends.

DIFFICULTY: Difficult. Requires route finding ability on steep terrain and is for experienced hikers only. Not recommended for horses. Elevation change is +232 and -1073 feet.

LENGTH and TIME: 1.7 miles, 1.5 hours one-way.

MAPS: Weavers Needle, Arizona USGS topo map. Superstition Wilderness Tonto National Forest map.

FINDING THE TRAIL: *Use Map 5.* This hike starts on top of Bluff Spring Mountain near the USGS 4041 elevation notation **[5-FF, 4041]**.

THE HIKE: *Use Map 5.* There are no trails on this route. From the end of the Ely-Anderson Trip **[5-FF, 0, 4041]**, walk south and then west taking advantage of the flat ridge as you walk toward the high point of Bluff Spring Mountain **[5-LL, 0.4, 4152]**. The ground is heavily marked by the hooves of deer along this route. From the top of Bluff Spring Mountain **[5-LL]**, you can look down into the canyons to see the spectacular colors and jagged rocks which aren't evident when looking up from the trails below. The view of Weavers Needle across to the west is impressive since this vantage point is almost 400 feet higher than Fremont Saddle and just 400 feet below the top of Weavers Needle.

Before descending Bluff Spring Mountain, visually locate the Terrapin Trail (234) in Needle Canyon and try to imagine where you will intersect the

---

trail **[5-OO]**. From the high point **[5-LL, 0.4, 4152]**, there is more than one way to descend into Needle Canyon, but the easiest is to walk south, then west through a break **[5-MM, 0.5]** in the ridge and rocks. Follow the contours of the terrain and select a route of your choice either along the ridge line or directly into the bowl of the ravine. The ridge line affords fine views into the valley, but dropping into the ravine at this point avoids some scrambling on steep slopes above the west facing cliffs. We didn't see any mine diggings along the ridge line, but there are numerous rock monuments that look like prospector claim markers. There is loose rock along the ridges and slopes so be careful not to slide off the cliffs. Sims Ely, Glenn Magill, Walter Gassler and others have had rock sliding experiences on Bluff Spring Mountain and all were lucky enough to be saved either by their companions or by a terrifying self-rescue.

The descent is slow due to the loose rocks and steepness of the terrain. Once you approach the bed of the ravine **[5-NN, 1.3]**, it is best to stay on the north side. You can avoid the brush and cliff areas by staying on the slopes just above the bed of the ravine. As the terrain begins to open up, pick a line of sight route over to the Terrapin Trail. The hike description ends at the Terrapin Trail **[5-OO, 1.7, 3220]**. See Trip 6 for directions back to Peralta Trailhead.

View from Bluff Spring Mountain above Needle Canyon toward the northwest.

Hidden Valley Loop

For experienced off-trail hikers, this long day-hike through Hidden Valley on Bluff Spring Mountain provides a challenging trek. From the sheer cliffs of Bluff Spring Mountain you can look down into the surrounding canyons. The high cliffs provide an ideal vantage point for photographs. The overhang at Magill's Camp on the north end of the mountain can still be seen.

ITINERARY: This hike starts on top of Bluff Spring Mountain at the summit of the Ely-Anderson horse trail (Trip 12). The hike descends into Hidden Valley toward the spring. From the spring area make a clockwise-loop over a pass to the west, then contour along the cliffs heading north to the Magill Camp. Return through the creek bed of Bluff Spring Mountain Canyon to the spring area. Retrace your route to the end of the Ely-Anderson trip on the ridge.

DIFFICULTY: Very difficult. Experts only. No trails. Requires route finding ability on steep, rugged terrain. Not recommended for horses. Elevation change is ±1361 feet.

LENGTH and TIME: 4.4 miles, 6.5 hours round trip.

MAPS: Weavers Needle, Arizona USGS topo map.
Superstition Wilderness Tonto National Forest map.

FINDING THE TRAIL: This hike starts on top of Bluff Spring Mountain near the USGS 4041 elevation notation **[5-FF, 4041]**.

THE HIKE: *Use Map 5.* There are no trails on this route. It is best to scout this route from a high point before dropping down into the valley. From the end of the Ely-Anderson Trip **[5-FF, 0, 4041]**, walk north down into the bed of Bluff Spring Mountain Canyon until you are about 0.25 mile south of the spring—near the site of Al Reser's 1984 camp **[5-PP, 0.7, 3400]**. The remains of old and recent camps are here—an old metal chair, wooden ax-handle, and the poles for a tee-pee made out of the stalks of five large century plants. When there is water in the wash this is a pleasant place to visit. A short but very steep climb up the pass **[5-QQ]**, to the east, takes you above the sheer cliff overlooking La Barge Canyon where you have a birds eye view of Charlebois Canyon and Music Canyon.

From Al Reser's Camp **[5-PP]**, this loop hike goes west, cross-country, up to the pass. From the pass, there are good views of Weavers Needle and the upper reaches of Needle Canyon. The route turns north and skirts the steep slopes of Hill 3999 where you may find some faint trails, one of which traverses a rocky area that has been blasted by prospectors. Some of the boulders along here contain thick bands of white quartz. Be careful on the steep slopes. Most of the rock is loose and the footing is not good. The early prospectors often had problems with loose rocks. Large masses of rock and dirt have been reported to slide down the slopes carrying people with them. Once around Hill 3999, there is a small saddle and the terrain tends to be less steep. Head west and north, to the edge of the cliffs, for more good views into Needle Canyon.

We looked for Magill's mine, *The Dutchman*, but could not find it. Greg Hansen of the Forest Service said the mine diggings were being restored to natural conditions. We don't advise you to climb around the cliffs looking for it. Most of the cliffs are a sheer drop into the canyon below. Continue to the north end of the mountain and work your way down to the lowest, wide flat terrace. No climbing is necessary, but you will have to look for breaks between the boulders. On the lower terrace, we found the overhang **[5-RR, 2.3]** that Magill and his partners used as their camp. The wide, flat terrace in front of the overhang provides a fine view to the north into Needle Canyon and La Barge Canyon.

The return route follows the bed of Bluff Spring Mountain Canyon, south, to the beginning of the loop. From Magill's overhang **[5-RR]**, walk south along the flat terrace until you see a ravine entering from the west. This is the best place to drop down into the bed of Bluff Spring Mountain Canyon. The canyon is narrow and full of boulders and vegetation. A few sections are easy walking but most of the canyon entails some of the roughest cross-country trekking in the Wilderness. The only good aspect of the thrash-through-the-vegetation-hiking is that it isn't that long. You will find a slightly overgrown trail to the east of the water course, after the canyon has turned due south. Just as the canyon begins to open up, an old wall crosses the water course at the spring area. Most of the wall has been washed away. It looks as though the rocks in the wall were set in cement.

From Al Reser's Camp **[5-PP, 3.7]**, the trip continues south to the ridge either by following the water course or heading cross-country to the start of

View looking north into Needle Canyon (left) and La Barge Canyon (right) from the overhang at Glenn Magill's camp on the north end of Bluff Spring Mountain.

the hike on Hill 4041 **[5-FF, 4.4 4041]**. Follow Trip 12 (Ely-Anderson Trail) or Trip 13 (Southwest Route) to connect with a Forest Service Trail.

HISTORY AND LEGENDS. Before you visit the top of Bluff Spring Mountain, it would be worthwhile to read Curt Gentry's book, *Killer Mountains*, which describes Glenn Magill's adventures. Although we can't verify their claims of discovery, Curt Gentry tells a fascinating story of the *Dutchman Mine* on Bluff Spring Mountain. On the cliffs below the mine, they reported a tunnel that was rigged with "rock traps" which would send huge boulders tumbling down if any rocks were moved. Surrounding the tunnel were four two-man guardhouses built of stone in the cliff. Also in the area were many tree stumps, assumed to have been cut for mine timbers.

To reach the mine above the tunnel, Magill's men used a helicopter on occasion but often just scrambled up the steep cliffs. We haven't explored Magill's trails. One route was described as being straight down. Another route to the top of the cliffs piqued the interest of some Lost Dutchman Mine searchers since it involved climbing through a hole in two rocks without the use of footholds.[68] Jim Bark reported a similar story credited to Joe Deering in the late 1800s. In describing the area where he found gold,

Deering said there was a trick to the trail where you had to go through a hole. As with many tellers of treasure stories, Deering died before revealing the location of his find.[69] Magill's *Dutchman Mine* on Bluff Spring Mountain did not produce any gold.

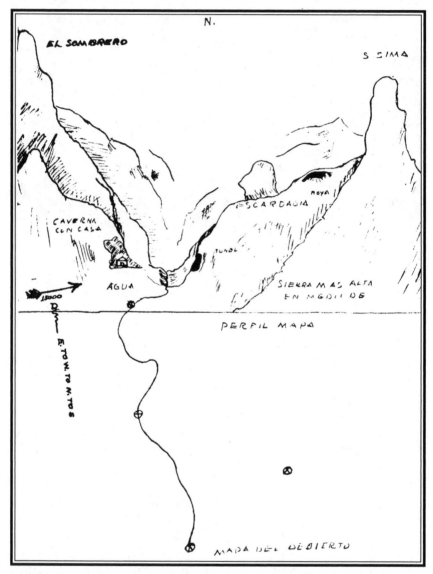

The Ruth-Gonzales Map (Peralta-Ruth Map) is one of the maps Glenn Magill used to locate his mine on Bluff Spring Mountain. COURTESY GREGORY DAVIS, SUPERSTITION MOUNTAIN HISTORICAL SOCIETY, DONS CLUB FILE.

Upper La Barge Area

The Upper La Barge Area begins south of Charlebois Spring and extends east, past La Barge Spring, to the Upper La Barge Box. All the hikes in this area can be accessed from La Barge Canyon via the Dutchman's Trail (104) or the Red Tanks Trail (107).

FINDING THE TRAILHEAD. *Use Maps 3, 5 and 6.* La Barge Canyon is one of the major drainages in the Superstition Wilderness. It runs northwest from La Barge Mountain through the heart of the Wilderness to Canyon Lake. The many small scenic canyons entering La Barge Canyon offer the hiker numerous enjoyable side trips. There is no specific trailhead for this area. All hikes are accessed from the Dutchman's Trail and/or Red Tanks Trail.

HISTORY AND LEGENDS. Barry Storm, in his book *Thunder God's Gold,* writes that La Barge Canyon and Spring are probably named after Phil La Barge who was cattleman Martin Charlebois' partner.[70] The 1984 book by Michael and Jan Sheridan, *Recreational Guide to the Superstition Mountains and the Salt River Lakes,* suggests that "La Barge Canyon was named after John Le Barge (sic) a gold prospector who was born in Canada in 1856."[71] Several of the old books on the Superstitions use the "Le Barge" spelling but most recent authors have been using La Barge as shown on the USGS topographic maps.

La Barge Spring is one of the more reliable springs in the Superstition Wilderness but you should always verify the water conditions with the Forest Service before you go. La Barge Spring is located in a grove of tall trees on the east side of La Barge Canyon near the junction with Bluff Spring Canyon. The spring and cement water trough are on the hillside and somewhat hidden under the trees. A faint path leads to the cement water trough which is sometimes overflowing with water. The date inscribed in the cement reads *7-1-39.*

Whiskey Spring Trail

Whiskey Spring may have water and makes a good destination for day hikes from Peralta Trailhead. Many loop hikes use the Whiskey Spring Trail to connect Miners Summit with La Barge Canyon. This is the site of a biplane wreck in the 1940s.

ITINERARY: Whiskey Spring Trail (238) is a short trail connecting Miners Summit with La Barge Canyon. The trail can be used as a side trip or as a connecting trail on longer loop hikes.

DIFFICULTY: Easy. All trail walking. Elevation change is +120 and -560 feet.

LENGTH and TIME: 2.0 miles, 0.75 hours one-way.

MAPS: Weavers Needle, Arizona USGS topo map.
Superstition Wilderness Tonto National Forest map.

FINDING THE TRAIL: The trail starts at Miners Saddle or in La Barge Canyon. See Trip 4 (Bluff Spring Loop) or Trip 10 (Charlebois Spring–Loop 2) for details.

THE HIKE: *Use Map 3.* From Miners Saddle **[3-0, 0]**, Whiskey Spring Trail (238) goes east along a ridge where it tops out in about 0.5 miles. From there it drops down into Whiskey Spring Canyon and turns north. Whiskey Spring **[3-W, 1.3]** is on the east side of the trail, up-canyon from the abandoned rectangular cement cattle trough. The spring always has had water when we hiked here in the cooler months, but check with the Forest Service for current water conditions. The last several times we were here, the short pipe in the cement box contained a hand carved wooden stopper. Take the stopper out of the pipe and a good flow of water comes out.

From Whiskey Spring, it is another 0.7 mile to the junction with La Barge Canyon **[3-X, 2.0]**. At La Barge Canyon the trail turns east, a short distance into La Barge Canyon, before it is easy to cross over the bed of La Barge Canyon where it meets the Red Tanks Trail (107). The Whiskey Spring Trail ends here **[3-X, 2.0]**.

HISTORY AND LEGENDS. In 1965 Glen Hamaker and O. E. Wagner found a metal whiskey still at Whiskey Spring and carried the whiskey still out of the Superstition Mountains via First Water Trailhead. Ray Ruiz has the whiskey still on display at the Blue Bird Mine and Gift Shop museum on North Apache Trail.[72]

In 1942 or '43, a Fleet Mark 7 PT-6 biplane crashed in Whiskey Spring Canyon directly west of Whiskey Spring. Bill Barkley reported that both pilots walked out to his Quarter Circle U Ranch after the crash. In 1946, Tom Kollenborn and his father hiked here and photographed the wreckage. The plane was removed in 1963 and later restored to flying condition.[73]

Fred Mullins, a stagecoach driver out of Pinal, told a story about a man who discovered gold on the west side of Picacho Butte in 1894. Picacho

Glen Hamaker and O.E. Wagner found this whiskey still at Whiskey Spring in 1965. It is on display at the Bluebird Mine and Gift Shop. COURTESY RAY RUIZ, BLUEBIRD MINE AND GIFT SHOP.

Butte is the hill east of Whiskey Spring. The man, named Wagoner (also spelled Waggoner), would board the stage in Pinal and depart in the desert on the south side of the Superstition Mountains near the Whitlow Ranch. After taking out hand picked rose-quartz gold ore he would meet the stage again for a ride back to Pinal. Wagoner told Mullins his route from Whitlow Ranch was up Randolph Canyon, up Red Tank Canyon, down La Barge, and around Picacho Butte. Wagoner said he concealed the outcropping with brush and rocks and planted a circle of trees around the site so he could locate it in the future. In 1952, gold in rose-quartz float was found by prospector and miner Ray Howland on the west side of Picacho Butte. No one has reported the exact location of Wagoner's diggings.[74]

In 1974 there was a large tent-camp on the north side of La Barge Canyon at the Whiskey Spring Trail and Red Tanks Trail junction. Author Jack Carlson recalls two large white-canvas wall-tents and some horses at the camp. One of the men from the camp was lying on an air mattress in a

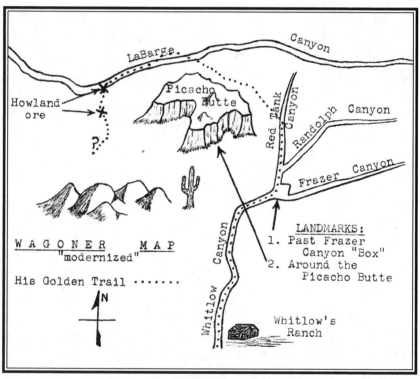

Barry Storm's "modernized" version of the Wagoner Map, with typewritten landmarks, from his 1945 book, Thunder God's Gold. Courtesy Robert Schoose, Schoose Publishing, Goldfield Ghost Town.

Hiker's Guide to the Superstition Wilderness

Typical mining claim marker made of rocks. In 1993 when we took this photograph, we found the March 1983 Certificate of Recording papers stuffed inside the beer can.

small pool in La Barge Creek. He was drinking beer and enjoying the sun. After a short conversation, our group walked back to Whiskey Spring. As we were returning, one of our fellow hikers asked us if we saw the other man, by one of the tents, pointing a rifle at us. We were a bit naive about the dangers in those years.

T R I P 1 6

Trap Canyon

Trap Canyon is a small canyon that has seasonal water. It is an easy walk to the seasonal spring. This intimate canyon is pleasant when there is running water.

ITINERARY: Starting from the Red Tanks Trail (107) in La Barge Canyon, this hike goes northeast into Trap Canyon. Return the same way.

DIFFICULTY: Easy. No trail. Not recommended for horses past the spring. Elevation change is ±280 feet.

LENGTH and TIME: 1.2 miles, 1 hour round trip.

MAPS: Weavers Needle, Arizona USGS topo map.
Superstition Wilderness Tonto National Forest map.

FINDING THE TRAIL: The hike starts in La Barge Canyon on the Red Tanks Trail (107) at Trap Canyon. See Trip 10 (Charlebois Spring—Loop 2).

THE HIKE: *Use Map 6.* From Red Tanks Trail **[6-Y, 0]** we often follow the trail on the bench of the wash up to the spring area **[6-Z, 0.3]**. From the seasonal spring, it is easy walking in the bed of the canyon. Normally we don't go much further than 0.6 miles up canyon **[6-H, 0.6]** from La Barge. We haven't hiked the entire length of Trap Canyon but others have told us the rocks and vegetation make it a rough trip. It is best to hike it in the downstream direction, from east to west.[75] On one trip we found mining claim markers, white wooden stakes in a pile of rocks, that still contained the location notice papers. When there is water running in Trap Canyon this is a pleasant place to visit.

Music Canyon

Music Canyon is a small canyon that has seasonal water. This is a seldom traveled area that is ideal for one or two people. It is possible to find a few flat places to camp, but you might have to look around a bit and maybe select a spot up on the lower cliffs.

ITINERARY: From the Dutchman's Trail (104) in La Barge Canyon walk up the bed of Music Canyon. Select a route to the north, hike up the slopes to Peters Trail (105), and then return to La Barge Canyon on Peter Trail.

DIFFICULTY: Moderate. No trail. Not recommended for horses. Elevation change is ±440 feet.

LENGTH and TIME: 1.3 miles, 1.5 hours one-way.

MAPS: Weavers Needle, Arizona USGS topo map.
Superstition Wilderness Tonto National Forest map.

FINDING THE TRAIL: The hike starts in La Barge Canyon on the Dutchman's Trail (104) at Music Canyon. See Trip 9 (Charlebois Spring–Loop 1).

THE HIKE: *Use Map 5.* From the Dutchman's Trail **[5-J, 0]** walk up the bed of Music Canyon. There are some trails of use here so pick one that looks good. Music Canyon Spring **[5-K, 0.2]** is seasonal. The canyon narrows as you continue north and eventually opens into a wide canyon with sloping hillsides. There may be seasonal water in the bed of the canyon or pot holes of water. Since there are no large campsites, this is not a place for large groups. Lone hikers can find some very small, scenic places to camp below the low cliffs.

One possible way out of Music Canyon is to head west over the ridge **[5-L]** to the Peters Trail (105). Follow Peters Trail south, to the Dutchman's Trail **[5-M, 1.3]** in La Barge Canyon where the hike description ends.

Carney Springs Trailhead

From Apache Junction go 8 miles east on U.S. Route 60. Turn left, north, between mileposts 204 and 205, onto Peralta Road, FS77. Continue 6.0 miles on FS77 to an unsigned dirt road and turn left (west) for 0.6 miles to an unsigned parking area.

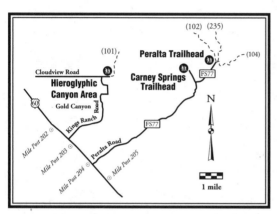

FINDING THE TRAILHEAD. Carney Springs Trailhead is very near the Peralta Trailhead. If you can't find the turnoff for the Carney Springs Road, drive all the way to the end of FS77 and retrace you route from the Peralta Trailhead parking lot. Carney Springs Road is 1.2 miles south on FS77 from the Peralta Trailhead parking lot. The Carney Springs Trailhead is on State Trust Land. If this land is sold to private owners we will lose access to this area.

FACILITIES. There are no facilities at this Trailhead. **Bring your own water.**

THE TRAIL. The trail from the Carney Springs Trailhead begins at the west end of the parking area. The trail starts out as a rough, rocky road and leads to the Wilderness boundary gate. There are no trailhead signs in this area.

HISTORY AND LEGENDS. The Carney Springs area was named for Peter and Thomas Carney who prospected and mined here in 1908.[76] A vein of copper was mined at Carney Springs and some gold and silver were also found.[77] A 1914 claim feud resulted in the death of one of Carney's miners.

From the Carney Springs Road, it is less than 1.0 mile to the mine at the base of the Dacite Cliffs. After leaving FS77 road, go northwest up Carney

Springs Road 0.4 mile and turn right (northeast). Continue another 0.1 mile and park at the end of the dirt road. Follow the deteriorated road across the wash and continue walking for about 15 minutes to the large alcove in the cliffs. The Dacite Cliffs Mine is located at the base of the cliff about 100 yards east of the large alcove. It won't be hard to miss since someone has painted red arrows all over the rocks. There is a lot of red and white graffiti at the entrance. Before 1930 the Dacite Cliffs were known as Lava Cliffs.[78]

Enter the mine at your own risk. Cave-ins and poisonous gas are always a danger. You can avoid these dangers by reading our description; let that be your "armchair tour" of the mine.

Dacite (pronounced "day-site") is a fine-grained igneous rock formed by the crystallization of molten rock material on the earth's surface from volcanic activity.[79] The color of dacite and the interior of the mine is mostly medium gray in contrast to the buff colored cliffs. The drift is about six feet wide and seven feet or more high with the first section extending straight back for over 200 yards. The shaft makes a 90 degree right turn for 50 yards and then a left turn for another 50 yards where it ends. On one wall, the hard rock mining technique is shown where seventeen dynamite charge holes in alternating rows of three and four have been drilled. The floor is dry and has a ribbed effect which might indicate a narrow-gauge-rail track was used to haul out the rock. The ceiling in one part of the mine shows evidence of the miners following a potential prospect near a quartz vein. The mine is home to bats so try not to disturb them since they are an essential link for pollination and insect control.

West Boulder Saddle

This is a pleasant hike that is less traveled than the nearby Peralta Canyon Trail. The seldom-used trail passes Carney Spring (often dry) and leads to West Boulder Saddle where there are good views of the north side of Superstition Mountain and West Boulder Canyon.

ITINERARY: From the Carney Springs Trailhead follow the West Boulder Trail to the saddle with West Boulder Canyon. Return by the same route or continue with Trip 19 (Superstition Mountain Ridge Line), Trip 20 (Dacite Mesa Loop), or Trip 21 (West Boulder Canyon).

DIFFICULTY: Moderate. Trail walking on steep trail. Not recommended for horses. Elevation change is ±1360 feet.

LENGTH and TIME: 3.6 miles, 2.5 hours round trip.

MAPS: Goldfield, Arizona USGS topo map.
Weavers Needle, Arizona USGS topo map.
Superstition Wilderness Tonto National Forest map.

FINDING THE TRAIL: The West Boulder Trail starts at the northwest end of Carney Springs Road. The trail starts out as a rough, rocky road and leads to the Wilderness boundary gate.

THE HIKE: *Use Map 1.* From the Wilderness boundary gate **[1-SS, 0, 2320]**, follow the old road north. The beginning of the trail is sometimes difficult to follow, but it is always worth the extra effort to stay on the trail as it turns north and works its way into the Carney Springs ravine. There are some signs of digging, cement footings, rusty cans, etc., along the trail. Fifteen minutes up the trail there is a fountain-like rock structure where the iron pipe from Carney Spring ends at a former picnic area. The concrete slabs once supported picnic tables.[80] The spring has been dry when we have been here. The old iron pipe from the spring is still visible along the left side of the trail, and this pipe is a good guide for following the faint and sometimes overgrown trail. The trail turns north into the ravine and stays on the west

This century plant (agave) has not yet produced a tall showy stalk. It takes many years, but certainly not a century.

side. If you lose the trail on the smooth rocks, it generally goes up. Staying on the trail is fairly easy because the terrain is so rugged you can't go far without it. The trail becomes more obvious as it ascends toward the saddle.

At the saddle **[1-TT, 1.8, 3680]**, you have a nice view down into West Boulder Canyon and the back slopes of the Superstition Mountain. Return by the same route or continue with Trip 19 (Superstition Mountain Ridge Line) or Trip 20 (Dacite Mesa Loop).

Superstition Mountain Ridge Line

This is a very demanding hike that rewards energetic hikers with fine views from the crest of Superstition Mountain. There is no trail, but the hike on the rocky ridge line is very enjoyable. It is easy to find solitude on this trip.

ITINERARY: From the Carney Springs Trailhead follow the West Boulder Trail to the saddle with West Boulder Canyon. The hike leaves the trail and goes up to the Superstition Mountain ridge line, following this ridge all the way to Siphon Draw. The route connects with the trail down Siphon Draw and ends at Lost Dutchman State Park.

DIFFICULTY: Very difficult. Route finding ability required. Options to abort hike are limited. Unpredictable weather. Not recommended for horses. Elevation change is +3980 and -4220 feet.

LENGTH and TIME: 10.5 miles, 8 hours one-way. Caution, some hikers require 17 hours or more to complete this hike. Vehicle shuttle is 20 miles one-way.

Maps: Goldfield, Arizona USGS topo map.
Weavers Needle, Arizona USGS topo map.
Superstition Wilderness Tonto National Forest map.

FINDING THE TRAIL: The West Boulder Trail starts at the northwest end of Carney Springs Road. The trail starts as a rough, rocky road and leads to the Wilderness boundary gate.

THE HIKE: *Use Maps 1, 4, 7, and 9.* The route finding will be much easier if you use the detailed Goldfield, Arizona USGS topographic map and follow the elevation benchmarks printed on that map. Since this is a one-way hike, park a shuttle vehicle at the Lost Dutchman State Park. See Trip 23 (Siphon Draw Trail) and the Lost Dutchman State Park Trailhead descriptions for more information.

This hike is quite different from most other hikes in the western Superstition Wilderness. The high altitude changes the local weather patterns. Rain, hail, sleet and low clouds are always a possibility. Always be pre-

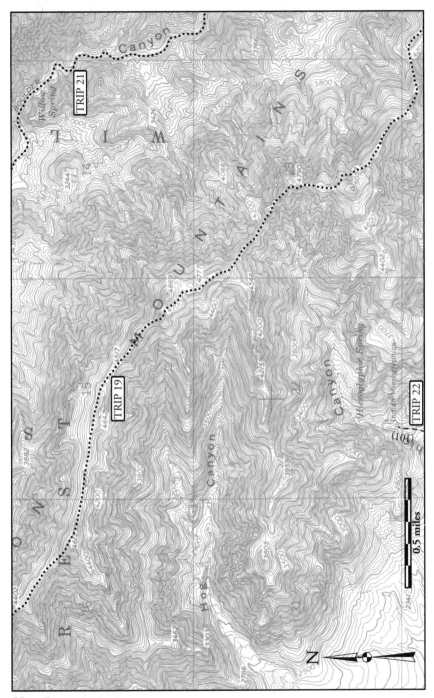

Map 7 - *Trip 19.*

pared for rain and wind. Make sure all the hikers in your party are capable of a sustained eight-hour strenuous hike. Carry your own water, and be sure to have some energy food in your lunch.

The hike begins at the northwest end of Carney Springs Road where the road turns into a trail at the Wilderness boundary gate **[1-SS, 0, 2320]**. Follow the West Boulder Saddle description (Trip 18) for the first 1.8 miles.

At West Boulder Saddle **[4-TT, 1.8, 3680]** there's an exceptional view both down into West Boulder Canyon and of the back slopes of Superstition Mountain. From the saddle, many of the high points on the Superstition Mountain ridge line are in view. This is a good time to identify the peaks on your topo map. Take the good trail heading left (southwest) from the saddle, which contours for a short distance, along the left slope of West Boulder Canyon. The trail crosses the corner section-marker at a big rock cairn **[4-UU, 1.9]**. The marker is a short iron post with a metal cap inscribed with *General Land Office Survey 1919 (R9E/R10E S24-S19-S25-S30 T1N)*. Continue in the same general westerly direction for about 15 minutes, until you have a clear view of the slopes heading up to the ridge, then pick an easy route and hike southwest up to the ridge line. You should be on the ridge line before the 4391 elevation benchmark shown on Map 4 **[4-VV, 2.6, 4391]**. The highest point on the ridge is the peak of Superstition Mountain, 5057 feet, which we go around on the right side (east).

Your hike navigator should follow a route defined by the elevation benchmarks shown on Map 7; left of 4790, across 4777, left of 4869, right of 4517, right of 4642, right of 4453, right of 4613, left of 4402, right of 4562, then stay level working your route south and then west, right of 4648, right of 4861, left of 5024 and down into Siphon Draw **[9-N]**. You can modify the above route for your own hiking style. The only critical part of the hike is finding the descent into Siphon Draw. It starts out very steep but no technical climbing is necessary. At least one person in your party should have hiked to the top of Siphon Draw (Trip 23) to check out the landmarks at the edge of the cliff.

Take some time to stop on the ridge line to enjoy the view to the south and north. In the north you can see the back slopes of the Superstition Mountain and the headwaters of West Boulder Canyon and First Water Creek. The Massacre Grounds are further to the northwest. These are some good places to hike where you rarely find many people.

Refer to the Trip 23 (Siphon Draw Trail) and the Lost Dutchman State Park Trailhead for the scramble down Siphon Draw and the hike over to your shuttle vehicle **[9-K, 10.5]**.

View of the Monument Canyon cliffs near the end of the Superstition Mountain Ridge Line hike.

HISTORY AND LEGENDS.

Hiking the Superstition Mountain ridge line is fairly straightforward but the weather can be unpredictable. On a hike across the ridge line in 1985 with the Arizona Mountaineering Club, we were surrounded by clouds in a powerful September thunderstorm. We couldn't see more than 100 feet for about an hour. Several mule deer came up over a saddle and almost ran us down in the blinding rain storm. Both the deer and our group were surprised by the other's presence. Surrounded by thick clouds, our group had a tendency to drift off the ridge line down into side canyons. A compass and map were essential in those low visibility conditions. We were lucky to have had a hike leader, Denis Duman, who knew the route from previous experience.

Tom Kollenborn in his 1982 story, *Al Senner's Lost Gold of Superstition Mountain*, wrote an interesting account of a man accused of high-grading gold ore from the Mammoth Mine in Goldfield around 1894. The man, Al Senner, took revenge on the owners of the Mammoth Mine for cutting him out of the claim he helped develop. As a miner at the Mammoth, he stole gold ore each day and then on Sunday would pack it up to the top of Superstition Mountain where it was cached. After he was run out of camp for his misdeeds, Senner made an attempt to remove his gold from Superstition Mountain. He died when his horse and pack animal fell off the steep cliffs. No one has ever located his cache which is estimated to hold 1250 pounds of gold ore. It is worth reading the complete story which tells of the doctor who found Senner's body. The doctor, many years later, fell in love with the woman Senner was planning to marry. Reprints are available at the Superstition Mountain Museum.[81]

A more recent account of Al Senner's story is given in Helen Corbin's *Senner's Gold*. Her 1993 book includes the story of Tom Kollenborn and Bob Corbin searching for Senner's cache of gold. The treasure map and

Kollenborn's famous topo map will interest everyone. We hiked to the site of the three piñon pine trees shown on Bob Corbin's rendition of the treasure map. There are four trees now. Three trees have a ten to twelve inch trunk diameter while the younger fourth tree has a branched trunk measuring seven inches.

Rancher Jim Bark held the grazing rights to much of the Superstition Mountains between 1891 and 1907 and always welcomed visitors to his ranch on the southeast side of the mountains. An 1899 *Arizona Daily Herald* newspaper article tells of a geological survey team that found arrowheads and other evidence of prehistoric Indians on the mountain. Later in 1899, a group of Mesa residents searched Superstition Mountain and recovered 106 arrowheads. Returning from the mountain, they stopped at Jim Bark's ranch, now the Quarter Circle U, and were surprised when Bark brought out a stash of 887 arrowheads he had recently found in an olla on Superstition Mountain. The rules have changed since those finds, and we must abide by the State and Federal laws that prohibit collecting artifacts.[82]

An account of a backpack trip across the Superstition Mountain ridge line is given in the *Arizona Highways* publication, *Outdoors in Arizona, A Guide to Hiking and Backpacking*, with photographs by John Annerino.[83]

View looking east from the top of Monument Canyon along the Superstition Mountain Ridge Line hike. Weavers Needle is in the distance below the horizon.

Dacite Mesa Loop

This is another rewarding hike that takes you to the top of a 4000 foot mesa with good views in all directions. You will enjoy the piñon pine trees, the hoodoo rock formations, and open spaces on top of this seldom traveled mesa.

ITINERARY: From the Carney Springs Trailhead follow the West Boulder Trail to the saddle with West Boulder Canyon. The hike then leaves the trail and goes right (northeast) on a cross-country route over to Fremont Saddle. Return by the Cave Trail (233) or Peralta Trail (102) to Peralta Trailhead parking lot. Continue 1.8 miles along Peralta and Carney Springs roads to your vehicle, or leave your shuttle vehicle at Peralta Trailhead.

DIFFICULTY: Difficult. Route finding ability required. Not recommended for horses. Elevation change is ±1875 feet.

LENGTH and TIME: 6.6 miles, 5 hours round trip.

MAPS: Weavers Needle, Arizona USGS topo map.
Superstition Wilderness Tonto National Forest map.

FINDING THE TRAIL: The West Boulder Trail starts at the northwest end of Carney Springs Road. The trail starts out as a rough, rocky road and leads to the Wilderness boundary gate.

THE HIKE: *Use Maps 1 and 2.* This hike can be done as a loop hike, or you can return by the same route. The hiking time is about the same. Depending on your hiking skills, finding a route from the top of the mesa down to Fremont Saddle could be difficult. Plan to leave plenty of daylight for returning by the same route if you can't get through the maze of pinnacles and rock formations to Fremont Saddle.

The hike begins at the northwest end of Carney Springs Road where the road turns into a trail at the Wilderness boundary gate **[1-SS, 0, 2320]**. Follow the Trip 18 (West Boulder Saddle) description for the first 1.8 miles.

On the trek up to West Boulder Saddle, you will probably be thinking how distant the sculptured rock formations look on the horizon to your right (northeast). They are distant, but in about two hours the hike will take you into this fairyland of rocks.

At West Boulder Saddle **[1-TT, 1.8, 3680]**, there's a nice view down into West Boulder Canyon and the back slopes of Superstition Mountain. From West Boulder Saddle **[1-TT]** the route over to Fremont Saddle begins by going right (northeast) following a faint trail marked by small cairns. (The well defined trail to the left is the start of the Superstition Mountain Ridge Line Trip.) Going right, the faint trail stays fairly level as it turns east into the ravine. The route crosses to the left side of the ravine near the first piñon pine trees. Less than 10 minutes further up the ravine there is a large piñon pine tree and small grassy area that would make a good place for a snack or rest **[1-XX, 2.0]**. From here the main ravine branches out into three smaller ravines. Hike up the ravine on the left heading north. There is no sign of a trail from here to Fremont Saddle, so pick your route carefully to avoid any major obstacles. Less than 10 minutes to the north you can take a wide ravine to your right (east) and continue to the summit. Another option maintains a route north, bringing you to a ridge overlooking a drainage into West Boulder Canyon. In either case, you are pretty much on your own from here.

Your objective is to enjoy the rock pinnacles, views from the ridges and the maze of rock formations. Leave yourself plenty of time for exploring and for working your way northeast toward Fremont Saddle. Spend some time exploring the ridge to the north since the interesting part of the hike is over once you drop down to Fremont Saddle **[1-D, 2.5, 3766]**. If you can see Weavers Needle, that is a good landmark. Note that Fremont Saddle is to the south of Weavers Needle.

The return trip either retraces your route or drops down to Fremont Saddle. There are several scrambles off the ridge to Fremont Saddle. All the scrambles require that you have a clear view from the ridge line into Peralta or East Boulder Canyon. Assuming you have found a route through the ridge line rocks to the Peralta or East Boulder side of the ridge, you will be able to see a direct scramble to Fremont Saddle. If not, you probably should stay up high until you can select the route. If you can't see a direct scramble to Fremont Saddle, there is a good chance you may "cliff-out" which requires you to climb back up to the top. Never descend anything that you can't easily climb back up. The Sheriff does not enjoy rescuing hikers from these cliffs. Try to descend the slope so you end up just behind the rock formation at the west side of Fremont Saddle (on the USGS Weavers Needle topo aim for the "e" in Saddle). The scramble down from the ridge to Fremont Saddle might take about 25 minutes since it is steep and rocky (no technical climb-

View from the Peralta Trail near Fremont Saddle looking west toward the hoodoos on Dacite Mesa.

ing is necessary). Loose rocks on the scramble to the saddle make this route very hazardous. Be careful.

From Fremont Saddle **[1-D, 2.5, 3766]**, the hike proceeds down the Peralta Trail (104) or the Cave Trail (233) to the Peralta Trailhead parking lot **[1-A, 4.8, 2400]**. See Trip 1 (Fremont Saddle) and Trip 2 (Cave Trail) for a description of those trails.

If you did not park a shuttle car at Peralta Trailhead parking lot, hike southwest on Peralta road for 1.2 miles, turn right (northwest) on Carney Springs road and continue another 0.6 miles to the Carney Springs Trailhead where the trip ends **[1-SS, 6.6]**.

West Boulder Canyon

This seldom traveled route takes you to the 1931 base camp of Adolph Ruth at Willow Spring. Seasonal water and smooth rock sections of this canyon make the rugged hiking worthwhile.

ITINERARY: From Carney Springs Trailhead follow the West Boulder Trail to the saddle with West Boulder Canyon. The hike then leaves the trail and goes down West Boulder Canyon.

DIFFICULTY: Difficult. Route finding ability required. Abandoned West Boulder Trail is overgrown with vegetation. Not recommended for horses. Elevation change is ±2180 feet.

LENGTH and TIME: 8.8 miles, 7.5 hours round trip.

MAPS: Goldfield, Arizona USGS topo map.
Weavers Needle, Arizona USGS topo map.
Superstition Wilderness Tonto National Forest map.

FINDING THE TRAIL: The West Boulder Trail starts at the northwest end of Carney Springs Road. The trail starts out as a rough, rocky road and leads to the Wilderness boundary gate.

THE HIKE: *Use Maps 1 and 4.* The hike begins at the northwest end of Carney Springs Road where the road turns into a trail at the Wilderness boundary gate **[1-SS, 0, 2320]**. Follow Trip 18 (West Boulder Saddle) description for the first 1.8 miles.

At West Boulder Saddle **[4-TT, 1.8, 3680]**, you have an exceptional view down into West Boulder Canyon and the back slopes of Superstition Mountain. The trail into West Boulder Canyon is overgrown and difficult to follow. This is pretty much a bushwhacking hike down the drainage. Sometimes it is easy to follow the water course and other times it is best to look for a game trail around obstacles. The last time we hiked this canyon was in the mid 1980s. We mostly followed the bed of the canyon so that is where we drew the dotted line on the map. We recall a stone corral **[4-YY]** south of Willow Spring, but that location is only approximate.

Adolph Ruth had his 1931 camp at Willow Spring **[4-WW, 4.4]**. See the First Water Trailhead description for Adolph Ruth's story. The hike description ends at Willow Spring. Return by the same route or continue down to the Dutchman Trail in Boulder Basin. Another return that Bill Sewrey suggests, which we haven't taken yet, is to go up and over the ridge to East Boulder Canyon and return on the Peralta Trail.

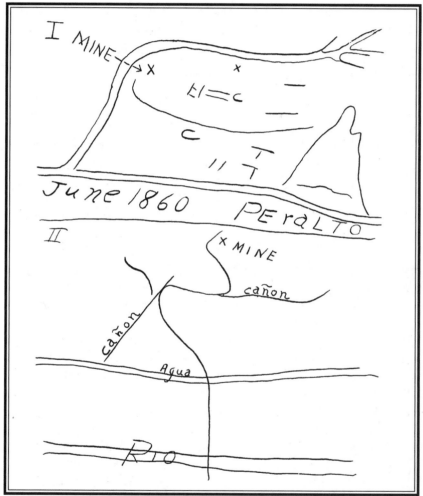

The Peralta Locator Map was used by Adolph Ruth, Glenn Magill and others in the search for the Lost Dutchman Gold Mine. COURTESY SUPERSTITION MOUNTAIN HISTORICAL SOCIETY.

Hieroglyphic Canyon Area

From Apache Junction go 6 miles east on U.S. Route 60 to Gold Canyon (3.3 miles from the end of U.S. Route 60 Superstition Freeway). Between mileposts 202 and 203, turn left (northeast) onto paved Kings Ranch Road. Follow Kings Ranch Road 2.8 miles to the cattle guard.

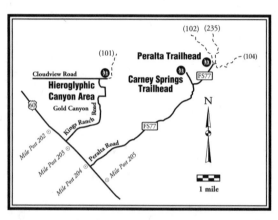

FINDING THE TRAILHEAD: There is no official trailhead for Hieroglyphic Trail. We describe an unofficial route that has been used by others to reach Hieroglyphic Canyon. The access to Hieroglyphic Trail traverses a portion of the Lost Goldmine Trail using a Pinal County right-of-way. Private land is very close to the trail and the unofficial parking area. Please respect the wishes and suggestions of the private property owners. Use your best judgement and manners when hiking in this area.

From the cattle guard at Kings Ranch Road and Baseline Avenue, turn right on Baseline Avenue and drive 0.25 miles. Turn left (north) on Mohican Road for 0.3 miles, then left (west) on Valleyview Road. Valleyview Road meanders north northwest, connecting with Whitetail Road which intersects Cloudview Road. Go right (east) on Cloudview Road for 0.5 miles. Park at the end of the road in a turnaround area.

Cloudview Road is a Pinal County road surrounded by private land. At the east end of Cloudview Road, follow a well-used path, the Lost Goldmine Trail, heading east across the Pinal County right-of-way for about 0.1 miles to a gate at the State Trust Land boundary. Continue through the livestock gate on the Lost Goldmine Trail and be sure to close the gate even if you see another party right behind you. Follow the Lost Goldmine Trail another 0.1

miles as it heads up to the top of the ridge to join the well-worn trail into Hieroglyphic Canyon.

HIKING NEAR PRIVATE LAND. Access to public lands near private property is always a difficult problem. Please obey all *No Trespassing* signs and *No Parking* signs. If a local resident requests you to leave their property, you must obey their wishes. The route description does not require you to walk in private driveways or close to houses. If you do, you are lost. Please clean up any trash that other people have left and report any acts of vandalism you see to the Pinal County Sheriff's Office. The portion of the Hieroglyphic Trail north of the Lost Goldmine Trail to the Wilderness gate is on Arizona State Trust Land. A hiking permit is required to use State Trust Land and the permit is available from the Arizona State Land Department. See Useful Address in the back of the book for their address.

LOST GOLDMINE TRAIL. The eastern portion of the Lost Goldmine Trail was completed in 2001 and it provides an important link in the trail system to reach Hieroglyphic Canyon from Cloudview Road. At its western end, the

Lost Goldmine Trail connects with the Jacobs Crosscut Trail (58) near Broadway Road, then skirts the Wilderness boundary as it goes east along the southern face of Superstition Mountain. The trail ends at the cattle guard and Forest boundary on Peralta Road near the Peralta Trailhead. The Lost Goldmine Trail is managed by Pinal County and is open for public use by hikers, horserid-

Petroglyphs in Hieroglyphic Canyon. This prehistoric rock art was carved on the cliffs over 800 years ago.

ers and bicycle riders. Pinal County, under the direction of Supervisor Sandie Smith, obtained the right-of-way easements across Arizona State Trust Land, private property and existing county roadway to provide a continuous trail for public enjoyment. The Superstition Area Land Trust, under the direction of Rosemary Shearer, was the lead organization in coordinating the volunteers and other groups that performed the trail design and construction.

FACILITIES. There are no facilities. **Bring your own water.** Parking is very limited at the turnaround on Cloudview Road, so don't bring a lot of vehicles. It might be wise to car pool the last several miles.

HISTORY AND LEGENDS. Author and historian Tom Kollenborn reports that Hieroglyphic Canyon was called Apache Springs Canyon before 1930. Kings Mountain was named after William N. King and later changed to Silly Mountain by Bud Elrod. King's Ranch Resort, formerly known as the Shadows at Kings Ranch,[84] is named for Julian and Lucy King who established the ranch in 1947.[85]

Hieroglyphic Canyon is a misnomer. The carvings and line drawings on the rock are actually petroglyphs, dated by most archeologists from A.D. 700 to A.D. 1100 during Hohokam habitation. Debate continues whether they depict hunt scenes or were used by shamans for teaching the origins of life.[86] Hieroglyphic Canyon was listed on the National Register of Historic Places in April of 1994.

Hieroglyphic Spring. PHOTOGRAPH BY RICHARD DILLON.

Hieroglyphic Trail

Hikers will enjoy the easy hike up to this special area with many Indian petroglyphs and pools of seasonal water. The trail follows a ridge line which offers good views in all directions.

ITINERARY: From an unimproved parking area, follow the trail up to the ridge to a wide track leading to the Wilderness boundary gate. From the gate, Trail 101 begins and heads north into Hieroglyphic Canyon where the petroglyphs are located. Return by the same route.

DIFFICULTY: Easy. Well-defined trail walking. Elevation change is ±560 feet.

LENGTH and TIME: 3.0 miles, 2 hours round trip.

MAPS: Goldfield, Arizona USGS topo map.
Superstition Wilderness, Tonto National Forest topo map.

FINDING THE TRAIL: Start at the east end of Cloudview Road and walk east on a well-worn dirt trail. Do not walk north up the private driveway.

THE HIKE: *Use Map 8.* This is a nice area for beginning hikers. There is a lot of green here. The surrounding desert abounds with many different kinds of healthy vegetation: jumping cholla, saguaro, palo verde, jojoba, brittle bush, bursage, etc. Views are good, both going up and back. There is much variety and something interesting to see at the hike's destination. The trail is easy to follow and it is hard to get lost once you are on it.

The hike starts on the Lost Goldmine Trail at the east end of Cloudview Road **[8-A, 0]**. There are no trail signs. Use this trail rather than bushwhacking through the surrounding private property. Following the well-worn trail is easy as it goes east to the gate at the State Trust Land boundary **[8-B, 0.1]**. In the years when we get a lot of rain we often see a nice display of spring wildflowers, poppies and lupines, growing near this gate. Close the livestock gate after you pass through and continue east as the Lost Goldmine Trail heads up a slope to intersect with a wide trail on the ridge **[8-C, 0.2]**. Since the trail intersection is not easily recognized when hiking down the ridge,

---

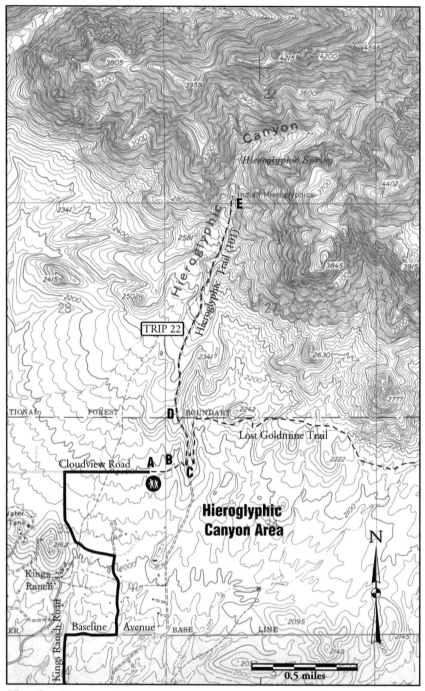

Map 8 - *Trip 22*

Wilderness boundary gate on Hieroglyphic Trail.

you need to mark the trail with a cairn or remember some landmark for the return trip. At the trail intersection **[8-C, 0.2]**, turn left (north) and continue to the Wilderness gate **[8-D, 0.4]**.

After you go through the Wilderness boundary gate be sure to close it. This is the start of the Hieroglyphic Canyon Trail 101. The trail follows the route of an old road across the top of the ridge where large patches of wildflowers bloom.

When the trail comes close to the wash you will cross over a large boulder in the trail. Take note of the large bed-rock mortars (grinding holes) in the boulder. Prehistoric people made these holes and used them to grind plants for food preparation.

A short distance beyond the bed-rock mortars, when the trail becomes very faint, you are at your destination **[8-E, 1.5]**. The petroglyphs you will probably see first are on the cliff face across the wash on an east facing wall. Also look around your feet for some others. There are at least three pools in the wash. After seasonal rains, there is quite a bit of water here, and you may have to go up the wash to get across to the west side. There are some recent graffiti markings on the walls which may be difficult to distinguish from the old petroglyphs. Down the wash (south) about 200 yards on the west side is another cliff face with more petroglyphs. The many drawings of animals might have some religious significance or represent the story of a successful hunt or the big one that got away! The hike returns by the same route to the parking area **[8-A, 3.0]**.

You can also continue up canyon as far as you like before returning. We have not hiked to the top, but a friend of ours, Dave Hughes, said it was a real bushwhack up the canyon when he did it in February 1981.

Local resident Larry Shearer likes to hike cross country to the top of Superstition Mountain in December when the weather is cool. On his trip in December 2000 he left the Hieroglyphic Trail at the petroglyphs and followed a ridge to the northeast. He does not go up the Hieroglyphic Canyon wash. On each trip he takes a slightly different route and plots a route through the cliffs above. It takes 4 hours to go up to the 5057 elevation mark on Superstition Mountain and another 3 hours to return.

Lost Dutchman State Park Trailhead

The Lost Dutchman State Park Trailhead is located 5.4 miles north of Apache Junction on State Route 88 (between mileposts 201 and 202). From State Route 88 turn right (east) on the paved road and drive into the State Park. State Route 88 is the famous Apache Trail, now designated as a National Forest Scenic Byway.

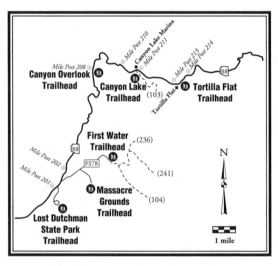

LOST DUTCHMAN STATE PARK. At the park entrance station there is a quarter mile native plant trail that identifies the cacti, trees and bushes seen throughout the Superstition Wilderness area. Even if you don't plan to start hiking from the State Park Trailhead, a short walk on the native plant trail is highly recommended. The park rangers have identified additional plants along the trails inside the 300 acre State Park. The park entrance station has a small selection of free and for sale literature. The rangers are happy to answer any questions you may have.

The State Park charges a $4.00 daily fee for parking and use of the picnic facilities. A $10.00 overnight camping fee is charged per vehicle. You may wish to use the State Park as a secure parking area while you are on an overnight hike. Park Manager Bob Sherman and Assistant Manager Steve Jakubowski told us that backcountry hikers can park their vehicles here for a nominal fee. Parking your vehicle at the State Park will minimize the problem of vehicle break-in and vandalism that is common at the other trailheads. The State Park has picnic tables, single and group ramadas, restrooms,

Lost Dutchman State Park entrance with Superstition Mountain in the background.

showers, drinking water, telephone, developed campsites, and an RV dump station, but no RV hookups. Rock climbers often use the State Park as the starting point for the climbs to *The Hand* (Praying Hands) and to the *Crying Dinosaur*. The Lost Dutchman State Park is a convenient location to park a shuttle vehicle for Trip 19 (Superstition Mountain Ridge Line) from Carney Springs Trailhead.

THE TRAILS. The Tonto National Forest borders the Lost Dutchman State Park on the east boundary of the State Park. The Superstition Wilderness boundary is about one mile east of the State Park. The Siphon Draw trailhead is located on the southeast side of the State Park near the camping area. After entering the park, follow the road signs for Siphon Draw Trail. Other trails leave from the northeast corner of the park. Printed information on all hiking trails is available at the Park Headquarters. *Day Hikes and Trail Rides in and Around Phoenix* by Roger and Ethel Freeman has a good trail description for the Lost Dutchman State Park.

HISTORIC MINING DISTRICT. North Apache Trail (State Route 88) near the Lost Dutchman State Park was once a booming gold mining district. The center of gold mining activity was in the former town of Goldfield near the

---

Weekes Station about 2 to 3 miles north of Apache Junction on the Apache Trail in 1905. COURTESY GREGORY DAVIS, SUPERSTITION MOUNTAIN HISTORICAL SOCIETY, WEEKES RANCH FILE.

Mammoth Mine. John Wilburn, in his 1990 book, *Dutchman's Lost Ledge of Gold*, documents the sites of fifteen gold mines, including the Mammoth, within a narrow corridor along Route 88.[87] Twelve of the mines are on the west side of Route 88 including the Bull Dog Mine, which John Wilburn suggests is the site of the Lost Dutchman gold mine. This mine was the district's second largest gold producer, yielding an estimated 6,700 ounces of gold. The 1892 Bull Dog Mine received its name from the shape of a nearby rock formation that resembles the head of a bulldog. A portion of the bulldog face was blasted away about a hundred years ago. If you look closely you can still see the image of a bulldog. The Bull Dog mine is located 1.7 miles west of the Lost Dutchman State Park just below the Pinal/Maricopa County line.

In his book, John Wilburn describes the operation and history of the mines and accounts for at least 58,620 ounces of gold removed from the mines in this region. Prospectors in Goldfield discovered the gold in veins of white quartz exposed on the surface. The Mammoth Mine accounted for about 43,300 ounces of gold and reached a depth of over 1000 feet.[88]

John Wilburn not only has written about the Lost Dutchman Mine but also has searched for the gold. The Black Queen Mine was first staked in 1892 and was mined by several operators over the past century. In March of 1977, Wilburn obtained a lease from Goldfield Mines, Inc. on the old Black Queen where he discovered new veins rich in gold. The new veins produced tons of high-grade ore. After the Mammoth and Bull Dog mines, the Black Queen was the third largest producer, yielding an estimated 6000 ounces of gold in all its years of operation.[89]

Ray Ruiz is the owner of the Bluebird Mine and Gift Shop on the North Apache Trail where John Wilburn and Louis Ruiz can often be found discussing all aspects of the Lost Dutchman legend with customers and friends.

Siphon Draw Trail

Siphon Draw is a scenic hike that takes you up a steep canyon under the towering cliffs of Superstition Mountain. Every spring the slopes are covered with wildflowers, dominated by the yellow brittle bush. You can walk by the site of the 1886 Palmer Mine and you may see rock climbers on the Crying Dinosaur in Siphon Draw and Praying Hands near trail #56.

ITINERARY: This hike starts at Lost Dutchman State Park. The wide track heads east up the slopes into Siphon Draw. The trail ends after 1.6 miles but a steeper and more difficult route continues another mile to the Flatiron. Return by the same route. From the Palmer Mine Road an alternate hike down the lower slopes goes past the Palmer Mine connecting with trail #57 and then trail #56 for a return to the northeast corner of the Lost Dutchman State Park.

DIFFICULTY: Easy if you turn around at the end of the trail, but the hike to the Flatiron is considered Difficult. Not recommended for horses. Elevation change is ±1030 feet. Elevation change to the Flatiron is ±2781 feet.

LENGTH and TIME: 3.2 miles, 2.5 hours round trip. Add 1 hour for alternate return. Allow 5 hours for the 4.8 mile round trip to the Flatiron.

MAPS: Goldfield, Arizona USGS topo map.
Lost Dutchman State Park Hiking Trail map.
Superstition Wilderness Tonto National Forest map.

FINDING THE TRAIL: The Siphon Draw Trail starts inside the Lost Dutchman State Park at the southeast corner near the camping area. There is a small paved parking area here and the trail is well marked.

THE HIKE: *Use Map 9.* This is a popular day hike and would be a nice hike for beginning hikers since it's difficult to get lost and turnaround is possible at anytime. We rated the hike *easy*, but it is all uphill and you will probably need to stop a few times to catch your breath. The view toward the Superstition Mountain cliffs is spectacular. We included this hike because some people prefer a less isolated hike; in addition, this is the exit route for

Lost Dutchman State Park Trailhead   **131**

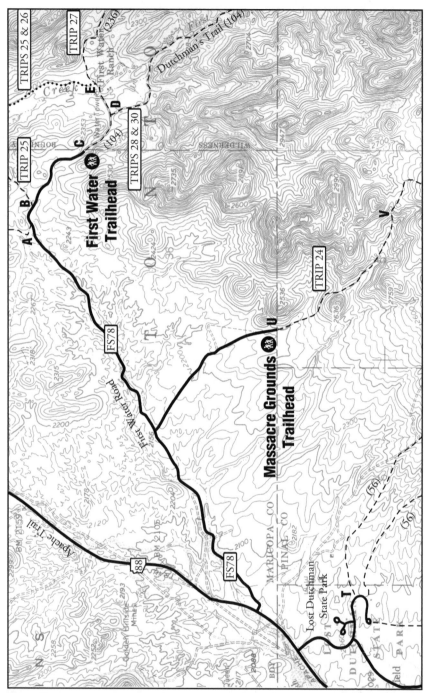

Map 9 - *Trips 19, 23 and 24.*

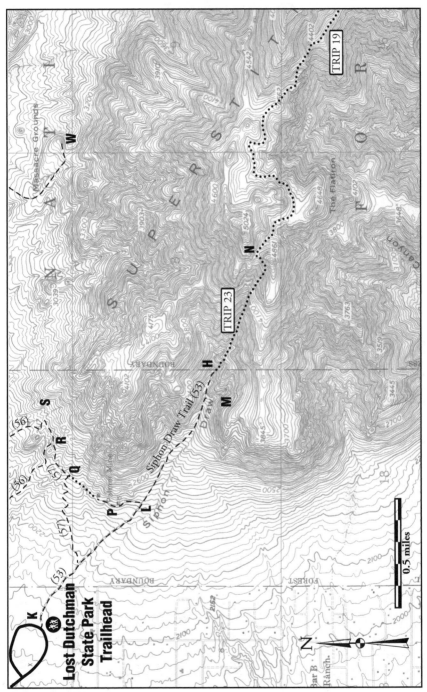

Map 9 continued - *Trips 19, 23 and 24.*

the dramatic and arduous Trip 19 (Superstition Mountain Ridge Line) from Carney Springs Trailhead. Although we rated the Siphon Draw Trail *easy* compared to other trips in our book, hikers should know the Lost Dutchman State Park rates this a *very difficult* hike compared to other hikes in their information pamphlet.

From the Lost Dutchman State Park Trailhead **[9-K, 0, 2080]**, hike east up the slope on the wide, well-traveled track. A trail from Barkley Road joins the main track and forms a smaller trail on the slope heading east toward the Superstition Mountain cliffs. Brittle bush is the dominate ground cover along the trail, and in the Spring, the mountain slopes are a vibrant yellow color. The Palmer Mine Road **[9-L, 0.8, 2420]** branches off to the left (north) about 25 minutes into the hike. There is an abandoned building foundation near the junction with the Palmer Mine Road.

Farther up the trail, Siphon Draw narrows. On the right (south) side of Siphon Draw is the Crying Dinosaur rock formation **[9-M]**. Continue up the trail through Siphon Draw as far as you like. After the trail goes into the

Goldfield area in the early 1900s with Superstition Mountains in the background. Photograph by Walter Lubken. Courtesy Salt River Project History Services.

Weekes Ranch on the west side of Superstition Mountain circa 1930. Left to right, Clover Dale, Tex Barkley, Margaret Weekes holding Phil Patterson (child), Fred Weekes, Merrel Weekes, Charlie Weekes (knelling) and Grant Peterson. COURTESY GREGORY DAVIS, SUPERSTITION MOUNTAIN HISTORICAL SOCIETY, WEEKES RANCH FILE.

wash, there is a smooth rock section where the official trail ends below a seasonal waterfall **[9-H, 1.6]**. Return the same way to the Lost Dutchman State Park Trailhead **[9-K, 3.2]**.

For those going to the top of the Flatiron, bypass the waterfall area on the right (south) side of the wash. Someone has painted big white arrows on the rocks, so it is easy to follow the route up Siphon Draw. There is no official trail here, but you can see where other hikers have established a path that takes you over a low ridge and back into Siphon Draw. Here someone has spray painted the cliff, *Best Way, Stay in Canyon All the Way*. Although the advice is good, painting the rocks is not appropriate in the Wilderness. Please don't paint the rocks. Most people hike up the bed of Siphon Draw. There is a trail on the south side of Siphon Draw which is easier to follow going downhill. The route goes around the north side of the Flatiron, the prominent buttress, and becomes very steep before reaching the top of the cliffs. Loose rocks make the Siphon Draw route very hazardous. Don't roll rocks down onto hikers below you.

There are several trails on top. One goes south across the top of the Flatiron (elevation 4861) and another goes up to a saddle **[9-N, 2.4, 4680]** below some weathered rock formations. You can easily spend several hours

---

Hoodoos on top of Superstition Mountain. This rock formation, one of several in the area, is located east of the saddle near the end of the hike to the Flatiron.

up here photographing the rock formations and enjoying the views in all directions. Whenever you decide you have had enough exercise, return using the same trail to the Lost Dutchman State Park Trailhead **[9-K, 4.8]**.

At the Palmer Mine Road, on the trail down the slope, consider hiking over to the former mine site and taking the alternate route back to the trailhead. The Palmer Mine Road is not marked and it looks more like a trail now. The green steel beam structures at the mine site were removed when the shaft **[9-P]** was covered and the area revegetated. Farther up an unmarked path, to the north, are some smaller mine workings. Continue north along the narrow unmarked path until it intersects trail #57 **[9-Q]**. Go north on Trail #57 until it intersects Trail #56 **[9-R]**. Trail #56 is a loop trail. Our trip follows Trail #56 in the counterclockwise direction.

To the northeast there are some interesting vertical rock formations that look like tall, thin fins. The farthest one to the north is named Praying Hands **[9-S]**. See History and Legends. Continue north on Trail #56 and follow the trail as it turns west down the slope and returns to the northeast corner of Lost Dutchman State Park **[9-T]**.

From the ramadas at the northeast corner of Lost Dutchman State Park, follow the Discovery Trail, inside the park, to the Lost Dutchman State Park

Trailhead parking lot **[9-K, 6.5]** where this trip description ends. The walk along the Discovery Trail is pleasant and several of the native plants are identified with name plaques.

HISTORY AND LEGENDS. The first mining claim in the Superstition District was the Buckhorn Claim, now known as the Palmer Mine. It was staked by W. A. Kimball in 1886. In 1900 and years prior to that, copper and gold ore were shipped from the mine. Dr. Ralph Palmer was a physician for the Roosevelt Dam construction site from 1903 to 1906 and mayor of Mesa in 1912. During this time, he became interested in gold mining. After Kimball's death, a group of businessmen and Dr. Palmer acquired the Buckhorn mine in 1917 and discovered small pockets of gold ore. In 1926, Dr. Palmer purchased the mine from his partners, but it wasn't until 1947 that the shaft was extended down from 215 feet to 265 feet. Unfortunately, only small traces of gold were found but nothing in commercial quantities. Dr. Palmer died in 1954. The Barkley Cattle company used the shaft as a water well from 1950 to 1962.[90] The area was revegetated and the mine

Government Well in the early 1900s, about seven miles northeast of Apache Junction on the Apache Trail. Photograph by Walter Lubken. Courtesy Salt River Project History Services.

Bill Sewrey rappelling from The Hand, February 1966. COURTESY
DESERT MOUNTAIN SPORTS, PHOENIX, ARIZONA.

shaft was covered, so you can't look down into the pit.

There are several technical rock climbs on the cliffs of Superstition Mountain. Two of the more popular crags are the *Crying Dinosaur* and *The Hand* (Praying Hands). The *Crying Dinosaur* rock formation **[9-M]** is on the right (south) side of Siphon Draw. The vertical head and neck of the dinosaur and V-shaped mouth are visible from the trail. A long crack in the rock near the dinosaur eye looks like a tear. Rock climbers rate this a 5.5 climb.[91] Technical climbing equipment is required. The rappel off the top is a spectacular free rappel to the ground.

To the northeast there are some unusual vertical rock formations that look like tall, thin fins. The farthest one to the north is named Praying Hands **[9-S]**. The "hand" formation is actually easier to see as you are driving from Apache Junction north on State Route 88. Rock climbers call this *The Hand*. Bill Forrest, Key Punches and Gary Garbert made the first ascent to the top of *The Hand* in 1965 on the Razor's Edge route. Later that same year Bill Sewrey and Dave Olson made a first ascent using the Chockstone Chimney route. A 150 foot freefall rappel from the top is quite exciting. Technical climbing equipment is required for these climbs which are both rated 5.6.[92]

The cactus wren, Arizona's state bird, has built many nests in the cactus and shrubs around the Lost Dutchman State Park. Watch for bird nests that look like bundles of hay woven between the branches of the cholla cactus and small trees in this area. Some of the nests are at eye level which makes it easy to inspect the narrow, foot-long bundles of grass. Look for the bird's round entrance on one end of the nest.

Massacre Grounds Trailhead

Massacre Grounds Trailhead is located off Forest Service Road 78 (FS78) near the First Water Trailhead. From Apache Junction, drive 5.6 miles northeast on State Route 88 to the First Water Trailhead Road (between mileposts 201 and 202). From State Route 88 turn right (east) on dirt FS78 and continue 1.0 mile to an unmarked dirt road where you turn right (southeast) onto the Massacre Grounds Road. Continue on the Massacre Grounds Road for 0.7 miles where the road ends in a small unsigned parking lot.

FINDING THE TRAILHEAD. The Massacre Grounds Road gets rocky near the end, but we have seen low clearance cars here. Drive cautiously and watch your oil pan. You will know you are at the right trailhead when you see an earthen cow tank across from the Wilderness boundary fence just south of the parking area.

FACILITIES. There are no facilities or signs at the Massacre Grounds Trailhead. There is no drinking water here. **Be sure to bring water**.

THE TRAIL. The Massacre Grounds Trail starts from the south side of the parking area as a wide dirt road at the Wilderness boundary fence.

HISTORY AND LEGENDS. The story of the Massacre is told by Sims Ely in his 1953 book, *The Lost Dutchman Mine*. George Scholey was a friend of an

Prospector Hermann Petrash at his cabin near Queen Creek. PHOTOGRAPH BY CARL BODERICK, COURTESY SUPERSTITION MOUNTAIN HISTORICAL SOCIETY.

Apache known as Apache Jack who related this episode to him. In 1848,[93] when Apache Jack was about 12 years old, he and other reinforcements from the Apache village near the Picket Post military camp were summoned by the warriors to join the running fight against the Mexicans. Some authors believe the Mexican miners were part of the Peralta family expedition making the last trip to the mountains to recover gold because the international boundary was being moved south to the Gila River at the end of the 1846-1848 Mexican/American war. Apache Jack joined the fighting on the third day. The miners were being driven south and west against the cliffs of Superstition Mountain. The last of the Mexicans to die were killed in the area now known as the Massacre Grounds on the northwest slopes of Superstition Mountain. Several of the Mexicans escaped around the west side of the mountain, but their mules were either killed or scattered. Apache Jack said his group cut the packs and bags of rock (gold ore) off the mules and left it on the ground before taking the animals to their camp on a flat-topped mountain. Apache Jack said the place where Silverlocke and Malm found their gold was the site of the massacre.[94]

Scholey said that during a deer hunting trip in the Superstitions, Apache Jack took him near a gold mine on Black Mountain but then had second thoughts about showing him the exact location. Apache Jack was worried he

Hiker's Guide to the Superstition Wilderness

would displease his tribal leaders by disclosing the location of a mine to a white man. George Scholey later learned that Apache Jack died from symptoms similar to arsenic or strychnine poisoning. Scholey attributed this poisoning to Apache Jack's medicine man who may have upheld the legend that a horrid fate would overcome anyone who divulged the site of any mine to a white man.[95] See History and Legends in the Peters Mesa Area description for more on the poisoning incident.

Although the exact dates vary depending on the source, Carl A. Silverlocke, also known as Silverlock,[96] and Carl Malm, also known as Goldlock, were prospecting in the Superstition Mountains from 1901 through 1917.[97] In 1912 they found $18,000 of gold ore on the northwest slope of Superstition Mountain at the Massacre Grounds.[98] They shipped their gold ore from a local express office in Mesa.[99] It is generally accepted that this gold was lost during the Massacre. After rumors of their find, others scoured the mountain slopes, but no reports of a gold discovery were made public. Silverlocke and Malm continued prospecting but were apparently not successful because, in their final years, they were receiving supplies in Mesa on credit. Silverlocke was committed to the State Mental Institution of Arizona in 1917[100] and died on July 18, 1929.[101]

Robert Garman, in his 1975 book, *Mystery Gold of the Superstitions*, writes about several others that have found gold ore in circumstances similar to Silverlocke. Legendary Lost Dutchman Mine hunter Hermann Petrach told Garman that a prospector came to his cabin with gold ore found in a pile next to a trail west of Weavers Needle. Another find was made about 1933 by two men, Mr. James and Mr. Ives. They found gold about 50 feet north of the trail in Needle Canyon on the pass going over to East Boulder Canyon. We believe this could have been the Upper Black Top Mesa Pass.

In his book, Garman drew a map that shows a possible trail that the fleeing Mexicans traveled during the Apache attack. The trail starts on the south side of the Wilderness, but it is unclear—due to misplaced landmarks on his map—how they arrived in East Boulder Canyon. From First Water, the Mexicans were fleeing west when the Apaches forced them south toward Superstition Mountain and the Massacre Grounds.[102]

Massacre Grounds Trail

This easy hike takes you up the foothills to the north side of Superstition Mountain and the historic Massacre Grounds. In the rainy season, you will find water in the washes and small waterfalls cascading from the lower cliffs of Superstition Mountain. Not many people hike here so you may have the area all to yourself.

ITINERARY: From the Massacre Grounds Trailhead follow the Massacre Grounds Trail south, up the back slopes of Superstition Mountain, to an area known as the Massacre Grounds. Return by the same trail. There are several longer, optional off-trail returns via First Water Trailhead.

DIFFICULTY: Easy. Trail walking except for the optional return routes. The difficulty of the optional routes are considered moderate since they require off-trail hiking and some route finding ability. Elevation change is ±980 feet.

LENGTH and TIME: 3.0 miles, 3 hours round trip.

MAPS: Goldfield, Arizona USGS topo map.
Superstition Wilderness Tonto National Forest map.

FINDING THE TRAIL: The trail leaves the south side of the parking lot and heads south up an old dirt road.

THE HIKE: *Use Maps 9 and 10.* From the Massacre Grounds parking lot **[9-U, 0]**, walk south up the old dirt road (now closed to vehicles by the Wilderness boundary fence). You'll immediately see a large earthen cow tank on the right. The trail goes up over a small pass between the hills then follows a wash. After about 30 minutes of hiking, the trail leaves the wash in a confusion of several trails **[9-V, 0.8]**. Look for the well-traveled trail and head left (northeast) out of the drainage up onto a flat area. If you take the wrong path up the drainage, it gets very narrow and rocky. Once you're on the flat area, the top of Weavers Needle appears with an interesting tower-like rock formation in the foreground.

Chainfruit cholla cactus on the northwest slopes of Superstition Mountain.

As you walk along the trail surrounded by unusual rock formations and the massive hulk of Superstition Mountain to the south, you have a sense of being far away from town. This is a very pretty area and is less traveled than the trails starting from the First Water Trailhead. Brittle bush, bursage, catclaw and Mormon tea are the prominent types of vegetation here.

The trail continues up hill and toward the south, with several trails of use, all marked by cairns, leading up and around the right side (west) of the low cliffs. All the trails of use seem to converge so there is little chance of getting lost. The trail crosses the wash that skirts the west side of the cliffs and continues up a sloping rock outcrop that ends at an impressive cliff that drops off to the east **[9-W, 1.5]**. This is the turnaround point for the hike and makes a good spot for a rest or snack. From the turnaround point **[9-W]**, the Massacre Grounds Area stretches east and west along the base of Superstition Mountain. After a rain, look for a waterfall pouring off the low red cliffs just to the south of here. There is a trail on the east side of the wash leading up to the cliffs below the seasonal waterfall. The cliff below the waterfall provides shade and makes a nice lunch spot even when there is no water here. Return the same way to the parking lot **[9-U, 3.0]** or try one of the optional return routes.

OPTIONAL RETURN ROUTES. Several optional return routes are possible, and they would be good for those desiring to experience off-trail hiking and route finding. Although we have not hiked all sections of these routes, they seem fairly straightforward. All of these off-trail routes start from the south side of the cliff where the Massacre Grounds Trail ends.

The first off-trail trek follows the drainage that heads directly north toward First Water Trailhead. You can proceed all the way to First Water Trailhead following the bottom of the wash or pick a shorter route, west over the hills back to the Massacre Grounds Trailhead.

A second off-trail route goes east after you drop down to the 2700 foot elevation. Follow the relatively flat terrain southeast toward First Water Creek drainage **[10-CC]** and return via First Water Creek or continue southeast and pick up the faint trail down O'Grady Canyon **[10-DD]**. Only experienced off-trail hikers should attempt the O'Grady Canyon route.

Refer to Trip 28 (Upper First Water Creek) for the return to First Water Trailhead. It is 2.3 miles by dirt road from First Water Trailhead **[9-C]** to the Massacre Grounds Trailhead **[9-U]**. Errors in route finding will generally result in your crossing First Water Road or Second Water Trail to the north. If you make this error, you can follow the FS78 road (west) to the Massacre Grounds road junction. In the case of O'Grady Canyon, route finding errors might put you in West Boulder Canyon, so don't try O'Grady if you are a novice.

Corral and buildings at First Water Ranch, circa 1975. PHOTOGRAPH BY RICHARD DILLON.

First Water Trailhead

First Water Road is 5.6 miles north of Apache Junction on State Route 88 (between mileposts 201 and 202). The First Water Road turnoff is just 0.2 miles north of the Lost Dutchman State Park entrance. From State Route 88 turn right (east) on dirt FS78 and continue 2.6 miles to the First Water Trailhead parking lot at the end of the dirt road.

FINDING THE TRAILHEAD. While driving along FS78 take note of the turnoff for a dirt road (right) to the Massacre Grounds at mile 1.0, the horse trailer parking area on the left at mile 2.1, and an unmarked dirt road (locked gate) to an abandoned corral and windmill on the left at mile 2.2. These will be useful landmarks for future adventures.

There is a small parking lot at the trailhead. If this is full you can drive back down the dirt road about 0.5 miles and park in a larger area where the outfitters saddle-up for their pack trips. Since January 1997 a $4 fee per vehicle per day is required for all parking. There is an unmarked dirt road leaving from this trailer parking lot that heads north and is useful as a route to the Hackberry Spring area. The unmarked dirt road (with locked gate) branching off to the northeast, between the trailer parking area and the main parking lot, goes down to a windmill and corral next to First Water Creek.

FACILITIES. There are toilet facilities, but no drinking water at the First Water Trailhead. **Be sure to bring your own water.** A seasonal Tonto

---

National Forest Service information board usually has a map posted with some other interesting facts about the area. Most of the year the information signs are put in storage, and the only sign in the area reads *No Parking on the Road*. Due to vandalism, the Forest Service displays the trailhead signs only when they have rangers at the trailhead tent-camp during February and March. You will know you are at the right place by recognizing the old dirt road (now the trail) heading east out of the parking area. In the prime hiking season, February and March, there are Forest Service rangers here taking hiker surveys and they are available to answer any questions you have.

Theft and vandalism are common at this trailhead so don't leave valuables in your vehicle. Thieves steal clothes, books, maps, camping gear, gasoline, tools, etc. Be sure everything is locked in the trunk or better yet, don't bring it to the trailhead.

THE TRAILS. The Dutchman's Trail and Second Water Trail both leave the east side of the parking lot and head east, down an old rough dirt road. The trailhead was originally at the end of this old road. About 0.5 miles down the old dirt road, the Dutchman's and Second Water Trails diverge. The Second Water Trail goes east crossing First Water Creek (a rocky creek bed usually dry or with little water), passing through Garden Valley, skirting Second Water Spring, and finally intersecting Boulder Canyon Trail (103) about 3 miles later. The Dutchman's Trail heads southeast and loops through

First Water Trailhead.

many interesting areas and finally ends at Peralta Trailhead 18 miles later. There is a lot of hiker traffic on the beginning portions of these two trails, so it is necessary to branch off the main trail if you prefer to experience the solitude of the wilderness.

Fifty feet from the trailhead there is a great view of Weavers Needle with the Superstition Wilderness sign in the foreground on the left side of the trail. The sign is only in place the months the rangers are present. From here most hikers expect to see Weavers Needle on the right side of the

Walt Upson. He accompanied Barry Storm on expeditions in the Superstitions. COURTESY SUPERSTITION MOUNTAIN HISTORICAL SOCIETY, JOHN BURBRIDGE COLLECTION.

Dutchman's Trail. Can you explain why Weavers Needle appears to be out of place—on the left side of the trail? Answer: The old road heads south here. Farther down the trail, the Dutchman's Trail turns east and Weavers Needle is visible on the right side.

HISTORY AND LEGENDS. On June 13, 1931, treasure hunter Adolph Ruth rode into the Superstition Mountains on the Dutchman's Trail from First Water Trailhead. At that time, First Water Creek was called Willow Creek as shown on the old maps. The story says that on June 13 he was led by Leroy F. Purnell and Jack Keenan, two cowboys/prospectors from Tex Barkley's outfit, up the trail in Willow Canyon (now First Water Creek) over Parker Pass and down into West Boulder Canyon to a permanent pool of water at Willow Spring. An extensive search was undertaken when Ruth was discovered missing from his camp on June 20. Ruth's skull was found near the Dutchman's Trail and Bull Pass Trail junction in Needle Canyon on December 11, 1931, by an expedition of the Arizona Archeological Commission, sponsored by the *Arizona Republic*. Holes in his skull appeared to be bullet holes. His body was found a month later about one-half mile away on the lower east slope of Black Top Mesa. The last entry in his notebook was *Veni, Vidi, Vici* (I came, I saw, I conquered) which led some investigators to believe he found what he was looking for—the Lost Dutchman Mine. His maps to the lost treasure were missing. Ruth's death was recorded as a natural death, but many believe he was killed for his maps and information. Sixty years later, the story of Adolph Ruth continues to be discussed and reviewed by the experts.[103]

Windmill Hike

This easy hike follows a dirt road down to an old corral and windmill just outside the Wilderness boundary. On the other side of the Wilderness boundary fence you may find small pools of seasonal water in the bedrock of First Water Creek.

ITINERARY: This loop hike starts at the locked-gate road near First Water Trailhead and follows a dirt road down to an old windmill and corral on First Water Creek. Three return routes are available. (1) Return by retracing your trip. (2) Hike south up the First Water Creek bed to Second Water Trail (236) then proceed to the First Water Trailhead. (3) Hike north down the First Water Creek bed to the first wash on the left and follow a well-used horse trail back to the horse trailer parking lot.

DIFFICULTY: Easy. Trail walking except for the alternate returns in First Water Creek bed. Not recommended for horses. Elevation change is ±180 feet.

LENGTH and TIME: 0.9 miles, 0.75 hours round trip.

MAPS: Goldfield, Arizona USGS topo map.
Superstition Wilderness Tonto National Forest map.

FINDING THE TRAIL: The Windmill Hike starts at an unmarked dirt road **[10-B]** that we refer to as the locked-gate road. You can see the locked gate a few feet from FS78. The unsigned locked-gate road is off FS78 about 0.1 mile east of the horse trailer parking lot **[10-A]** on the north side of FS78. If you park at the First Water Trailhead parking lot, walk west on FS78 about 0.4 miles and you will see the locked-gate road on your right (north).

THE HIKE: *Use Map 10.* Climb over the locked gate **[10-B, 0]** or under the barbed wire fence and walk northeast up the dirt road. From the top of the ridge, the road drops down into the First Water Creek drainage. Visible from the road are an old metal water tank, barbed wire corrals, a broken windmill and tin-roofed ramada **[10-P, 0.3]**. The blades and gear box of the windmill had toppled off the tower and were lying at the foot of the structure in

December 1992, but in November 1993 we noticed they had been removed from the area. After looking around the corral, continue down one of the many paths (east) to First Water Creek **[10-O, 0.4]**. The barbed wire fence is the Superstition Wilderness Boundary. If there is water running in First Water Creek or if the potholes have water, stop on one of the large rocks and eat lunch or have a snack. Even without water, this is probably the best place to take a break.

There are three possible routes back to the start of the hike. The easiest is to return the same way (less than 20 minutes) **[10-B, 0.9]**.

The second return route takes you south up First Water Creek bed to Second Water Trail **[10-E, 1.1]**. There is an old trail on the east side of the creek, but it is obscure and not easy to follow. We have often seen mule deer in this area. Continue west on Second Water Trail to the First Water Trailhead parking lot **[10-C, 1.7]** and then west down FS78 to the locked-gate road **[10-B, 2.2]**. This return adds 35 minutes and 1.3 miles to the hike.

For the third route, hike north down the First Water Creek bed to the first wash on the left (before First Water Creek narrows into a small canyon) **[10-N, 0.7]**. Proceed up the wash and look for a well-defined horse trail that follows the bottom of a narrow ravine **[10-R, 0.8]**. This horse trail connects with a dirt road **[10-M, 1.5]** leading south to the horse trailer parking lot **[10-A, 1.7]**. Walk east on FS78 to the locked-gate road **[10-B, 1.8]**. This return adds about 30 minutes and 0.9 miles to the hike description.

The abandoned windmill near First Water Creek, December 1992.

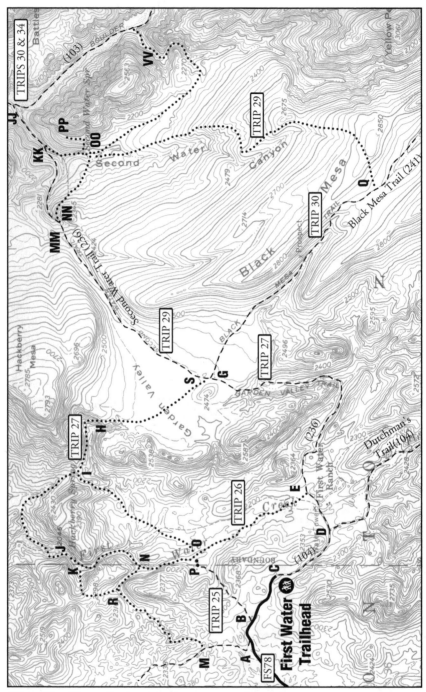

Map 10 - *Trips 24, 25, 26, 27, 28, 29, 30 and 31.*

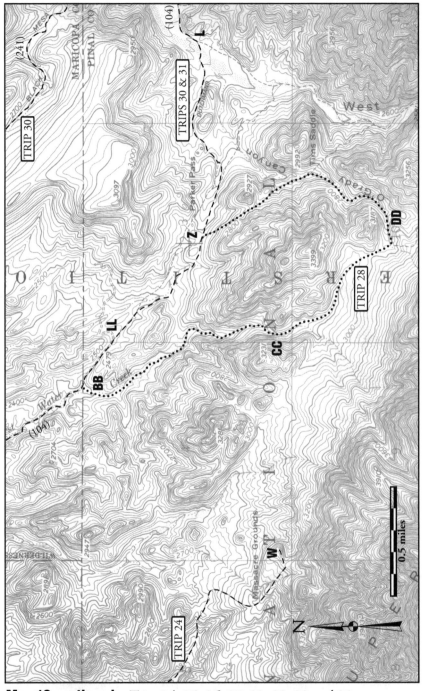

Map 10 continued - *Trips 24, 25, 26, 27, 28, 29, 30 and 31.*

Hackberry Spring

This easy hike takes you to Hackberry Spring which often has water when everything else is dry. Easy walking in the First Water Creek bed leads you through a narrow section of canyon to the well-shaded and pleasant Hackberry Spring.

ITINERARY: This hike starts at the locked-gate road near First Water Trailhead and follows a dirt road down to an old windmill and corral on First Water Creek. The hike continues down First Water Creek to Hackberry Spring. Return the same way or see Trip 25 for alternate return routes.

DIFFICULTY: Easy. Some easy off-trail creek-bed walking. Not recommended for horses. Elevation change is ±274 feet.

LENGTH and TIME: 2.2 miles, 2.0 hours round trip.

MAPS: Goldfield, Arizona USGS topo map.
Superstition Wilderness Tonto National Forest map.

FINDING THE TRAIL: This hike starts at the locked-gate road described in Trip 25. There is no trail signpost here. The locked-gate road is off FS78 about 0.1 mile east of the horse trailer parking lot on the north side of FS78. If you park at the First Water Trailhead parking lot, walk back up FS78 (west) about 0.4 miles and you will see the locked-gate road on your right (north).

THE HIKE: *Use Map 10.* Refer to Trip 25 (Windmill Hike) for the first section of this trip. At First Water Creek **[10-O, 0.4]** continue, north, down First Water Creek to Hackberry Spring. There is no trail here, but it is easy walking along the creek bed. In 0.4 miles the creek goes through a section of narrows with high cliffs on both sides. Just on the other side of the narrows you will see signs of a well-traveled horse trail coming down a ravine from the west **[10-K, 1.0]**. This is the trail that leads back to the horse trailer parking lot on road FS78. You can use the horse trail as an alternate return route. Hackberry Spring **[10-J,1.1]** is a few hundred yards farther north on the east side of First Water Creek in a small hand-carved niche at the bottom of the

---

First Water Creek at Hackberry Spring.

cliff. From the stream bed you can see a metal pipe extending over the dirt bank. Some water collects in the rubble-filled cement tank at the edge of First Water Creek. There is often water at Hackberry Spring in the dry season. This is a pretty canyon with sheer cliffs on the east and abundant greenery on the canyon floor. Fremont cottonwoods and willows grow in the water course, and on the bench there are large netleaf hackberry, honey mesquite and oak trees.

Return the same route to the start of the hike **[10-B, 2.2]**. Refer to Trip 25 (Windmill Hike) for alternate return routes. Trip 27 (Garden Valley Loop) describes some other trails in the Hackberry Spring area that you might want to explore.

To avoid the narrow rocky-canyon south of Hackberry Spring in First Water Creek, horseback riders can take the road (north) from the horse-trailer parking lot to Hackberry Spring. A popular horse-ride follows Trip 27 (Garden Valley Loop) in reverse.

Garden Valley Loop

Garden Valley is the site of a prehistoric Indian ruin where pot sherds litter the ground under a forest of chain fruit cholla cactus. Several trails traverse this level expanse with Weavers Needle and Four Peaks rising above the surrounding low hills. The horse trail to Hackberry Spring is seldom used so you may find solitude along this part of the trip. Hackberry Spring often has water in the dry season and there may be seasonal pools of water in First Water Creek.

ITINERARY: From First Water Trailhead follow the Second Water Trail (236) east to Garden Valley. From Garden Valley an unmarked horse trail heads northwest to Hackberry Spring. Three alternate return routes are available from Hackberry Spring: take First Water Creek bed south to Second Water Trail; follow an unmarked trail leading west then south to the horse trailer parking lot; or hike south in First Water Creek bed and out the windmill/corral road to the locked gate.

DIFFICULTY: Easy to Moderate. Trail walking except for the section along First Water Creek bed. Elevation change is ±454 feet.

LENGTH and TIME: 5.4 miles, 3.5 hours round trip.

MAPS: Goldfield, Arizona USGS topo map.
Superstition Wilderness Tonto National Forest map.

FINDING THE TRAIL: The Second Water Trail and Dutchman's Trail both leave the southeast side of the First Water Trailhead parking lot and head east, down an old rough dirt road where you will see the wooden trail sign.

THE HIKE: *Use Map 10.* From the parking lot **[10-C, 0]**, walk east about 0.4 miles down the old dirt road to the trail intersection where the Dutchman's and Second Water Trails diverge **[10-D, 0.4]**. Take the Second Water Trail which goes left (east) and crosses First Water Creek (a rocky creek bed usually dry or with little water). Just after crossing the First Water Creek bed, look to the left (north) and remember the lay of the land. One of the possible return routes will be through the creek bed or on an abandoned trail on the east bank near the barbed wire fence. Continue east following Second Water Trail over to Garden Valley **[10-G, 1.9]**. The USGS map appropriately refers to this trail as the Garden Valley Trail.

Garden Valley is a very flat area covered with mesquite trees and chain fruit cholla cactus. There is a sign at the trail intersection showing the Black Mesa Trail branching off to the right (southeast). The Second Water Trail continues left (northeast) going over to Second Water Spring, Boulder Canyon and La Barge Canyon. For this hike, you want to look for the unmarked trail that branches left, off the Second Water Trail, about 100 feet north of the Black Mesa Trail and Second Water Trail intersection **[10-S, 2.0]**. This unmarked horse trail has a well-defined track across the flat valley floor and begins just north of the small knoll identified as 2474 on the USGS Goldfield topo map. The knoll, which is on your left (west), is not shown on the Superstition Wilderness Tonto NF map. The unmarked trail goes northeast across Garden Valley where it drops down into a ravine and continues on to Hackberry Spring.

The prehistoric Indian ruin is about 50 feet north of the Second Water and Black Mesa Trail sign. The ruin is covered with grass and palo verde trees and looks like a big mound of rocks. There are pottery sherds all over Garden Valley. Look at them, take some photographs, but leave the pottery sherds on the ground for the next visitor.

The hike resumes on the unmarked horse trail **[10-S]**, continuing northwest to Hackberry Spring. From the northwest corner of Garden Valley, the well-defined horse trail drops down into an unnamed ravine. There is a small hole in the hillside (below the trail), evidence of old mine diggings **[10-H, 2.7]**. A few hundred yards down the trail it is easy to look up canyon to see the small mine in the eroding bank, dug by Barry Storm in the late 1930s or early 1940s.[104] At the trail junction **[10-I, 2.9]**, on the saddle, a horse trail to the left heads down to First Water Creek, but this hike continues on the right branch. The landscape in this area is dominated by jojoba, mesquite and saguaro cactus. Four Peaks can be seen through a break in the hills to the north. From the saddle the trail heads north, then west over another low saddle before dropping down into First Water Creek just north of Hackberry Spring.

Hackberry Spring **[10-K, 3.4]** often has water in the dry season. It is located in a small hand carved niche at the bottom of the cliff on the east side of First Water Creek. See Trip 26 (Hackberry Spring).

ALTERNATE RETURN ROUTES. From Hackberry Spring there are three possible routes to First Water Trailhead. About 200 yards south of Hackberry Spring, the first route follows a horse trail **[10-K, 3.5]** up a steep hill to a ridge on the west side of First Water Creek. This is a quick return route but not that interesting. It is used for easy access by horse riders to avoid the narrow section in First Water Creek. From the ridge, follow this trail north, down a ravine, until it crosses a small wash **[10-R, 3.8]**. Here the trail splits. The left branch goes down to First Water Creek. This hike takes the right branch heading southwest and follows the sandy wash. In about 15 minutes a short trail goes west, out of the wash, up to the dirt road **[10-M, 4.4]**. Follow the dirt road south to the horse trailer parking lot at FS78 **[10-A, 4.6]**. Turn east on FS78 and walk another 15 minutes back to the First Water Trailhead parking lot **[10-C, 5.1]**.

A more interesting variation of this return is to connect with the dirt road by hiking up First Water Creek 0.4 miles from Hackberry Spring to the first wash on the right (west) **[10-N, 3.8]**. Proceed up the wash and look for a well-defined horse trail that follows the bottom of a narrow ravine. This horse trail connects with the dirt road **[10-M]**, horse trailer parking lot **[10-A]**, and trailhead parking lot **[10-C, 5.3]** as described above.

From Hackberry Spring, the other two alternate routes continue up the First Water Creek bed (south) toward the Second Water Trail. One route follows the east bank of First Water Creek on one of several meandering game trails until it crosses Second Water Trail **[10-E, 4.8]**. We sometimes get a fleeting glimpse of several deer in the brush along this trail. Take the Second Water Trail right (west) back to the main parking lot **[10-C, 5.4]**. This is the same trail used at the start of the hike.

The other route leaves First Water Creek **[10-O, 4.1]** about 0.7 miles south of Hackberry Spring, heading west toward an old dirt road visible on the hill on the western horizon. Starting at the old windmill and corral **[10-P]**, this dirt road takes you to the locked gate near FS78 **[10-B, 4.5]** and on to the trailhead parking lot **[10-C, 4.9]**. This route will normally have the least hiker traffic. See Trip 25 (Windmill Hike) for a description of this area.

HISTORY AND LEGENDS. The Goldfield USGS map still shows buildings at the First Water Ranch site. Bill Barkley, son of Tex Barkley, and his wife Betty built a house, a barn and some out buildings here on the south side of the Second Water Trail near First Water Creek.[105] The Forest Service removed the structures, and all that remains today are some concrete footings. Greg Hansen and Russ Orr of the Forest Service recall that about 1972

Elizabeth Stewart inspecting the grinding holes in Garden Valley.

the cattle operation was moved about 0.7 miles north along First Water Creek, just outside the Wilderness boundary fence. This is the site of the old abandoned windmill.

The *Arizona Daily Gazette*, in 1893, reported the ruins of a prehistoric stone house in Garden Valley. They estimated the structure to be at least three stories with a large stone-paved courtyard in the center. The outside dimensions were estimated to be 300 by 500 feet. On the southeastern and upper side of Garden Valley there was evidence of irrigation canals.[106] The ruin is still there today, but is easy to miss since it is covered with grass and palo verde trees. The ruin is only 50 feet north of the intersection of the Second Water and Black Mesa Trails, just west of knoll 2474. You can still see the remains of a few walls, but it mostly looks like a big mound of rocks. The 1893 report seems to overestimate the size. By our estimate the ruin is probably closer to 75 feet wide, 150 feet long, and 10 feet high. We couldn't find the irrigation canals, but we did find two large and two small metates (grinding bowls) in the rocks on the southeast side of knoll 2474—about half way to the top. The grinding holes are carved into flat rock and measure six to eight inches in diameter and two to ten inches deep. We found these in two locations. There are parts of broken manos (grinding stones) on the valley floor.

The pottery sherds in Garden Valley are usually about an inch to an inch and a half square with one side finished in a smooth, solid red color and the other side an unfinished desert-sand color. A few sherds have designs painted in red (red on buff). Specks of mica in the unfinished side sparkle in the sun. Some of the sherds have the smooth edged feature of a vessel lip. This pottery was probably made by the Salado Indians between A.D. 1100 and 1400. Don't take any of the pottery sherds away from the site.

Watch for the jumping cholla cactus. The literature inconsistently refers to both chain fruit cholla (Opuntia fulgida) and teddy bear cholla (Opuntia bigelovii) as jumping cholla. Both plants drop spiny segments to the ground, but the teddy bear cholla has the reputation for being strongly barbed and more difficult to remove when embedded in your skin. It is easy to step on a cholla segment and transfer the spines from your shoe to your leg.

In 1866, Garden Valley was the site of a major skirmish between the Apache and Yavapai Indians, and the U.S. Infantry led by army commander Lt. Dubois from Fort McDowell. Note that these were foot soldiers, not cavalry soldiers. Thirty Indians were killed and many taken prisoner.[107]

In some areas of Garden Valley you can see both Four Peaks and Weavers Needle. Some of the Lost Dutchman Mine maps show a reference line between these two peaks. Garden Valley lies to the west of that reference line. There is another clue that proposes the Lost Dutchman Mine lies on a line drawn from Four Peaks when the four peaks are viewed as one peak. Four Peaks has that orientation when viewed from the Tortilla area.

Upper First Water Creek

This enjoyable hike follows First Water Creek to its headwaters where you may find seasonal pools of water in the bedrock. There is a chance to find solitude here as you view the broad expanse of the Superstition Mountain north slopes. Parker Pass provides a good view of Weavers Needle.

ITINERARY: From First Water Trailhead, follow the Dutchman's Trail (104) southeast. The route leaves the Dutchman's Trail and continues up First Water Creek bed, climbs though a small canyon and out onto the back slopes of Superstition Mountain. The return continues south to O'Grady Canyon where a seldom used trail circles north to Parker Pass, connects with the Dutchman's Trail and retraces the Dutchman's Trail northwest back to the First Water Trailhead parking lot.

DIFFICULTY: Moderate. Trail walking except for the sections along First Water Creek bed and route finding in O'Grady Canyon. Not recommended for horses. Elevation change is ±960 feet.

LENGTH and TIME: 7.2 miles, 6 hours round trip.

MAPS: Goldfield, Arizona USGS topo map.
Superstition Wilderness Tonto National Forest map.

FINDING THE TRAIL: The Second Water Trail and Dutchman's Trail both leave the southeast side of the First Water Trailhead parking lot and head east down an old rough dirt road where you will see the trail marker.

THE HIKE: *Use Map 10.* From the First Water Trailhead parking lot **[10-C, 0]** walk east about 0.4 miles down the old dirt road to the trail intersection **[10-D]** where the Dutchman's and Second Water Trails diverge. A wooden signpost marks this junction. Take the Dutchman's Trail right (southeast) and continue past at least six stream or dry creek bed crossings. There are some nice rock formations in the low cliffs on the right side of the trail. After walking about 20 or 30 minutes the Dutchman's Trail crosses over First Water Creek for the last time. This is the place where the hike leaves the

Prospector and treasure hunter Barry Storm, author of Thunder God's Gold. COURTESY SUPERSTITION MOUNTAIN HISTORICAL SOCIETY, JOHN BURBRIDGE COLLECTION.

Dutchman's Trail **[10-BB, 1.4]**. At this point the Dutchman's Trail heads southeast, away from the creek and up a small hill. If you continue up the hill for another five minutes on the Dutchman's Trail **[10-Z]**, you will see the top of Weavers Needle. This is the turnaround point for the easy hike. You will then know that the last creek crossing was back down the trail and that you must return to the creek. From the bottom of the hill **[10-BB]**, near a stone water diversion bar on the trail, this hike continues south up First Water Creek. You can walk up the creek bed if it is dry or on either side of First Water Creek since there is no trail. The most interesting portion of the hike begins where First Water Creek makes a bend due south, and the creek bed climbs through a small narrow canyon. There has been water in the pools **[CC, 2.8]** here even when the lower creek bed was dry. This would be the best place for lunch or a snack.

Continuing to the top of the narrow canyon, the creek bed opens out into a large sloping plane on the backside of Superstition Mountain. Just to the west is Trip 24 (Massacre Grounds). Could the Mexicans have passed here on their ill-fated escape from the Apache Indians in 1848? Is there lost gold dropped by the retreating Mexicans miners still lying on the ground? It might be worth a few minutes to walk around and check the ground for gold nuggets revealed by recent erosion.

Continue walking on the relatively open desert southeast along the low hills for about 0.6 miles until you see the narrow ravine of O'Grady Canyon on your left. Look for the O'Grady trail at the start of the ravine on the right side (south) **[10-DD, 3.6]** and continue down the ravine in a northeasterly direction where a trail comes in from the southeast off Tims Saddle. The O'Grady trail is not well-defined so you must take your best guess for trail direction in some places.

After the intersection with the Tims Saddle Trail, continue northwest on the O'Grady Trail up through a small pass and then down to the Dutchman's Trail near Parker Pass **[10-Z, 4.9]**. This is a good place to view Weavers Needle which is 2.5 miles to the southeast. The site of Aylor's Caballo Camp is about 1.5 miles directly east, just north of Palomino Mountain. Descend the Dutchman's Trail into the First Water Creek drainage. The return route continues northwest, retracing the hike on the Dutchman's Trail back to the First Water Trailhead parking lot **[10-C, 7.2]**.

HISTORY AND LEGENDS. In their 1978 *Hiker's Guide to the Superstition Mountains*, Dick and Sharon Nelson noted an abandoned vehicle **[10-LL]** along the north side of the Dutchman's Trail about 0.7 miles northeast of Parker Pass.[108] It has been rumored that the car may have belonged to an old time prospector, either Chuck Aylor or Obie Stoker.[109] Forest Service Wilderness Ranger George Martin disassembled the car with a cutting torch and enlisted the help of the Sierra Club to pack it out of the Wilderness in March of 1980 or 1981.[110] While recognizing the need to restore and preserve the Wilderness, some Superstition Mountain aficionados felt a sense of loss when this rusty old landmark was removed.

U.S. Forest Service camp at First Water Trailhead in 1993.

Second Water Spring

This hike takes you beyond Garden Valley to a seasonal spring with cattails and reeds. Above the spring is the site of an old mining camp. An easy walk up the hill takes you to the caved-in mine shaft. From the mine there are good views of the canyons and surrounding mountains. Ten minutes east of Second Water Spring is Boulder Canyon where you may find seasonal water.

ITINERARY: From First Water Trailhead, follow the Second Water Trail (236) to Second Water Spring. A short loop hike can be made down and out of Second Water Spring. Return by Second Water Trail (236). An alternate approach takes the Black Mesa Trail (241) to the summit, then drops northwest down an off-trail route into the ravine of Second Water Canyon, ending at Second Water Spring. Return by the Second Water Trail (236).

DIFFICULTY: Moderate. Mostly trail hiking except in Second Water Spring area. Alternate approach involves moderate off-trail hiking. Elevation change is ±740 feet.

LENGTH and TIME: 7.2 miles, 3.5 hours round trip.

MAPS: Goldfield, Arizona USGS topo map.
Superstition Wilderness Tonto National Forest map.

FINDING THE TRAIL: This trip begins at the wooden trail sign in Garden Valley **[10-G, 1.9]**.

THE HIKE: *Use Map 10.* From the First Water Trailhead parking lot **[10-C, 0]**, follow Trip 27 (Garden Valley Loop) to the junction of the Black Mesa Trail in Garden Valley **[10-G, 1.9]**. From the trail sign **[10-G, 1.9]**, follow the Second Water Trail (236) northeast across the flat expanse of Garden Valley. At the north end of Garden Valley the trail skirts a earthen cow tank. From here the trail begins to descend and, after a short distance, the trail becomes rocky again.

After walking about 30 or 40 minutes from the Garden Valley trail-junction sign, you pass the old road **[10-MM, 2.8]** going over to Cholla cow tank on the left. Another 5 minutes down the trail there is a rock cairn on the right marking a faint trail **[10-NN, 2.9]** that leads to an old mining camp above the Second Water Spring. Take this trail heading west and follow it for 10 minutes until you reach Second Water Canyon. Trash from some mining work is still at the camp **[10-OO, 3.3]** on the west side of the ravine—rusty buckets, kitchen gear, bed frames, etc. At the north end of the camp, if you look closely, you will see a trail heading steeply up the hill. After heading east it contours around to the north and ends at an old mine shaft **[10-PP]** filled in with rock and timber. It takes less than 10 minutes to reach the mine from the camp. At the mine, you are rewarded with a fine view of the surrounding area.

Back at the camp, hike down the bed (north) of Second Water Canyon. It is easy walking over the bedrock. The quantity and quality of water here will depend on the season. It is best to bring your own drinking water. Grasses, reeds, and cattails are usually growing in small catch basins of water. Farther down, there are some larger bushes and trees. Continue down Second Water Canyon until the ravine crosses the main trail (236). This is the turnaround point for this hike **[10-KK, 3.6]**. Boulder Canyon **[10-JJ, 3.8]** is another 10 minutes down the trail (northeast), but you want to turn left

Remnants of a former mining camp above Second Water Spring.

here and follow the trail southwest to Garden Valley where the trip description ends **[10-G, 7.2]**.

ALTERNATE ROUTE DIRECTIONS. The alternate route for this hike begins at the junction **[10-G, 1.9]** of Second Water Trail and Black Mesa Trail in Garden Valley. Add an extra hour and 1.4 miles to the hike totals for this route. When we hiked this route, from Garden Valley, it took us almost 2 hours (3.8 miles) to reach Second Water via Black Mesa. Follow the Black Mesa Trail (241) to the top of Black Mesa **[10-Q, 3.0]**. Leaving the flat area on top of Black Mesa, walk west through the forest of cholla—no trail. When you reach the ridge, locate Second Water Canyon and descend northwest into the canyon via your choice of a route. The canyon at this point is more like a shallow ravine and never becomes very deep, even at the spring area. The terrain along this cross-country route is mostly easy walking, and you can find a few flat spaces for camping on the saddle to the east. In 1993 there were many old and new cow trails here. Don't feel that you have to follow our suggested route. We normally select a cross-country route by visually scouting the easiest path. On another trip you might want to check out a short canyon, east and north of elevation mark 2270 **[10-VV]**, where you can find seasonal water in smooth rock basins. Continuing down Second Water drainage you will eventually arrive at the old mining camp **[10-OO, 5.7]** on the right side of the ravine. Follow the main hike description from here.

Jack Carlson in the cholla cactus forest on top of Black Mesa.

Black Mesa Loop

This popular loop hike takes you from Garden Valley to the top of Black Mesa then down into West Boulder Canyon. You may find seasonal water in West and East Boulder Creek. A short side trip takes you to East Boulder Canyon to the site of Aylor's Caballo Camp, Aylor's Arch, Horse's Head With A Laid Back Ear, and wonderful views of Weavers Needle.

ITINERARY: This hike starts at First Water Trailhead and follows the Second Water Trail (236) east to Garden Valley. In Garden Valley, the Black Mesa Trail (241) heads southeast up and over Black Mesa, descending into West Boulder Canyon. A short hike takes you to the site of Aylor's Caballo Camp in East Boulder Canyon. From West Boulder Creek, there are two possible return routes. The shortest and easiest goes west on the Dutchman's Trail (104), over Parker Pass to First Water Trailhead. The alternate return goes east on the Dutchman's Trail, north on the Boulder Canyon Trail (103), and finally west on the Second Water Trail (236) back to the First Water Trailhead.

DIFFICULTY: Moderate. Trail walking. The alternate return on Boulder Canyon Trail requires numerous, but easy, creek crossings. Elevation change is ±900 feet.

LENGTH and TIME: 9 miles, 5 hours round trip. Plan for an additional 2.8 miles plus 2 hours for the alternate return via Boulder Canyon Trail and Second Water Trail.

MAPS: Goldfield, Arizona USGS topo map.
Superstition Wilderness Tonto National Forest map.

FINDING THE TRAIL: This trip begins at the wooden trail sign in Garden Valley **[10-G, 1.9]**.

THE HIKE: *Use Maps 10 and 11.* This is a favorite loop hike with many people. It is a nice, moderate hike for people who prefer trail hiking and for those who are still building their off-trail route-finding skills. It is also a good

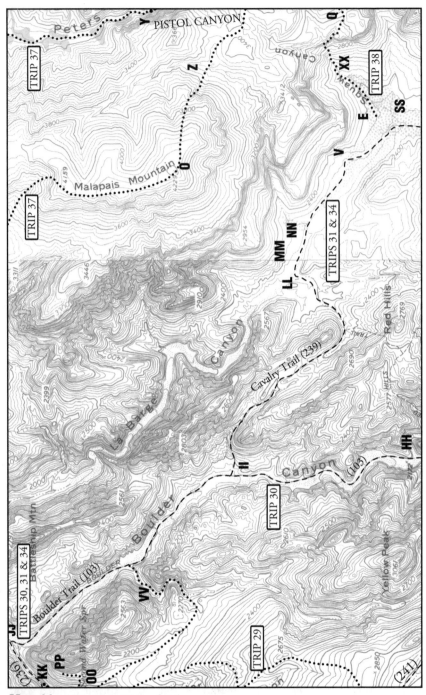

Map 11 - *Trips 30, 31 and 34.*

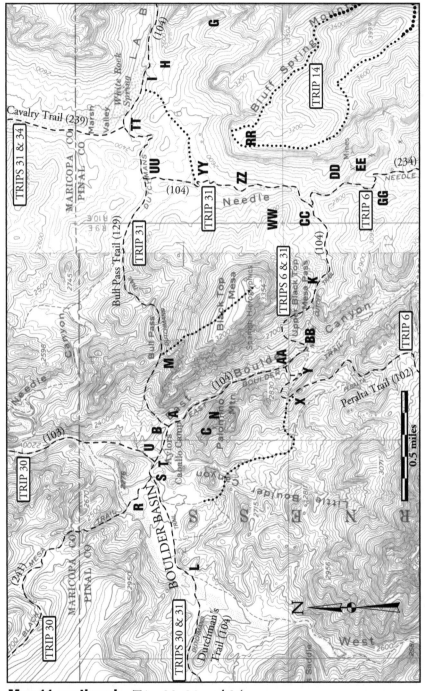

Map 11 continued - *Trips 30, 31 and 34.*

introduction to many of the trails that branch off to other parts of the Superstition Wilderness.

From the First Water Trailhead parking lot **[10-C, 0]**, follow Trip 27 (Garden Valley Loop) to the junction of the Black Mesa Trail in Garden Valley **[10-G, 1.9]**.

Garden Valley is a very flat area covered with mesquite trees and jumping cholla cactus. There is a sign at the trail intersection, next to the Indian ruin, showing the Black Mesa Trail (241) branching to the right (southeast). If the trail sign **[10-G, 1.9]** is missing, the intersection is just east of the small knoll (elevation 2474) on your left.

Take the Black Mesa Trail, and hike southeast up to the pass over Black Mesa. The trail passes under some towering saguaro cactus before leveling off at the pass **[10-Q, 3.0]** where there is a large forest of jumping cholla cactus. The trail doesn't go to the top of Black Mesa so, for a better view of the valleys below, you must take a short walk to the left or right, off the main trail. There are no trails to the ridge lines so you need to carefully wind your way through the thick forest of cholla. From the ridge on the left (north) side of the trail, the panorama is Battleship Mountain and Geronimo Head overlooking La Barge Canyon. Four Peaks is farther in the distance. If you have binoculars, you can get some even better close-up views. Second Water Canyon begins here on Black Mesa and drains north. It is possible to make a cross-country route from the ridge down to Second Water Spring (Trip 27). The panorama from the ridge on the west side of the trail overlooks First Water Creek drainage. To the west, the Dutchman's Trail can be seen going up and over Parker Pass.

As the trail begins to descend, the vista to the south opens up and you can begin to see West and East Boulder Canyons (Boulder Basin) with Weavers Needle in the distance. To the southeast, Bull Pass Trail goes up the low pass just to the north of Black Top Mesa. The steep and eroded Bull Pass Trail is well-defined but difficult to see from here. Black Top Mesa is recognized by its tan cliffs, topped by a small band of black volcanic rock. Palomino Mountain, just to the west of Black Top Mesa, also has impressive tan cliffs but no black top.

Continue to follow Black Mesa Trail southeast as it drops into the wide West Boulder Canyon area. As you are hiking, look out into the flat, wide valley of Boulder Basin for the Dutchman's Trail intersection and West Boulder Creek crossing. Once in the valley it will be difficult to get the big picture of the trail layout. Boulder Basin has endless flat places for tent camping and picnicking but only a very few small trees for shade. The trail crosses West Boulder Creek **[11-R, 4.7]** and quickly intersects the Dutchman's

Boulder Creek at the Calvary Trail junction with Boulder Creek at flood stage in December 1992.

Trail at a wooden trail marker **[11-S, 4.9]**. This is the point where the easy return hike goes right (west) and follows the Dutchman's Trail back to First Water Trailhead. The alternate return goes left (east) on the Dutchman's Trail for the longer trek via Boulder Canyon and Second Water Spring.

Whichever return route you select, you should take the short, quarter-mile side trip up the Dutchman's Trail, over the small hill, to the former site of Aylor's Caballo Camp in East Boulder Canyon. From the Black Mesa and Dutchman's Trail intersection **[11-S]**, take the Dutchman's Trail east. After about 10 minutes, the Boulder Canyon Trail branches off to the left **[11-T, 5.0]**. The Boulder Canyon Trail is the longer return route. Continue on the Dutchman's Trail east for 5 minutes to the Bull Pass Trail sign **[11-B]** and on another 5 minutes to Aylor's Caballo Camp **[11-A]**. Caballo Camp is marked on the Goldfield USGS topo map by a small black rectangle just above the "p" in Camp along the Dutchman's Trail in East Boulder Canyon.

The view of Weavers Needle up East Boulder Canyon is superb. A few minutes walk south of Aylor's Camp on the Dutchman's Trail there is a view of Aylor's Arch **[11-C]** on the skyline of east-facing Palomino Mountain. On the cliff face to the left of the arch is the outline of a *Horse's Head With Laid Back Ear* **[11-N]** which is said to be a landmark for a lost mine. The mine is believed to be on the hill under the head.[111] If you first locate the shape of the horse's eye, you will see the nose sloping off to the left and the ear defined by a dark desert varnish on the cliff face.

Another side trip in the area is to the site of an old arrastra used for grinding ore [11-U]. See History and Legends for the story of the arrastra.

Back at the Dutchman's Trail and Black Mesa Trail intersection [11-S, 4.9], the easiest return trip takes the Dutchman's Trail east. It is about 4.1 miles (2 hours) to the First Water Trailhead. Hike west through the relatively flat Boulder Basin area following the Dutchman's Trail on the south side of West Boulder Creek. If you have extra time you might want to leave the trail and walk through the desert for a change of pace. If you are planning a future camping trip, there are many flat areas for tent camping in Boulder Basin.

Twenty minutes up the Dutchman's Trail, the trail crosses West Boulder Creek [10-L, 5.5] and heads up to Parker Pass [10-Z, 6.5]. It's downhill from the top of Parker Pass to First Water Creek. Looking left (south) [10-BB, 7.6] up First Water Creek, you can see the route (no trail) of the Upper First Water Canyon hike. The Dutchman's Trail follows the First Water Creek drainage back to the parking lot [10-C, 9.0]. The creek is narrow and the several creek crossings are well-defined by heavy use.

ALTERNATE RETURN DIRECTIONS. The alternate return hike using the Boulder Canyon and Second Water Trails is about 6.9 miles (4 hours) back to the First Water Trailhead. This hike requires many crossings on boulders in the creek. Of course, if you don't mind wet feet, you can just wade across. The water is seasonal, so Boulder Canyon Creek might be just a dry creek bed which makes the hiking easier but the scenery is not as pleasant. Boulder Canyon Trail (103) starts from the Dutchman's Trail just 10 minutes heading east, over the low hill, from the Black Mesa Trail intersection. There should be a wooden sign here [11-T, 5.0]. The start of Boulder Canyon Trail goes north and follows East Boulder Canyon Creek. The trail soon passes West Boulder Canyon Creek entering on the left. This is the beginning of Boulder Canyon.

Boulder Canyon Trail continues down the Boulder Canyon water course on a trail marked by large rock cairns at each crossing. Needle Canyon enters on the right [11-HH, 5.7] and is marked by a naturally whitewashed, needle-shaped rock on the low cliff to the north. There are several flat sandy camping places here, formed by high water flowing through the canyon after heavy rains. Camp on high ground if it looks like it will rain.

The Cavalry Trail (239) comes in on the right (east) side of the creek. If you have been following the rock cairns, the trail will pass by the wooden trail sign **[11-II, 6.8]** on the east bank which marks the intersection with the Cavalry Trail. The Cavalry Trail is a convenient trail to use for trips over to La Barge Canyon and Marsh Valley. Across Boulder Canyon Creek from the Cavalry trail sign there are some flat, sandy campsites.

Continue downstream for about 40 minutes until you see Second Water Canyon **[10-JJ, 8.2]** break the horizon on the west side of Boulder Canyon. Map 10 shows the Second Water Canyon area better than Map 11. Second Water Trail (236) goes up this small drainage. There is a trail sign on the west bank, but the large, smooth, flat white rocks in the middle of the creek are a better indicator of the trail intersection. The Boulder Canyon Trail continues downstream on the west bank, but for this trip, you want to take the Second Water Trail west up the ravine for the final two hours of the trip. Follow the Second Water Trail to Second Water Spring drainage **[10-KK, 8.4]**, to Garden Valley **[10-G, 9.9]** and to First Water Trailhead **[10-C, 11.8]** where the trip description ends. See Trips 27 and 29 for more information about this trail.

If you have time, you might want to explore Second Water Canyon and spring. There are some mine diggings up on the hill to the east. Continue up the Second Water Trail until Second Water Canyon crosses the trail. About 200 feet up the trail you can drop down into Second Water Canyon and proceed up the terraced rock, through the seasonal water pools. For those who enjoy the reeds, cattails, and willows, this is an ideal spot. When the canyon branches, stay to the left (east) and continue up to a flat area that was a former camp. There are some old (and not so old) remnants of a camp here where a faint trail leads out of the west side of Second Water Canyon (which now looks like a wash). This trail goes up and then contours over to the Second Water Trail. Follow the description above for the return trip to First Water Trailhead.

HISTORY AND LEGENDS. Boulder Basin was commonly referred to as Brush Corral Basin in the 1970s and earlier. Greg Hansen of the Forest Service said Brush Corral was located near the Black Mesa and Dutchman's Trail junction **[11-S]**. It was a large wooden corral which burned sometime around 1965. Swanson and Kollenborn, in their book, *The History of Apache Junction, Arizona*, show a 1948 picture of Brush Corral with rancher William T. "Bill" Barkley overlooking the branding operation.[112] Bill was William A. "Tex" Barkley's son.

A quarter mile southeast of Brush Corral, Charles "Chuck" and Martha "Peg" Aylor located their camp in East Boulder Canyon **[11-A]**. From the late 1930s to the late 1960s, they were actively prospecting for gold and enjoying the beauty of the Superstition Mountains. Their camp, located just south of the junction where East and West Boulder canyons meet, had a fine view up East Boulder Canyon toward Weavers Needle with the sheer cliffs of Palomino Mountain on the west and Black Top Mesa on the east. They named their camp *Caballo Camp* which is still shown on the Goldfield USGS topographic map. Since the arch **[11-C]** on Palomino Mountain doesn't have a name, we wanted to identify it for easy reference in our hike descriptions. Tom Kollenborn suggested *Aylor's Arch* which we think is an appropriate name. He also said some story tellers call it the *Eye of the Horse* or *Caballo Ojo*. Caballo Camp was removed by the Forest Service in the early 1960s, but you can still see the flat terrace beside the black basalt boulders where it was located. The Aylors also built a stone house in lower La Barge Canyon below the Lower Box. After it was discovered by the public, their stone house was dismantled by the Forest Service in the 1960s. Permanent structures are not permitted in the Wilderness Area. Chuck Aylor died in 1967 and Peg Aylor died in 1969.[113]

An arrastra is a fifteen-foot circular arrangement of flat rocks upon which large rocks are dragged to crush gold ore. A horse or mule was attached to a beam to supply the power that moved the rocks (similar to a children's pony ride). The Blue Bird Mine and Gift Shop along the Apache Trail has an arrastra on display behind the store. After a heavy rain in 1940, Brownie Holmes found an arrastra a few hundred yards south of the East and West Boulder Canyon junction **[11-U]**. After another heavy rain in 1944, he noted that it was covered with dirt again. We have not seen the arrastra, but it may appear again, so we will keep looking.[114]

The Superstition Mountain Museum has an arrastra drag rock on display that was packed out of the mountains by Tex Barkley and his ranch hand "Boog" Barnett in the early 1930s. The drag rock was found at the junction of East and West Boulder Canyon. Nancy Barkley McCollough (granddaughter of Tex Barkley) and her husband Ken donated the drag rock to the Museum. The rock had been part of a wall at the Three R's Ranch and later it was taken to Gertrude Barkley's home in Kings Ranch. The museum display notes that George Scholey packed the sweep pole, from the same arrastra, out of the mountains. The location of the sweep pole is unknown.[115]

Barry Storm claimed to have found gold ore in Boulder Canyon about a mile and a half north of the reported site of the arrastra. His February 27, 1940, assay report showed 28.64 ounces of gold valued at $1002.40 when gold was $35 an ounce. From Barry Storm's topo map[116] it appears that he found the ore in Boulder Canyon just south of the small canyon we marked **[11-VV]**.

Marsh Valley Loop

This is a classic hike that loops through the interior of the Wilderness. While hiking on portions of four established trails, you discover seasonal water, cottonwood and sycamore trees, a large stone holding corral, former mining camps, unusual claim monuments and markings, stone walls, extraordinary views of Weavers Needle, the site of the Adolph Ruth stories, Aylor's Arch and more.

ITINERARY: From the First Water Trailhead, follow the Second Water Trail (236) to Boulder Canyon. Take Boulder Canyon Trail (103) to Cavalry Trail (239) and follow the Cavalry Trail to La Barge Canyon. Explore La Barge Canyon north to the White Spring area. The return route takes the Dutchman's Trail (104) around Black Top Mesa, down East Boulder Canyon, over Parker Pass to First Water Trailhead. An alternate route goes from La Barge Canyon into Needle Canyon on Bull Pass Trail (129), over Bull Pass, connecting with the Dutchman's Trail to First Water Trailhead.

DIFFICULTY: Difficult day hike if you explore all the special attractions or moderate overnight backpack. All trail hiking. Off-trail hiking required to explore most of the special attractions. Elevation change is ±1540 feet.

LENGTH and TIME: 15.6 miles, 9 hours round trip.

MAPS: Goldfield, Arizona USGS topo map.
Weavers Needle, Arizona USGS topo map.
Superstition Wilderness Tonto National Forest map.

FINDING THE TRAIL: The hike starts in Boulder Canyon at the junction of the Second Water and Boulder Canyon Trails. See Trip 29 for the trail description starting from First Water Trailhead.

THE HIKE: *Use Maps 10 and 11.* This is one of our favorite hikes. It takes you into the Boulder and La Barge drainages where you have spectacular views of the open valleys and mountain peaks. The trip provides majestic views of Weavers Needle at many points along the trail. Lots of folks make the loop hike in one day but plan ahead if you want to do much off-trail exploring. Many people camp for several days near Marsh Valley and take hikes to the surrounding mesas and canyons.

Start the hike from the First Water Trailhead **[10-C, 0]** by following Trip 29 (Second Water Spring) beyond Second Water Spring to the junction of Boulder Canyon **[11-JJ, 3.6]**. At the Boulder Canyon and Second Water Canyon signed trail junction **[11-JJ, 3.6]**, take the Boulder Canyon Trail to the right (south) and follow it along the bed of the creek. The trail crosses Boulder Canyon Creek many times, and is usually easy to follow if you spot the rock cairns at each crossing. The amount of water in Boulder Canyon varies with the season. The creek can be bone dry or, on occasion, it can be at flood stage and impassable. Most often, it has seasonal water and is easily crossed on the many rocks that dot the stream bed. There are flat camping places on the low bench along the creek bed, but don't camp here when it rains due to the danger of flash flooding. From Second Water Canyon, proceed south, up the Boulder Canyon Trail, to the signed Cavalry Trail **[11-II, 5.0]** which enters on the left (east). Follow the Cavalry Trail (239) as it goes over a pass just north of the Red Hills and drops down to La Barge Creek **[11-LL, 6.4]**.

La Barge Canyon offers many places for camping and exploring. A few hundred yards south on the east side of La Barge Creek is a small hill which has signs of an old camp on its flat top **[11-MM]**. Trash is buried in a large pit, and a stone wall forms a corral against the south-facing rocks. This is a good vantage point from which to locate the larger stone corral a few hundred yards to the south **[11-NN]**.

From the creek bed, go upstream about a quarter mile, or less, from the junction of La Barge Creek and the Cavalry Trail to visit the old stone holding corral **[11-NN, 6.7]**. It is on a low bench on the northeast side of La Barge Creek. From a cluster of Fremont cottonwood and Arizona sycamore trees growing in the bed of La Barge Creek, go directly east about 100 yards to locate the stone structure. The corral is U-shaped, without a roof, about 30 feet square with walls three to four feet thick. The rock walls are about four feet high with the back wall missing. The back wall was probably closed with a movable fence. We haven't been able to determine when it was constructed. We originally thought this was some kind of building, but Tom Kollenborn suggested it is more likely a holding corral. Clay Worst said that the corral was built by Bob Jacob (Crazy Jake).

Evidence of Salado occupation in this area of La Barge Canyon, probably between A.D. 1100 and 1400, is present, but traces of contemporary Lost Dutchman Mine seekers are more prevalent. Robert S. Jacob, or "Crazy

View from Jake's Trail in Squaw Canyon looking south across La Barge Canyon toward Weavers Needle. The large saguaro skeleton is next to the trail on the Squaw Canyon Route.

Jake" as he liked to be called, had several camps in the area, most notably in a rock grotto north of Squaw Canyon **[11-V]**, in Squaw Canyon **[11-XX]**, and up on Peters Mesa.[117] In the rock grotto area, north of the trail, there are still some piles of trash, rocked-in terraces, and bolts in the rock. A steep trail named the "Z" trail or "Jake's Trail" **[11-XX]** goes up Squaw Canyon to Peters Mesa.[118]

At the mouth of Squaw Canyon on the high bench is a well-constructed seven-foot rock monument **[11-SS]**. Looking southwest from the monument is a fine view of Weavers Needle. The Cavalry Trail (239) ends at a signed junction **[11-TT, 8.2]** with the Dutchman's Trail (104) near Marsh Valley. This hike takes the Dutchman's Trail west, but there are several other interesting attractions to see along the east branch of the Dutchman's Trail.

If you opt for the side trip, go left (east) on the Dutchman's Trail up La Barge Canyon about 0.3 miles to the first wash coming in from the south **[11-I]**. There is a good horse trail a few yards west of the wash **[11-I]** that cuts southwest across the low ridge to Needle Canyon. Just past the wash is an old rock wall **[11-H]** built across the trail. The wall is most evident on the south side of the trail. It runs toward the cliff and is extended by a decomposing barbed wire fence bolted to the cliff face. Continuing up the wash, you will see a 1967 prospector's claim marker painted on an east facing cliff **[11-G]** in three-foot-high white numbers, 6+5. Back on the trail in La Barge Canyon, you will find nice shady Arizona sycamore trees growing in the creek bed near some quiet pools of water. This is always a pleasant place to stop for a snack and rest. If you have time, it is an easy one mile walk up to Charlebois Spring. See Trip 9 for the attractions near Charlebois Spring.

Continuing the hike from the signed Cavalry Trail junction **[11-TT, 8.2]**, go west on the Dutchman's Trail to the signed intersection **[11-UU, 8.6]** with the Bull Pass Trail (129). The sparsely vegetated area at this trail junction is relatively flat with Weavers Needle rising high on the southern horizon. The Spanish Race Track is presumed to be in this area, but we haven't found it. Also at this trail junction, Adolph Ruth's skull was found on December 11, 1931. A month later his body was found to the east on the lower slopes of Black Top Mesa[119] **[11-WW]**.

The alternate trail takes the Bull Pass Trail (129) east into Needle Canyon and then over Bull Pass to Aylor's Caballo Camp. Both the Bull Pass and Dutchman's Trails attain the same elevation, but the Dutchman's Trail is not as steep and as a consequence it is 1.5 miles longer. The trail to the top of Black Top Mesa branches off the Bull Pass Trail (129) to the south at Bull Pass **[11-M]**.

On this hike, with the spectacular view of Weavers Needle ahead, we continue on the Dutchman's Trail going south from the signed intersection **[11-UU, 8.6]** with the Bull Pass Trail. The shortcut horse trail **[11-YY, 8.9]** from La Barge Canyon comes in from the left (east), and a shady camp under the canopy of sugar sumac trees is nearby on the left. Farther down the trail is a large stand of trees growing among house size boulders **[11-ZZ, 9.2]**. We believe this was Al Morrow's lower camp.[120] The Terrapin Trail (234) **[11-CC, 9.5]** comes in on the left (south) and leads to Needle Canyon which is an interesting place to explore if you have time. Needle Canyon has seasonal water. The Dutchman's Trail continues over Upper Black Top Mesa Pass **[11-K, 9.8]** and drops into East Boulder Canyon via a long switchback. The Dutchman's Trail crosses East Boulder Canyon **[11-BB, 10.5]** and heads northwest on the west side of the canyon to Aylor's Caballo Camp area **[11-A, 11.2]**. East Boulder Canyon has seasonal water. See Trip 30 (Black Mesa Loop) for the attractions in this area which include Aylor's Arch and an image of a horse's head on Palomino Mountain.

The final leg of the hike follows the Dutchman's Trail back to First Water Trailhead from the Black Mesa Trail junction **[11-S, 11.5]**. Hike up West Boulder Canyon **[10-L, 12.1]**, over Parker Pass **[10-Z, 13.1]** and then down First Water Creek to First Water Trailhead **[10-C 15.6]** where the trip description ends. See Trip 30 (Black Mesa Loop) for the trail description from Aylor's Camp to First Water Trailhead.

HISTORY AND LEGENDS. Over the years, the Superstition Mountains have attracted many prospectors and treasure hunters. One of these men was Robert S. "Crazy Jake" Jacob, a colorful character who maintained a large camp of men in La Barge Canyon to search for the Lost Dutchman Mine. Local rancher Bill Barkley gave him the name Crazy Jake, because he was likely to be the only one crazy enough to find the Lost Dutchman Mine. Between 1963 and 1986, Crazy Jake had several camps in the La Barge area. The most notable were in a rock grotto north of Squaw Canyon **[11-V]**, in Squaw Canyon **[11-XX]**, and on Peters Mesa.[121] Unfortunately, his keen ability to raise grubstakes led to his demise. Crazy Jake's search for the Lost Dutchman Mine ended in 1986 when he was convicted of fraud and sentenced to 10 years in prison for bilking investors out of $135,000 in his treasure hunting adventures.

Prospector and treasure hunter Barry Storm had several camps. This camp was somewhere in La Barge Canyon.
COURTESY SUPERSTITION MOUNTAIN HISTORICAL SOCIETY, JOHN BURBRIDGE COLLECTION.

Newspaper articles reported that Crazy Jake swindled prominent investors of $7 million over a period of 20 years while leading them to believe he had found the Lost Dutchman Mine.[122] In the rock grotto area, north of the trail, there are still some piles of trash, rocked-in terraces, and bolts in the rock. In December 1992, at the site of one of his camps near the head of Squaw Canyon, we found some recent stores of gasoline and camping equipment. The Forest Service said that this new prospector has been given orders to remove the equipment from the Wilderness. On a February 1994 trip, we found the camp restored to natural conditions. Although there is no water nearby, this site would make a nice camp for those wanting to get away from the trail in La Barge Canyon. Don Van Driel said the wire cable stretched out near that camp **[11-XX]** was used as a picket line for horses.[123]

Black Top Mesa, often called the Peralta Mapped Mountain, has interested treasure seekers over the years because of the Spanish Hieroglyphics found there and its proximity to Weavers Needle. In 1949, Clay Worst with the help of Nyle Leatham performed a survey on top of Black Top Mesa to evaluate the clues of an 1854 Peralta survey. In 1924 Perfecto Salazar, acting as an interpreter for a Peralta family member, was shown some survey data of a mine in the Superstition Mountains. He memorized some of the survey figures which are now commonly referred to as the Salazar Survey and passed the information on to Frank Swento. Local prospector Chuck Aylor was grubstaked by Swento, and later Clay Worst was brought into the deal. Clay Worst set up a surveyor's transit on Black Top Mesa using the Spanish symbols (petroglyphs not hieroglyphics) on the northwest and southeast as the survey baseline and then triangulated a mine site which was located in the Red Hills area. All of this excellent work was to no avail, probably because the Salazar clues were incomplete. The lost Salazar Survey Mine remains undiscovered today.[124]

More recently, in 1989, Black Top Mesa was in the news when Patricia Kuhl (formerly Patricia Kuhl Murray) of Troy's Gallery in Scottsdale hid a bronze sculpture on the mesa. Artist Harland Young created the sculpture *In Search of the Dutchman* depicting Jacob Waltz and his two burros. Kuhl wanted to generate publicity so the public would buy the limited edition bronzes. The proceeds would benefit the town of Apache Junction in the effort to commission a life-size sculpture. Since the Wilderness rules prohibit certain commercial activities, Don Van Driel of the Forest Service advised Kuhl to move the bronze sculpture outside the Wilderness which she did. Larry Hedrick, finder of the Hiram Walker Whiskey cache in 1978, said he discovered the place where the bronze had been hidden on Black Top Mesa a day after it was moved outside the Wilderness. The 76-pound bronze sculpture was found on February 20, 1989, at a new, undisclosed, hiding place outside the Wilderness by Andy Tafoya of Mesa, Arizona. Eddie Basha donated an identical bronze sculpture by Harland Young, to the Superstition Mountain Museum where it is now on display. From our observations, these men show that the competence of the treasure hunters is not in question. It's the obscurity of the clues to the Lost Dutchman Mine that seem to cause the problems.[125]

Trips 31 and 34, on the Cavalry Trail, take you by an area known as the Red Hills. The earth here is a reddish-brown color. One of the clues for the Lost Dutchman Mine refers to three red hills. The clue states that you have

Harland Young's bronze sculpture, "In Search of the Dutchman," is now on display at the Superstition Mountain Museum. COURTESY GREGORY DAVIS, SUPERSTITION MOUNTAIN HISTORICAL SOCIETY.

gone too far when you pass the three red hills. Even a simple clue like this is complicated by the fact that there is more than one group of three red hills in the Superstition Wilderness. One group is south of the Cavalry Trail, and another group is east of Upper La Barge Box.

Jim Bark tells a story about Mexican miners in the mid 1800s who were reputed to hold two-horse races along a dirt track in the Marsh Valley area. A bandit gang led by Joaquin Murietta would join the Peralta camp for mutual security and during their stay in the mountains would wager on the horse races. In the early 1900s, Jim Bark observed the race track to be one-hundred and fifty-yards long. We searched the elevated flat area north of Bluff Mountain several times and have not been able to locate the impression of the race track, although, if you use your imagination, there are two eroded areas that may qualify as a two-horse race track. When Adolph Ruth's skull was found in 1931 at the junction of the Dutchman's and Bull Pass Trails, this area was referred to as the Spanish Race Track.[126] One Lost Dutchman enthusiast recently said the race track is there but overgrown with vegetation, but others feel that this talk about the Spanish Race Track is just a myth.

Canyon Overlook Trailhead

The Canyon Overlook Trailhead is actually two different vehicle pullouts along the east side of State Route 88, about 12 miles northeast of Apache Junction between mileposts 207 and 208.

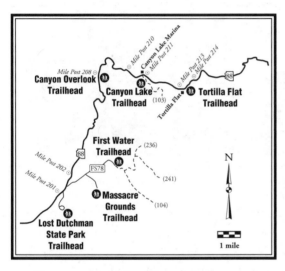

FINDING THE TRAILHEAD. The pullout for Trip 32 (First Water Creek Overlook Trail) is almost halfway between mileposts 207 and 208 on the east side of the paved road (State Route 88). There is a metal electric tower at the vehicle pullout with the painted identification "#174." Follow the well-worn trail that heads south into the wash.

The second vehicle pullout is farther north on State Route 88 exactly at milepost 208. This is the start of Trip 33 (Lower First Water Creek). The trail into the wash to the southeast is not well-defined, so the easiest place to start is a few feet east of the guy-wire anchor for the wooden electric power pole. The power pole is next to the paved road. Stand beside the power pole so that the 208 milepost is behind you, and look straight ahead for the start of the trail.

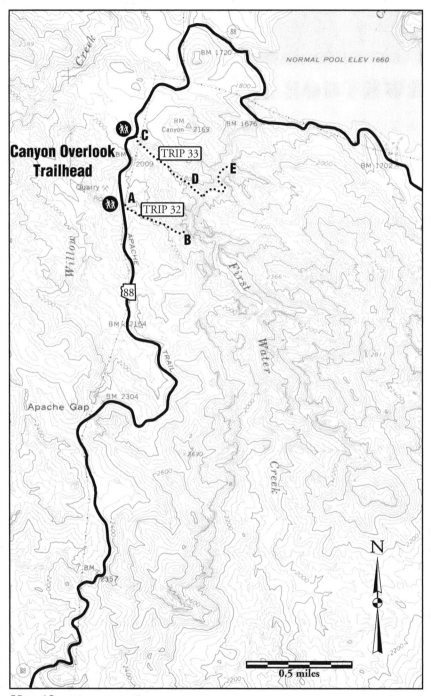

Map 12 - *Trips 32 and 33.*

First Water Creek Overlook Trail

This is an easy hike close to the paved road. You can experience the rugged beauty of the canyons just minutes away from your car. This short walk leads you to a nice scenic overlook of First Water Creek Canyon. In the spring wildflowers cover the slopes on both sides of the trail.

ITINERARY: This is a short trail to a scenic overlook that starts at a vehicle pullout, between mileposts 207 and 208 on State Route 88 and takes you to an overlook into First Water Creek Canyon.

DIFFICULTY: Easy. Trail ends at a point where rain pours off a seasonal water-fall into First Water Creek. Don't fall off the cliff. Not recommended for horses. Elevation change is ±160 feet.

LENGTH and TIME: 0.8 miles, 0.8 hours round trip.

MAPS: Mormon Flat Dam, Arizona USGS topo map.
Superstition Wilderness Tonto National Forest map.

FINDING THE TRAIL: From the vehicle pullout between mileposts 207 and 208 on State Route 88, the trail heads south from metal electric tower #174.

THE HIKE: *Use Map 12.* From the vehicle pullout **[12-A, 0]**, the well-defined trail goes south, descending into the wash. After a few minutes the trail leaves the wash and stays high, going east as it crosses a small ridge and heads toward First Water Creek. To the left (north) are nice views of Canyon Lake. In the spring, wildflowers are abundant. After about 10 minutes beyond the ridge, the trail becomes faint. Views to the north look into First Water Canyon and beyond to Canyon Lake. You can turn around here or continue a few minutes down the faint trail leading east to a cliff where the water (when there is water) pours off a 150 foot drop into First Water Creek. The view from the seasonal waterfall into the canyon is very scenic **[12-B, 0.4]**. Be careful not to fall off the cliff.. The rocks are smooth here. Wet smooth rocks and loose gravel can pose a footing hazard. Return via the same trail.

Lower First Water Creek

This short walk quickly takes you from the paved road, across the Wilderness boundary, into First Water Creek with its narrow canyon and pools of seasonal water. This is one of the fastest and shortest ways to get into a rugged canyon from the paved road.

ITINERARY: The hike starts at a vehicle pullout exactly at milepost 208 on State Route 88 and follows a series of poorly defined trails into First Water Canyon. You can hike down the canyon to Canyon Lake or up the canyon as far as you like.

DIFFICULTY: Moderate. Loose stones and poorly defined trail. Not recommended for horses. Elevation change is ±320 feet.

LENGTH and TIME: 0.5 mile into canyon one-way, 2 hours round trip.

MAPS: Mormon Flat Dam, Arizona USGS topo map.
Superstition Wilderness Tonto National Forest map.

FINDING THE TRAIL: Start a few feet east of the guy-wire anchor on the wooden electric power pole. The power pole is next to the paved road, State Route 88, and milepost 208 is right behind you.

THE HIKE: *Use Map 12.* From the vehicle pullout **[12-C, 0]**, the hardest part of the hike is getting down into the wash that heads east toward First Water Canyon. At first, the route is steep with many loose stones. There are many trails of use, so just pick one that looks well-traveled and follow it until you find a better one. The idea is to stay in the bottom of the wash when it is clear of brush—otherwise walk to either side. After walking about 20 minutes, scramble down some solid rock in the center of the ravine. Walking another 10 minutes brings you to a barbed wire fence—the Wilderness Boundary. Go under the fence and you are in First Water Canyon **[12-D, 0.5]**.

It is a short 15 minute hike down canyon, north, to Canyon Lake **[12-E]**. Here there are several small cottonwood trees growing in the bed of the

---

Canyon Overlook Trailhead

Crawfish shell found in First Water Creek near Canyon Lake.

canyon. When Canyon Lake is near full capacity, the water comes up the canyon near the cottonwood trees. We have seen many crawfish shells on the canyon floor, left behind after the water receded.

You can also hike up the canyon as far as you like. Less than ten minutes up the canyon you can see the water stain from the dry waterfall on the cliff above. The top of the dry waterfall is the end of Trip 32 (First Water Creek Overlook). Lots of boulder hopping is required if you go very far. When there is water in the canyon, you will probably want to wear shoes that are good for walking in water.

Return the same way to your vehicle **[12-C, 1.0+]**. After crawling under the barbed wire fence, you will notice two small ravines ahead to the west. Take the one to the right (north) and retrace your original route.

Canyon Lake Trailhead

The Canyon Lake Trailhead is on State Route 88, about 15 miles northeast of Apache Junction between mileposts 210 and 211.

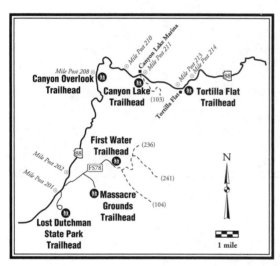

FINDING THE TRAILHEAD. There are two single-lane bridges along this stretch of road. The trailhead is on the east side of the second bridge as you come from Apache Junction. The trailhead is across the paved highway from the Canyon Lake Marina complex where free trailhead parking is provided inside the fenced area. At the Canyon Lake Marina entrance gate, ask the security guard where to park for the Canyon Lake Trailhead. The marina provides this parking service free of charge as part of its contract with the Forest Service. When the restaurant is closed you might have to wait up to an hour at the marina gate until the 24-hour security guard completes his rounds.

FACILITIES. The Canyon Lake Marina has a restaurant, marina, beach area and fenced parking. In addition to the Canyon Lake Marina, there is a large USFS picnic area and paved parking on the southwest side of the bridge where you can park your vehicle. There are ramadas, picnic tables and toilets, but no water. **Bring your own drinking water.**

THE TRAILS. The Boulder Canyon Trail starts from the paved road, State Route 88, on the east side of the bridge. There is a big sign reading *Boulder Canyon Trail 103.*

Boulder Creek crossing on the Roosevelt Road (Apache Trail) in 1907. PHOTOGRAPH BY WALTER LUBKEN. COURTESY SALT RIVER PROJECT HISTORY SERVICES.

If you want to enter the mouth of La Barge Creek (often incorrectly called Boulder Canyon), start on Boulder Canyon Trail (103). After hiking 15 or 20 minutes, take a spur trail down to the bed of La Barge Creek. See Trip 35 for more details. Trying to contour around the cliffs into La Barge Creek with Canyon Lake at normal water level is usually not possible. The dirt road on the east side of the lagoon eventually connects, after some bushwhacking, with the Boulder Canyon Trail 103, so it is much easier to start hiking on Trail 103.

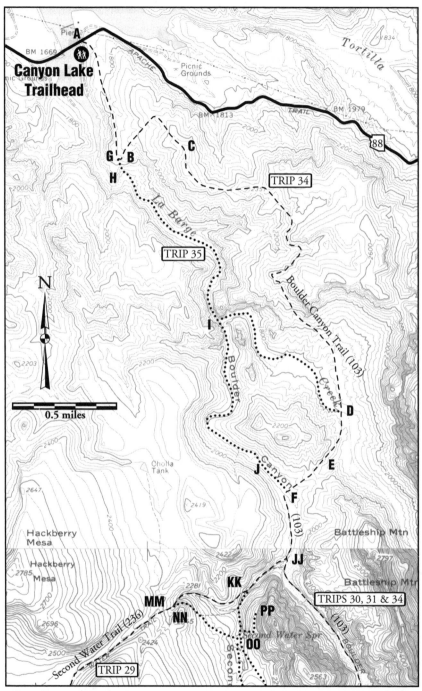

Map 13 - *Trips 34 and 35.*

Boulder Canyon Trail to Marsh Valley

Boulder Canyon Trail is a unique trail because there's a fine view of Weavers Needle and Battleship Mountain within the first half-mile of the trip—an easy walk for almost everyone. The Indian Paint Mine, stone holding-corral, and the seasonal water and vegetation along La Barge and Boulder Canyons make this a good choice for an overnight trip.

ITINERARY: From the Canyon Lake Trailhead on Route 88, Boulder Canyon Trail (103) starts next to the paved highway, heads up to a ridge east of La Barge Creek, then drops down into La Barge Creek. The trail goes over Paint Mine Saddle to Boulder Canyon and continues up Boulder Canyon. From Boulder Canyon, the trip takes the Cavalry Trail (239) over to La Barge Creek and follows La Barge Creek south to Marsh Valley. Return same way or plan a trans-wilderness hike to another trailhead or a loop hike back to the Canyon Lake area.

DIFFICULTY: Difficult day trip because of length, or moderate overnight. Elevation change is +1940 and -1220 feet one-way.

LENGTH and TIME: 8.4 miles, 6 hours one-way.

MAPS: Mormon Flat Dam, Arizona USGS topo map.
Goldfield, Arizona USGS topo map.
Weavers Needle, Arizona USGS topo map.
Make your own composite copy of the 3 USGS map corners.
Superstition Wilderness Tonto National Forest map.

FINDING THE TRAIL: The Boulder Canyon Trail (103) starts from the paved road, State Route 88, on the east side of the single-lane bridge across from the Canyon Lake Marina complex.

THE HIKE: *Use Maps 11 and 13.* From the paved road **[13-A, 0]**, Boulder Canyon Trail heads south, up the hill. After hiking about 15 or 20 minutes, a faint spur trail **[13-G, 0.6]** continues straight while the main trail bends left. The spur trail continues south and goes into the bed of La Barge Creek

[13-H, 0.7] which has seasonal water. Another 3 minutes on the main trail brings you to the wooden Superstition Wilderness sign **[13-B, 0.6]** and a great view of Weavers Needle and Battleship Mountain to the south. About 30 feet north of the Wilderness sign is a jumping cholla cactus with an abandoned cactus wren nest. It is built at eye level so it is easy to inspect. Boulder Canyon Trail is a good choice for those who want to take a short hike to a scenic vista and then return by the same trail. Hikers can turn around after reaching the Wilderness sign or the top of the ridge, or they can take the spur route into La Barge Canyon.

At the Wilderness sign, Boulder Canyon Trail makes a sharp left turn as it heads up to the ridge east of La Barge Creek. From the top of the ridge **[13-C, 1.6]**, the trail drops down into La Barge Creek at about the 3 mile point **[13-D, 3.0]**.

If you are making this trip in the opposite direction or hiking along La Barge Creek, it would be easy to miss the (103) trail junction with La Barge Creek **[13-D]**. One landmark is an eroded cut bank of reddish dirt and boulders. It is on the east side of the creek bed on a right bend (when going up canyon). The trail crosses La Barge Creek 100 yards or so north (downstream) of the eroded bank. Battleship Mountain and a smaller butte, to the north, are also good landmarks. The small butte viewed from the creek bed,

View from Boulder Trail looking south toward Battleship Mountain and Weavers Needle.

resembles a miniature Battleship Mountain. Trail 103 crosses La Barge Creek below these two buttes.

After the trail crosses La Barge Creek, it follows the west bench for a short distance. There are several flat camping places here. Some iron mining equipment is lying about, probably from the Indian Paint Mine. The trail quickly goes over a low saddle named Paint Mine Saddle[127] **[13-E, 3.3]**. Indian Paint Mine is next to the trail on the west side of Paint Mine Saddle.

From Paint Mine Saddle, the trail drops down into Boulder Canyon. There may be water at the trail crossing **[13-F, 3.5]** or down canyon (north) 0.1 mile beyond a small grove of Fremont cottonwood trees **[13-J]**. Continuing on the trip, look for trails of use on the west bench of Boulder Canyon that lead south to the intersection with Second Water Trail (236). A section of smooth, white bedrock in the floor of Boulder Canyon marks the Second Water Canyon **[11-JJ, 3.8]**. A wooden trail sign is posted on the west bank for Second Water Trail. Continuing south, Trail 103 crosses Boulder Canyon many times and may be difficult to follow if the rock cairns have been washed away by high water. Horses and pack animals help maintain a reasonable path up Boulder Canyon, but the occasional flash floods clean out many of the obvious crossing points. Even when the canyon bed is dry,

Ralph Morris building the cabin at Indian Paint Mine in 1956. COURTESY GREGORY DAVIS, SUPERSTITION MOUNTAIN HISTORICAL SOCIETY, DAN HOPPER COLLECTION.

Typical rock cairn marking the trail in Boulder Canyon.

it is sometimes easier hiking the trails on the low bench rather than boulder hopping up the main channel.

Traveling south, 1.4 miles up Boulder Canyon from Second Water Canyon, take the Cavalry Trail (239) which enters on the left (east) **[11-II, 5.2]**. Follow the Cavalry trail as it goes over a pass just north of the Red Hills and drops down to La Barge Creek. Since the hike crosses the corners of all three USGS topo maps, keeping track of your progress may not be easy. If you make a composite copy of the corners of all three USGS topo maps, you can use it as a quick reference to find landmarks in this area.

Before the Cavalry Trail reaches La Barge Canyon, there are some flat camping places **[11-LL, 6.6]**. Cavalry Trail goes up the bed of La Barge Creek for a short distance and eventually stays on the east side of the canyon. La Barge Canyon has seasonal water and may have water after Boulder Canyon has gone dry. About a quarter mile from the junction of La Barge Creek and the Cavalry Trail, look for an old stone holding corral **[11-NN, 6.9]**. It is on a low bench on the northeast side of La Barge Creek. From a cluster of Fremont cottonwood and Arizona sycamore trees growing in the bed of La Barge Creek, go directly east about 100 yards to locate the stone structure—a U-shaped wall about 30 feet square with walls 3 to 4 feet thick. The rock walls are about 4 feet high with the back wall missing. See Trip 31 for more information about the corral and other attractions in the area.

The Cavalry Trail ends at the Dutchman's Trail (104) in Marsh Valley **[11-TT, 8.4]**. The hike description ends here. Return the same way to the trailhead **[13-A, 16.8]** or plan a loop trip back to the Canyon Lake area.

HISTORY AND LEGENDS. The Indian Paint Mine ruin is easy to inspect since most of the diggings are within 100 yards of the trail. Greg Davis, Director of Research and Acquisitions for the Superstition Mountain Historical Society, said early stories indicate that the Indians may have mined the red rock for paint, and the mine has been referred to as Indian Paint Mine as far back as 1911.[128] There are some stone walls, building foundations and a carved area in the cliff where a building may have stood. Greg Davis suggests, "When seeing an old mine shaft, tunnel, tailing or mine dump try not to look at it as a scar, but visualize an old miner searching for his golden dream. Think of the endless stories those old mines could tell if they could talk."

Ralph Morris is reported to have erected buildings at the Indian Paint Mine site in 1956.[129] A deep shaft was observed at the mine by Barry Storm in 1937[130] and by Dick and Sharon Nelson about 1978.[131] Greg Hansen and Russ Orr said the Forest Service filled in the mine shafts sometime in 1991 or 1992. Rancher Jim Bark told of a tunnel, without timbering, that John Chuning blasted out near the Indian Paint Mine, 150 feet long, along a boulder-filled 18 inch crack.[132] The Chuning Mine is across from the Indian Paint Mine three-fourths of the way to the top of the hill, north of the old building foundation.[133] There are several other holes and prospects near the Indian Paint Mine ruins. The first is about 50 feet south of Paint Mine Saddle. Two more are on the north side of Paint Mine Saddle; one is filled with mining camp trash—bed springs, cookware, and mining equipment. Another set of holes is across the ravine about 100 yards north-northwest of the main ruins. Some iron pipe fittings and iron bars are still there. All the mines that we saw have either collapsed or have been filled in. Robert Schoose in his 1986 reprint of Barry Storm's, *Thunder God's Gold*, describes several hand-picked Spanish mines not far from this area. He located the mines using Hank D'Andrea's map—shown in the book along with a picture of one of the mines. One of the mines has fire pits and beds carved into the walls.[134]

In December 1992, during a rain storm, Jack Carlson was trapped on the Cavalry Trail when both La Barge Creek and Boulder Canyon were flooding. The normally placid (often dry) creeks were raging with a force that recalled memories of white-water rafting rivers. Another hiker and Jack worked their way cross-country, to the southern end of Weavers Needle, using Dutchman's Trail (104) to enter East Boulder Canyon and then hiked to First Water Trailhead. At Aylor's Caballo Camp two other hikers were drying out after a soaking in a creek-crossing attempt. Their offer of hot chocolate and coffee made a pleasant pause in our adventure to escape the flood waters.

Lower La Barge Creek Loop

La Barge Canyon offers a good opportunity for hikers to explore a canyon that often has seasonal pools of water. Boulder Canyon Trail provides an easy return to the trailhead. A detour to Indian Paint Mine is a worthwhile side trip.

ITINERARY: From the Canyon Lake Trailhead on State Route 88, hike up Boulder Canyon Trail (103). From a spur trail off Trail 103, enter the creek bed at the mouth of La Barge Creek and hike south, up the creek bed, to the intersection with Boulder Canyon Trail (103). Return on the Boulder Canyon Trail.

DIFFICULTY: Moderate. No trail in La Barge Creek. Not recommended for horses. Elevation change is ±1220 feet.

LENGTH and TIME: 5.6 miles, 4 hours round trip.

MAPS: Mormon Flat Dam, Arizona USGS topo map. Superstition Wilderness Tonto National Forest map.

FINDING THE TRAIL: Use the Boulder Canyon Trail (103) which starts from the paved road, State Route 88, on the east side of the single-lane bridge across from the Canyon Lake Marina complex. The narrow canyon and cliffs at the south end of the lagoon block hiker access to the mouth of La Barge Creek. Trying to contour around the cliffs into La Barge Creek at normal Canyon Lake water levels is usually not possible. The dirt road, at lake level, on the east side of the lagoon eventually connects, after some bushwhacking, with the Boulder Canyon Trail 103, but it is much easier to start your hike on Trail 103.

THE HIKE: *Use Map 13.* From the paved road **[13-A, 0]**, Trail 103 heads south up the hill. After hiking about 15 or 20 minutes, a spur route continues straight on a faint trail **[13-G, 0.6]** while the main trail bends left. This route takes the spur trail and goes into the bed of La Barge Creek **[13-H, 0.7]** which has seasonal water. A recommended side trip of an additional 3 minutes on

---

Canyon Lake Trailhead   **193**

the main trail brings you to the wooden Superstition Wilderness sign **[13-B]** and a great view of Weavers Needle and Battleship Mountain. Although the trail is not well defined, following the spur trail down into La Barge Creek **[13-H]** is fairly easy—it is harder to follow the trail going uphill. There is no trail in this stretch of La Barge Canyon so you just walk up the bed of the creek. Wear appropriate shoes so you can walk through the water when that becomes necessary.

Hiking up the creek bed is slow going. Estimate a 1.0 mph hiking speed along the creek bed. Leisurely day hikers may want to walk up the creek a short distance and return the same way. About 1.0 mile up canyon, La Barge Creek makes a left bend (east) and Boulder Canyon officially begins **[13-I, 1.7]**. Boulder Canyon heads south, but this trip follows La Barge Creek to the left. The intersection with Boulder Canyon Trail (103) in La Barge Creek is another 0.9 miles up canyon **[13-D, 2.6]**.

After La Barge Creek makes the sharp left turn to the east, start looking for Boulder Canyon Trail on the east slopes. If you walked south more than 45 minutes from the junction with Boulder Canyon, you probably passed the Trail 103 intersection **[13-D, 2.6]**. There are no trail signs here. See Trip 34 for more help in finding this trail intersection.

The return on the Boulder Canyon Trail takes about two hours. From La Barge Creek **[13-D, 2.6]**, follow Boulder Canyon Trail (103) up to the ridge line and continue down to the Boulder Canyon Trailhead **[13-A, 5.6]**.

SIDE TRIP TO INDIAN PAINT MINE. If you have time, from La Barge Canyon **[13-D, 2.6]**, you could hike up to Paint Mine Saddle **[13-E]** to inspect the Indian Paint Mine site. From the trail junction **[13-D, 2.6]** in La Barge Creek, the round trip will take you less than 1.0 hour (about 0.7 miles). From the Trail 103 crossing **[13-D, 2.6]**, hike south on the west side of La Barge Creek on a trail heading up to Paint Mine Saddle. The mine site is on the west side of the saddle and on the south side of the trail. Trip 34 describes the Indian Paint Mine area.

ALTERNATE ROUTE TO INDIAN PAINT MINE. As an alternate route from the creek junction **[13-I, 1.7]**, you could hike up Boulder Canyon (south) and connect with Boulder Canyon Trail (103) **[13-F, 2.9]** as it comes down from Paint Mine Saddle **[13-E]**. The alternate route allows you to hike by the Indian Paint Mine site. Allow 2 hours for this detour (estimated 1.8 miles), and a little extra time for getting lost. The detour may take some map and compass work or skill at reading the terrain.

The cabin at Indian Paint Mine was constructed by Ralph Morris in 1956. COURTESY GREGORY DAVIS, SUPERSTITION MOUNTAIN HISTORICAL SOCIETY, DAN HOPPER COLLECTION.

Begin the alternate route from the junction with Boulder Canyon **[13-I, 1.7]**. Walk up the bed of Boulder Canyon 1.7 miles and look for the Boulder Canyon Trail (103) going east over the Paint Mine Saddle **[13-E]**. The trail may be difficult to find since there are no trail signs here. Start looking for the trail on your left (east) several hundred yards or more up canyon from a green area **[13-J]** and small clump of Fremont cottonwood trees growing on the canyon floor. There may be water here. Paint Mine Saddle is just north of Battleship Mountain. The Indian Paint Mine is on the west side of Paint Mine Saddle. See Trip 34 for the Indian Paint Mine story. From Paint Mine Saddle continue, east, down to La Barge Creek. Turn left (north) and hike down La Barge on the trail to the creek bed crossing **[13-D, 3.4]**. The trail crosses La Barge Creek and continues up the slope. See the main hike description for the return to the trailhead **[13-A, 6.4]**.

THE BIG FISH STORY. One early-spring day in 1984 we hiked the lower section of La Barge Canyon encountering many large pools of water. Several pools contained fish that were trapped when Canyon Lake receded or the spring runoff ended. As we approached each pool, the fish darted into the shadows of the bank. John Stickney, a friend from Colorado, said we could easily catch one of these fish for closer inspection. He talked us through the exercise. The technique—lay spread eagle on the ground, with head almost in the water, move both hands in the water until you touch the fish, then hold the fish against the bank and slide it to the surface. And then, you have a fat, 18-inch trout looking you straight in the eye.

Tortilla Flat Trailhead

The Tortilla Flat Trailhead is on State Route 88, about 17 miles northeast of Apache Junction between mileposts 213 and 214.

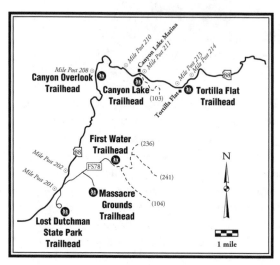

FINDING THE TRAILHEAD. Tortilla Flat Trailhead is located about a hundred yards northeast of the Tortilla Flat Store, where Tortilla Creek crosses State Route 88 in the town of Tortilla Flat. From the south side of the paved highway, the hike goes up the bed of Tortilla Creek or on either bank, depending on your preference. We often start the hike from one of the vehicle pullouts about a half mile east of Tortilla Flat and walk down the slope to Tortilla Creek. This saves about four-tenths mile of creek bed walking which, as you will find, can be tedious and time consuming.

FACILITIES. The town of Tortilla Flat is a row of old-west buildings on the south side of Apache Trail. There is a general store, restaurant, bar and gift shop. Restrooms are available when the stores are open. Bring your own water since there is no public access to water. The parking area at Tortilla Flat is posted, *No Overnight Parking.* The parking on both sides of the road is on private property. Do not park here without permission from the owners. If you need to leave your vehicle overnight, or even for a day hike, talk to the friendly owners in the restaurant. They try to be accommodating and may make special arrangements for you.

There are other options for parking your vehicle. We sometimes park in the small vehicle pullouts along the road east of Tortilla Flat. Also, east on the paved road you can park along the dirt roads in the Mesquite Flat vicinity. Mesquite Flat seems farther away, but if you start hiking at the first bend in Tortilla Creek from the paved road, it is about the same distance from Tortilla Flat. From October through May, you can reserve a campsite ($8 per night) at Tortilla Campground where they have restrooms and running water. The most secure area for free parking is at the Canyon Lake Marina which is two miles west of Tortilla Flat.

HISTORY AND LEGENDS. L. L. Lombardi in her 1994 book, *Tortilla Flat, Then and Now*, describes the history of Tortilla Flat. In the late 1800s, Tortilla Flat was used as a camp along the Yavapai Trail (Tonto Trail) which was only a footpath then. The Yavapai Trail was renamed the Apache Trail in the early 1900s after the road to Roosevelt Dam was constructed. In 1942, Tortilla Creek flooded and washed away most of the structures north of the road. Few of the families living there decided to rebuild. Jerry and Mary Jo Bryant have been owners of the town since 1988. Yes, they own the whole town. The iron crucifix on the bar inside the Tortilla Flat Restaurant is reported to have been found in the Superstitions in 1952 and is thought to be from the San Pedro Mine.[135]

Here at Tortilla Flat in the early 1940s, Barry Storm wrote his famous book, *Thunder God's Gold*, which includes the Gonzales treasure map. Canon Fresco appears on the Gonzales map and is considered an important clue in locating the lost Peralta mines. La Barge Creek and Fish Creek have been proposed as Canon Fresco, but Barry Storm considers Tortilla Creek to be a more logical choice. Possibly the junction of Tortilla Creek and Peters Canyon marks the location of the mines.[136] A copy of the Gonzales map is on display at the Superstition Mountain Museum. The Gonzales map is also printed in the January 1982 issue of the *Superstition Mountain Journal*. Robert Schoose, co-owner of the Goldfield Ghost Town, republished Barry Storm's out-of-print book, *Thunder God's Gold*, in 1986.

Lower Tortilla Creek Loop

After difficult hiking and bouldering in this narrow canyon, you will be rewarded by many refreshing seasonal pools of water shaded by giant cottonwood trees. It is possible to find water here in the summer, but the surrounding country can be unbearably hot.

ITINERARY: The hike starts at Tortilla Flat and follows the bed of Tortilla Creek east, past the junction with Peters Canyon. The route leaves Tortilla Creek drainage at a break in the northern ridge. Descending from the ridge to the north, the route follows several washes westward and connects with a jeep road that intersects the paved State Route 88 near Mesquite Flats. Return to Tortilla Flat on the paved road—State Route 88.

DIFFICULTY: Very difficult due to bouldering in the creek bed. Not recommended for horses. Elevation change is ±1040 feet.

LENGTH and TIME: 7.4 miles, 10 hours round trip.

MAPS: Horse Mesa Dam, Arizona USGS topo map.
Mormon Flat Dam, Arizona USGS topo map.
Superstition Wilderness Tonto National Forest map.

FINDING THE TRAIL: The route starts northeast of the town of Tortilla Flat where Tortilla Creek crosses the paved highway—State Route 88.

THE HIKE: *Use Maps 14 and 17.* There are no trails on this hike except for the 2.4 miles of jeep road and paved highway at the end of the trip. The route takes you through Tortilla Creek which may have water or pools of water—depending on the season. If you wear shoes that can get wet, the hiking will be much easier. You will need some experience in bouldering since some sections of the creek bed are blocked by large boulders that you must scramble over. No technical climbing equipment is required.

The hike starts in the bed of Tortilla Creek at State Route 88 **[14-A, 0]**. If you like, you can bypass the first 0.4 miles and drop down to the creek bed from the paved road near the first bend **[14-T, 0.4]** in the creek. After the

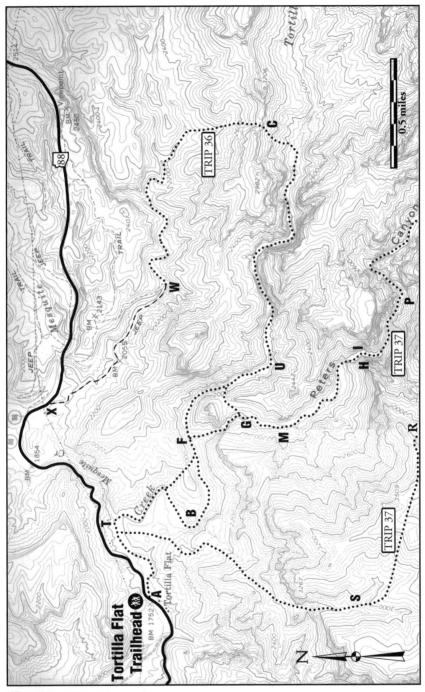

Map 14 - *Trip 36.*

creek turns south, it makes a big turn to the east **[14-B,1.1]**, signaling the approaching junction with Peters Canyon **[14-F, 1.6]**. Use this landmark to check your location on the map and to calculate an approximate hiking speed. In this area 1.0 mph would be a typical pace for the authors. Hikers on an easy day hike should turn around along this stretch of creek.

As Tortilla Creek turns southeast, the walls of the canyon change to sloping hills, cut by many small ravines. At the bend to the east, the stream bed is full of vegetation: grasses, reeds, Fremont cottonwood trees and velvet ash trees. Hells Hole Spring **[14-U, 2.2]** is located in this area. In May of 1866, fifteen Yavapai and Apache Indians were killed here in a battle with the U.S. Infantry from Fort McDowell.[137]

The canyon immediately narrows with steep walls on both sides. Large Arizona sycamore trees are wedged in between the massive boulders that litter the stream bed. Pools of water make the hiking slow. A good estimate for hiking speed here would be less than a half mph. This is another canyon that you would want to avoid if you expected a flash flood. There are very few places to camp, and most of them would not be secure in a flash flood.

Depending on the season, the water may be intermittent. The canyon floor alternates between dry, white boulders and heavily overgrown areas of vegetation. About one mile upstream, past the creek's bend to the east **[14-U]**, the canyon opens with broad (but steep) sloping hills on either side. Farther up canyon, two high points on the north ridge (elevations 2982 and 3206) silhouette a pass **[14-C, 3.5]** in the cliffs. It is possible to hike up and over the north side of the canyon in several places here. That is the route this hike takes.

As an alternate to leaving the canyon at this location, you can continue up Tortilla Creek (east) and exit the creek bed near the Tortilla Ranch dirt road (FS213). It might take another five hours just to reach the dirt road. Then, take the Tortilla Ranch dirt road north to the junction with State Route 88, which is gravel at this point **[17-E]**. This junction is a parking area for Tortilla Ranch Trailhead. As a second alternate route, you can return the same way you came, although the hike through the pass **[14-C]** would be one to two hours shorter.

To approach the pass in the cliff, pick the easiest uphill slope and head directly toward the pass **[14-C]**. The authors crossed the ridge just west of the pass through a small notch, but the approach was steeper and we had to climb higher than the pass. The best plan is to stay in the creek bed until you are parallel with the pass through the cliff, then head up the slopes. Even though this is remote and rough country, others have been here. We found

After 8 to 25 years the century plant (agave) shoots up a tall flower stalk, produces seed and then the plant dies. The yellow flowers bloom in the summer months of June, July or August.

two old sleeping bags stashed under a palo verde tree on a flat area about a quarter of the way to the top.

At the top of the ridge, you can see Four Peaks Mountain to the north and a small slice of Canyon Lake to the west. Descend the slope on the north side and drop into one of the washes. All the washes eventually lead west, connecting to a larger wash which intersects with the jeep road. The jeep road is easy to recognize from the bottom of the wash because it once spanned the ravine on a bridge **[14-W, 5.0]**. The bridge is gone, but the cement and stone foundations are still there. Climb out of the wash on the west side, and follow the jeep road to the intersection of the paved State Route 88 **[14-X, 5.9]**. Along this jeep road, just at dusk, we saw a coral snake, with the distinctive red and black bands separated by wide bands of white. The white on the coral snake is sometimes a cream or yellow color. In contrast, the non-poisonous king snake mimics a similar coloration, but there is no separation between the red and black bands. Coral snakes are poisonous and should not be handled. At State Route 88 turn left (northwest) and walk 1.5 miles on the paved road to Tortilla Flat where the trip description ends **[14-A, 7.4]**.

Peters Canyon Loop

Peters Canyon is a pleasant canyon with seasonal water and sheer cliffs. The loop trip goes up to historic Peters Mesa where many Lost Dutchman Mine searchers uncovered evidence of nearby mines. The return trek across Malapais Mountain and Geronimo Head offers a spectacular view into the canyons below and then takes hikers down a steep and narrow break in the cliff above Tortilla Flat. Many day hikers enjoy a short walk up Peters Canyon and return the same way.

ITINERARY: The hike starts northeast of Tortilla Flat where Tortilla Creek crosses State Route 88, and follows the bed of Tortilla Creek east to the junction with Peters Canyon. Follow the bed of Peters Canyon southeast to Peters Mesa. Return across the ridge line hiking southwest via Malapais Mountain and Geronimo Head. Descend the cliffs to the north, through a narrow break, 0.7 miles south of the Tortilla Flat store.

DIFFICULTY: Very difficult due to length of hike. Not recommended for horses. Elevation change is ±3140 feet.

LENGTH and TIME: 13.9 miles, 11 hours round trip.

Maps: Horse Mesa, Arizona USGS topo map.
Mormon Flat Dam, Arizona USGS topo map.
Weavers Needle, Arizona USGS topo map.
Goldfield, Arizona USGS topo map.
Make your own composite copy of the four USGS map corners.
Superstition Wilderness Tonto National Forest map.

FINDING THE TRAIL: The hike starts northeast of Tortilla Flat where Tortilla Creek crosses paved State Route 88.

THE HIKE: *Use Maps 15 and 16.* There are no trails on this hike. The route takes you through Tortilla Creek and Peters Canyon which may have water or pools of water—depending on the season. If you wear shoes that can get wet, the hiking will be much easier. Map reading is awkward since the hike crosses the corners of four USGS topo maps. For a handy reference, make a composite copy of the corners of all four USGS maps. Drawing the water courses in blue will make the copied map more readable.

The hike starts in the bed of Tortilla Creek at State Route 88 **[15-A, 0]**. If you like, you can bypass the first 0.4 miles and drop down to the creek bed from the paved road near the first bend **[15-T, 0.4]** in the creek. After the creek turns south, it makes a big turn to the east **[15-B,1.1]**, signaling the approaching junction with Peters Canyon. We often avoid the big bend by taking a cross-country route over the low pass to the south. A steep game trail takes you over the pass to Tortilla Creek just downstream from the mouth of Peters Canyon. The entrance of Peters Canyon comes in from the right (south) **[15-F, 1.6]**. Across from the mouth of Peters Canyon the cliff, at creek level, is penetrated by a six-foot hole. At high water, part of Tortilla Creek flows through this hole.

From Tortilla Creek, turn right (southeast) and proceed up the bed of Peters Canyon. The beginning of Peters Canyon is blocked with house-sized boulders and large pools of seasonal water. There is a rugged route around the boulders on the east bank below the cliffs. After the canyon turns southwest the walking becomes easier. A long stretch of smooth potholed bedrock begins here **[15-G, 1.9]**. This is the turnaround place for leisurely day hikers.

Tortilla Flat in the early 1900s. Photograph by Walter Lubken. Courtesy Salt River Project History Services.

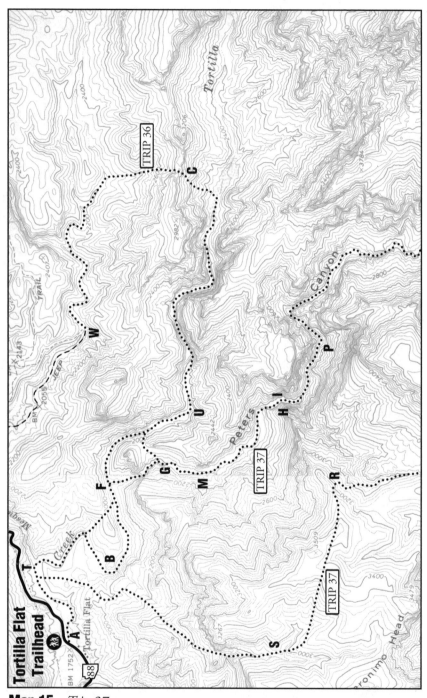

Map 15 - *Trip 37.*

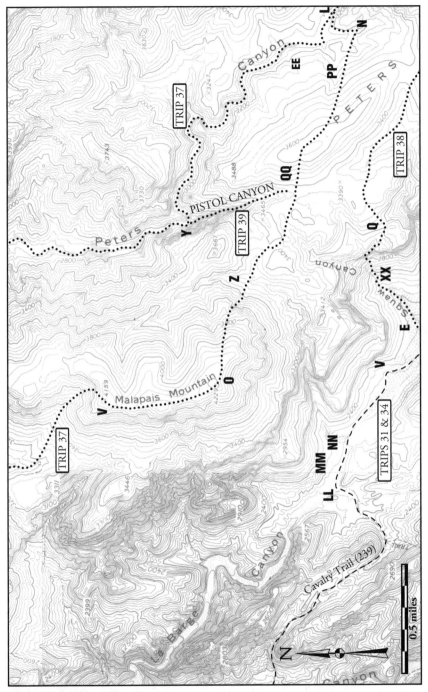

Map 15 continued - *Trip 37.*

Hikers can proceed up canyon as far as they like and return the same way, or return on a cross-country route that goes over the low pass to Tortilla Creek. The pass is located south of the butte below the junction of Peters Canyon and Tortilla Creek.

The image of a face, with a large nose, is nestled among tall rock spires on the west side of the canyon **[15-M]**. About one mile up from the mouth of Peters Canyon **[15-I, 2.6]**, on the east side of the canyon, is the rock formation Estee Conatser describes as the Indian Head. The profile of the face is very flat. When you see the large cave **[15-H, 2.6]** on the west side of the canyon, the Indian Head profile will be visible on the opposite side of the canyon on a tall, free-standing rock. The large cave on the west bank contains stone walls and makes a good shelter high above the canyon floor.

Farther up canyon there is another cave on the right bank (south) that is only about ten feet above the creek level. When we were there in December 1993, we saw an old sleeping bag, pots and dishes, a five-gallon plastic bucket and a lot of trash. Someone had been excavating the floor of the cave.

A few hundred feet upstream, the water flows over a low, slick rock waterfall into a deep pool **[15-P]**. It is possible to bypass the waterfall by climbing the broken cliff on the right side (south) of the canyon. A long, narrow pool, upstream of the waterfall, can be bypassed on the left cliff (north). Be careful when climbing around these obstacles. A fall here could easily result in a serious injury or death. After the waterfall, the canyon heads northeast for a short distance, then makes a sharp turn to the right. This is a pretty section of canyon with sheer walls on both sides.

The potholes, deep pools and caves are all landmarks connected to the Lost Dutchman Mine story as told by Walter Gassler. See History and Legends below for the complete story.

When the canyon narrows for the second time, Pistol Canyon **[15-Y, 5.4]** is due south and Peters Canyon makes an abrupt turn to the east. Trip 39 describes Pistol Canyon.

When the steep cliffs give way to gently sloping hills there is ample opportunity to make a cross-country trek up to Peters Mesa **[15-EE]**. Thick vegetation along the creek bed may restrict your access to the Peters Mesa. Although some 1880 feet higher than Tortilla Flat, the top of Peters Mesa is now only 520 feet above the canyon floor. There are several trip options from here. Continue up canyon (southeast) to the trail sign **[15-L, 7.2]**, then follow the unnamed trail up to Peters Mesa. Our trip heads cross-country (northwest) when you see the stone dam **[15-N, 3200]** along the unnamed trail. Or, remaining in Peters Canyon, proceed farther up canyon to another trail sign **[16-0, 8.0]** where Peters Trail (105) heads west to the saddle on

Peters Mesa. Read the Peters Mesa Area hike descriptions (Trips 38 and 39) for a good orientation to this interesting mesa.

There won't be much time to look around on Peters Mesa if you are doing this trip as a loop day hike, so continue northwest over the hill on Peters Mesa and set a course toward the high point on the south side of Malapais Mountain **[15-O, 4229]**. This is the section of the hike where a copy of the corners of all four topo maps comes in handy. On the eastern slope, there is a stone, well-like, structure **[15-PP]**. Pistol Canyon **[15-QQ]** drains to the north and Squaw Canyon drops off to the south. In February of 1982, we saw the remains of an abandoned tent camp on the saddle **[15-QQ, 8.7]** and some water in the wash to the west **[15-Z]**.

Getting to the top of Malapais Mountain is not difficult, although slow going, if you follow one of the ravines on the eastern side of the mountain. Toward the west, Malapais Mountain is not accessible because of the basalt cliffs. From the top of Malapais Mountain **[15-O, 9.4, 4229]**, the trek continues north across the ridge line **[15-V, 4159]** where you descend the mountain into a ravine running north-south. Cross this north-south ravine where it is shallow and head up to a low ridge line. Go northwest on the ridge until you cross the high point **[15-R, 3509]**.

View of Battleship Mountain and La Barge Canyon from the top of Malapais Mountain.

It is important to find the ravine that ultimately leads to the break in the cliffs **[15-S, 12.3]**. From the 3509 elevation point **[15-R, 3509]**, hike west to intersect the north-running ravine (near the 3000 elevation notation on the USGS map). Pick a line of sight route that avoids large ravines. Looking northwest, at some point you will see a large butte to the west of the cliffs above Tortilla Flat. Your hike will take you between the butte and the sheer cliffs on the east. Continue hiking north toward the large butte, and stay on the eastern side of the ravine. When the ravine narrows between two rock outcrops, an overgrown trail takes you along the east side of the steep ravine and eventually the trail heads up to the saddle on the east side of the large butte.

We finished the hike here in the dark one day and were surrounded by many snorting javelina that had either just walked down the same ravine or were waiting for a clear path to head up to the top. It was quite a confusing scene as we stood in the middle of the chaos and moving shadows. From the saddle, pick the easiest route down the slopes to Tortilla Creek or your vehicle **[15-A, 13.9]** where the trip description ends. Descending to the northeast was easier than descending to the northwest. On a decent to the northwest, we bushwhacked though a lot of vegetation, although we did find a trail near the bottom. Respect the private property at Tortilla Flat by taking an appropriately wide course around the developed land.

HISTORY AND LEGENDS. Peters Canyon was named after Gottfried Petrasch, known as Peter or Old Pete, who searched here for the Lost Dutchman Mine.[138] Gottfried Petrasch was the father of Herman and Reiney Petrasch.[139] Reiney, also called Old Pete,[140] and Julia Thomas were Jacob Waltz's friends. Jacob Waltz is reported to have told Reiney and Julia where his mine was located. Neither Gottfried nor his sons were ever successful in locating Waltz's mine. Gottfried died in 1914,[141] Reiney in 1943, and Herman in 1953.

Geronimo, a leader of the Chiricahua Apache, allegedly talked about a cave that held a large amount of gold. The cave, located somewhere in the Superstition Mountains, was supposedly marked by a large rock that resembled the head of an Indian. A similar rock formation in Peters Canyon, about a mile up canyon (south) from the junction with Tortilla Creek, piqued the interest of Estee Conatser. In her book, *The Sterling Legend*, Conatser describes the rock and the cave under the nose. The profile of the face is very flat and the nose points in a westerly direction. The rock stands almost one hundred feet high in the middle of Peters Canyon with nothing

Jack Carlson inspecting large cave in Peters Canyon. According to Walter Gassler this cave could have been the site of the Peralta headquarters.

else around it **[15-I]**. After a thorough investigation and checking with a metal detector, Conatser found no gold.[142]

In his 1983 manuscript, *The Lost Peralta-Dutchman Mine*, Walter Gassler describes the findings of his research at the Berkeley Library, Berkeley, California, between 1932 and 1935. The mine was in a north-south running canyon with hundreds of potholes **[15-G]**. A large cave **[15-H]** with a house in it served as the Peralta headquarters. A water hole **[15-P]** was a short distance up canyon from the cave. The mine was reported to be 1.5 miles up canyon which places the mine near Pistol Canyon[143] **[15-Y]**. All of these landmarks are still here today, but the most important landmark, the Lost Dutchman Mine, remains undiscovered.

Gassler wrote that an Indian friend of rancher Tex Barkley took Tex up Peters Canyon to a large water hole at the waterfall **[15-P]**. At that point, the Indian became nervous and decided to turn around. The Indian pointed up canyon and indicated to Tex that the mine was in that direction. Tex should take the next right hand canyon—Pistol Canyon.[144] Gassler also recalls Tex describing a cave in Peters Canyon that had posts and rafters. That might have been the remains of the two-room Peralta headquarters.[145]

Peters Mesa Area

The hike descriptions for Peters Mesa Area start on top of Peters Mesa. The shortest trail to Peters Mesa is Peters Trail (105) starting from the Tortilla Trailhead. The next shortest trail is the Bluff Spring Trail (235) connecting with the Dutchman's Trail (104) and Peters Trail (105) from Peralta Trailhead. Another popular approach, from First Water Trailhead, is the Dutchman's Trail (104) connecting with the Peters Trail (105).

FINDING THE TRAILHEAD. *Use Map 16.* Peters Mesa is about one mile north of Charlebois Spring (as the crow flies). Only one maintained trail crosses Peters Mesa—Peters Trail (105). There are several off-trail approaches to Peters Mesa and those routes are described below. Peters Trail (Trip 42) from Tortilla Trailhead is the shortest trail (5.0 miles) to Peters Mesa even if you have to walk the extra 3.2 miles on four-wheel-drive road FS213 (8.2 miles).

Trip 9 describes the next shortest trail which uses the Dutchman's Trail to connect with the Peters Trail. The total one-way mileage is 8.6 miles.

From First Water Trailhead, it is 9.7 miles to Peters Mesa using the Dutchman's Trail, the Bull Pass (129) shortcut, and the Peters Trail.

The Squaw Canyon Route (Trip 38) described below and the Peters Canyon Loop (Trip 37) provide more options for off-trail approaches to Peters Mesa. There is no water on Peters Mesa except for some seasonal runoff in the ravines. The closest water would be Charlebois Spring or seasonal pothole water in Peters Canyon.

HISTORY AND LEGENDS. Peters Mesa is an historic area that has been explored and prospected since the early 1900s. Some Lost Dutchman aficionados believe the area was mined in the mid 1800s. Many of the early books and manuscripts of the former prospectors describe the physical evidence and legends of Peters Mesa. A summary of the stories appears below but additional reading on your own will greatly enhance your trip to this historic mesa.

About 1911, Sims Ely made a trip to Peters Mesa where he discovered evidence of about forty Mexican fires northeast of Black Mountain. These fire beds were six-by-four foot areas in which coals were used to heat the

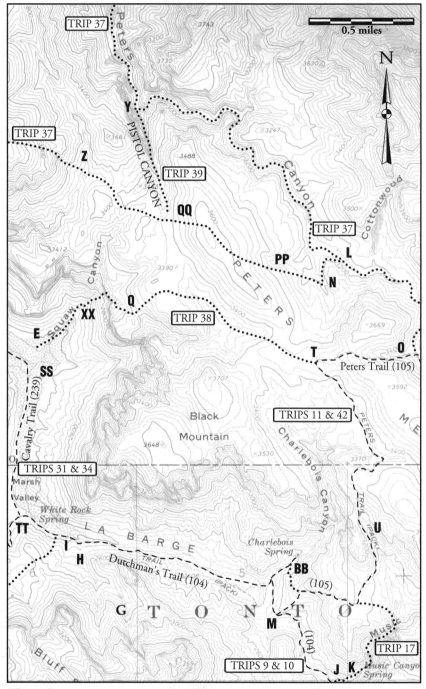

Map 16 - *Trips 37, 38, 39 and 42.*

ground and to surround a person sleeping there. Ely assumed they were used by Mexican miners. A year later, George Scholey and an Indian friend named Apache Jack hunted for game on Peters Mesa. Scholey was a miner and good friend of the local rancher, Jim Bark. Apache Jack's intent (disguised as a hunting trip) was to indirectly show Scholey where the gold mine was located. When they approached the northeast corner of Black Mountain, overlooking the fire beds, Apache Jack became nervous and headed back to First Water Trailhead. Shortly after this hunting trip, Apache Jack died from what Scholey thought was arsenic or strychnine poisoning by his medicine man—punishment for talking too much.[146] It is not clear to us why Scholey could not identify the type of poison, since the symptoms of arsenic and strychnine poisoning are very different. Arsenic poisoning results in severe gastric pain. Strychnine poisoning attacks the central nervous system causing dramatic and exaggerated convulsions of the body. For whatever reason the poisoning account was included in the story, it tends to cast suspicion on the validity of the episode.

Walter Gassler searched the Superstition Mountains from 1936 to 1984 for the lost mines and treasures. He documented his ideas and experiences in the 1983 manuscript, *The Lost Peralta-Dutchman Mine*. From Gassler's writings, it is clear that he considered Peters Mesa an important link in the mystery of the lost mines. Gassler describes the physical evidence such as the Mexican fire beds, the Spanish saddle, spurs, a pistol, a water hole in Peters Canyon, a cave on Malapais Mountain and cut timber to support his theory that Mexican miners were on the mesa. The Apache reportedly covered the mines and restored the landscape to prevent further mining there. Stories of the mine closures by several Indians included descriptions of three tee-pee-shaped boulders laid out in a semicircle, added more evidence to the exact location on the mesa. Tex Barkley's observation of the mescal pit and numerous grinding stones on Peters Mesa provided support for the mine closure theory. Although it is possible to develop other scenarios using this same physical evidence, most authors of the Lost Dutchman Mine legends have avoided those discussions.[147]

When Gassler first investigated Peters Mesa in 1936, he described a herd of horses on top of the mesa led by a large white stallion. Later, Gassler realized Tex Barkley referred to Peters Mesa as Horse Mesa because of these horses.[148] This and his many other stories of the mesa revealed his fascination with the region. On his last trip to Peters Mesa in May 1984, Walter Gassler died of a heart attack while walking on the Peters Trail near Charlebois Spring. He never found the mine, but like many others, received great satisfaction in the search for the unknown.[149]

Squaw Canyon

For expert hikers, who enjoy rugged hiking, the Squaw Canyon route offers a challenge to retrace the steps of former prospectors. This shortcut, cross-country trek provides another route to Peters Mesa.

ITINERARY: From La Barge Canyon, the Squaw Canyon route takes you up a steep ravine of Squaw Canyon to the top of Peters Mesa.

DIFFICULTY: Very difficult. No trail and very steep. Not recommended for horses. Elevation change is +1000 feet.

LENGTH and TIME: 1.0 miles, 1.25 hours one-way.

MAPS: Weavers Needle, Arizona USGS topo map. Superstition Wilderness Tonto National Forest map.

FINDING THE TRAIL: The route starts from the Cavalry Trail (239) in La Barge Canyon at the mouth of Squaw Canyon.

THE HIKE: *Use Map 16.* From the Cavalry Trail (239) walk northeast up the slopes on the north side of Squaw Canyon toward some large house-sized boulders **[16-E, 0]**. Look carefully on the uphill side of the boulders until you find a well-worn trail heading northeast up the north side of Squaw Canyon. It is worth the extra effort to find the trail since bushwhacking up the canyon is very difficult. Follow the trail northeast up to a flat camp area **[16-XX, 0.3]**. There is a long metal cable strung between two posts at this camp that was used by the prospectors as a pack-animal picket line. At the camp the route crosses Squaw Canyon Wash to the south side. There is no defined trail where the route crosses the wash.

On the south side of the wash a faint trail heads up the steep slope toward a dead, multi-armed saguaro cactus. If you look at the horizon line of the cliffs on Peters Mesa you can judge where the route goes. This route goes up a break to the north of the cliff that forms a ninety-degree angle against the background of the sky. The faint trail ends near some large boulders that look like they would make good shelter except for the fact that they are in the wash. From here, head right (east) up the steep slope to an obvious break in the cliff. There is no trail here. Be careful of the loose rocks while climbing though the thick vegetation. Within 100 feet you will come to a steep sloping cliff face pockmarked with lots of smooth hand and foot holds.

Only expert hikers with climbing experience should attempt this part of the hike. Although no technical climbing equipment is required to climb up or down the 100 foot cliff, it is dangerous and a fall could be fatal. An old hemp rope lying at the bottom of the cliff was used as a hand hold to get up and down the cliff. Going up the cliff may be more difficult than going down because the direction of the route is not obvious. Going up, the route tends to turn right. Staying on the less steep part of the cliff will lead you in the right direction. The wash above the cliff contains many loose rocks. Dislodging a rock above could injure someone below.

Once above the cliff, the route goes up the narrow wash. When you can easily walk out of the right (west) side of the wash, you will find a well-worn horse trail within 50 feet. There is an old camp here with some new and old trash scattered about. The small hill behind the camp provides a good view of Weavers Needle. Be careful. It's a sheer drop off the cliff.

Once you find the horse trail, follow it up to Peters Mesa. The route tops out on Peters Mesa **[16-Q 1.0]** where this trip description ends. The horse

View of La Barge Canyon from the Squaw Canyon Route. Weavers Needle is on the horizon.

Wedding picture of William A. "Tex" and Gertrude Barkley in 1905. COURTESY GREGORY DAVIS, SUPERSTITION MOUNTAIN HISTORICAL SOCIETY, BARKLEY COLLECTION.

trail continues south and eventually connects with Peters Trail (105) where Peters Trail makes a sharp turn **[16-T]** on Peters Mesa.

HISTORY AND LEGENDS.

Prospector Robert "Crazy Jake" Jacob had camps in La Barge Canyon and on top of Peters Mesa between the years 1963 and 1986. He used Squaw Canyon as a shortcut between camps, and some expert packers reportedly ran horses down the drainage of the canyon. Don't attempt this route on horseback. Don Van Driel and Greg Hansen of the Mesa Ranger District refer to the Squaw Canyon route we describe as the "Z" trail. Van Driel recalls the steel cable at the bottom of the steep section near a camp being used to tie up the horses. He also remembers riderless horses being driven down Squaw Canyon, also known as Squaw Box Canyon,[150] from Peters Mesa and then being rounded-up at the bottom of the cliffs. Tom Kollenborn has always known the trail up Squaw Box Canyon as "Jake's Trail."

The Squaw Canyon route may have been used by the cattlemen in the early 1900s since rancher Tex Barkley is reported to have found a Spanish saddle and spurs at the bottom of the cliffs here. Walter Gassler wrote about his concerns of possible conflicts with Robert "Crazy Jake" Jacob when Gassler was exploring the top of Peters Mesa in 1983, but he encountered no problems. Gassler, who searched for the Lost Dutchman Mine from 1936 to 1984 and wrote about Tex Barkley's discoveries, never mentions the route up Squaw Canyon.[151]

Pistol Canyon

Pistol Canyon is an area known to many Lost Dutchman Mine searchers. Some think that the lost mine is somewhere in this vicinity. This pretty canyon is a rugged route to Peters Mesa and can be included in your loop hikes from Peters Canyon.

ITINERARY: The Pistol Canyon Route starts on Peters Mesa and goes down Pistol Canyon to the bed of Peters Canyon.

DIFFICULTY: Very difficult. No trail. Not recommended for horses. Elevation change is -520 feet.

LENGTH and TIME: 0.5 miles, 1 hour one-way.

MAPS: Weavers Needle, Arizona USGS topo map.
Superstition Wilderness Tonto National Forest map.

FINDING THE TRAIL: Start from the top of Peters Mesa at the saddle between Squaw Canyon and Pistol Canyon.

THE HIKE: *Use map 16.* This is a very strenuous short hike that requires a lot of bushwhacking through the trees. From the top of Peters Mesa **[16-QQ, 0]**, hike north into the wide ravine of Pistol Canyon. Near the top of Peters Mesa, you can look north down Pistol Canyon and get a good view into Peters Canyon. Start in the bed of the wash and then contour along the eastern bank until it becomes too steep. Drop down into the bed of Pistol Canyon. Once in the bed of the canyon, the hiking is very slow and tiring so stay out of the water course as long as possible. There are several places where you must crawl under the branches of large trees. In contrast to the almost treeless mesas, this canyon supports some large groves of sugar sumac, oak and juniper. We saw several signs of an old trail in the bed of the canyon, but it was overgrown many years ago. The bushwhacking is difficult, and just about the time you wish you hadn't taken this hike, Peters Canyon **[16-Y, 0.5]** comes into view where this trip description ends. Trip 37 describes Peters Canyon.

HISTORY AND LEGENDS. Pistol Canyon is not shown on the Weavers Needle USGS topographic map, but Lost Dutchman Mine searchers and authors commonly refer to the north-draining canyon from Peters Mesa as Pistol Canyon. Clay Worst of the Superstition Mountain Historical Society told us that Pistol Canyon received its name in the early 1930s. Roy Bradford lost his six-shooter in the area and it was later found and returned by Chet Dickerson. Since then, everyone calls the small drainage Pistol Canyon.[152]

On one trip to Peters Mesa, Walter Gassler was accompanied by a friend, Tom Reis. After looking around Peters Mesa, Reis, who was an experienced mining engineer, commented that if there was a mine here, it would be on the north slope, possibly facing down Pistol Canyon.[153]

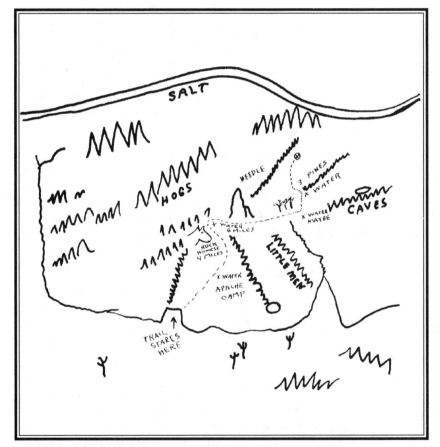

The Dutchman's Map may be a copy of one of the maps Julia Thomas sold to Lost Dutchman Gold Mine hunters. COURTESY SUPERSTITION MOUNTAIN HISTORICAL SOCIETY.

Tortilla Trailhead

From Apache Junction, go 23.8 miles northeast on State Route 88 to milepost 221, turn south onto four-wheel drive FS213 for 3.2 miles to the Tortilla Trailhead.

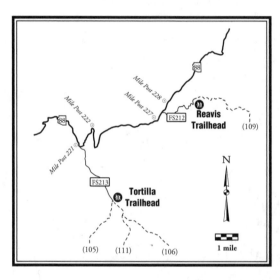

FINDING THE TRAILHEAD. There is parking along State Route 88 where you can leave your vehicle if you decide 4WD FS213 is too rugged. If your vehicle can negotiate the beginning of FS213, you might be able to drive to the end of FS213. The first 0.1 mile is the roughest part of the road. If you decide to walk, it is an easy hour and a quarter hike (3.2 miles), past the site of the Tortilla Headquarters buildings, to the end of FS213. The Forest Service is considering improvements to FS213 that will upgrade it to a high-clearance road. Check with the Mesa Ranger District for the latest road conditions.

Tortilla Well windmill is not in operation so don't count on it for water. Tortilla Creek is often dry. Even when there is water in Tortilla Creek at Tortilla Flat on State Route 88, the creek at Tortilla Ranch may be dry. **Bring your own water.**

Little remains of the Tortilla Ranch site. Just past a large honey mesquite tree along the road, there's a broken windmill and some old corrals. One corral has seen recent use. The old barn was torn down in the late 1970s and all that remains is the cement-slab floor. Several big, netleaf hackberry trees grow here next to the large parking area. Down the road, where the trail starts, is a small turnaround area but no parking lot. About 0.1 mile west of the vehicle turnaround is the old Tortilla Well windmill and metal water tank which mark the start of the Peters Trail.

FACILITIES. There are no facilities at this trailhead except for a corral. Bring your own water. Theft and vandalism are common both at this trailhead and at the parking area along State Route 88, so don't leave valuables in your vehicle. Thieves steal clothes, books, maps, camping gear, gasoline, tools, etc. Be sure everything is locked in the trunk, or better yet, don't bring it to the trailhead.

THE TRAILS. Three trails start near the Tortilla Trailhead. Peters Trail (105) begins at the Tortilla Well windmill and water tank. The small wooden *Peters Trail* sign marks the start of the trail. Peters Trail heads southwest up the bed of Tortilla Creek, then goes over a pass to Peters Canyon, and ends near Charlebois Spring.

From the end of FS213 (0.1 mile east of Tortilla Well windmill) the JF Trail (106) goes southeast (up the hill) across the Wilderness to the Woodbury Trailhead and nearby JF Headquarters. There are no trailhead signs here. The first trail sign is at the top of the hill where the Hoolie Bacon Trail (111) branches off the JF Trail. The Hoolie Bacon Trail proceeds south through Cedar Basin and Horse Camp Basin to La Barge Canyon where it connects with the Red Tanks Trail (107).

Tortilla Ranch before the buildings were removed. PHOTOGRAPH BY TOM KOLLENBORN. COURTESY SUPERSTITION MOUNTAIN HISTORICAL SOCIETY.

HISTORY AND LEGENDS. Although, for many years, Weavers Needle was the focus of the Lost Dutchman Mine searches, there was also considerable activity in the Tortilla region of the Wilderness. West of Horse Camp Basin near the Peters Trail (105) is an area considered to be the site of one Mexican mining camp and the source of cut timber for the unfound mines (Trip 42). The diggings at the Miller mines and the drift discovered by Estee Conatser about a mile and a half to the southeast of Tortilla Trailhead are evidence of more recent searches for mineral wealth (Trip 43). Before he died at Tortilla Flat on November 11, 1910,[154] John Chuning made extensive searches for the Lost Dutchman Mine in the Tortilla area using ladders to climb the sheer cliffs, but he, along with the others, was not successful in unlocking the mystery of the Lost Dutchman Mine.[155]

Without divulging names author Estee Conatser, in *The Sterling Legend*, writes that two men in the early 1950s located a sizable cache of gold south of Tortilla Ranch. She believes this discovery may be connected to stories related to Indians having buried gold in that region. She also recounts a story about a large cache of gold supposedly guarded by a band of Apache known as the Black Legion. This gold is presumed to be in the Black Cross Butte area, but the clues and treasure map are rather vague.[156]

John A. Bacon and Charlie Upton ran a cattle operation out of Tortilla Ranch. They also operated the Reavis Ranch in the 1940s and 1950s. The Hoolie Bacon Trail (111) is named for John Bacon who was nicknamed "Hoolie." John was not related to Vance Bacon, the geologist who worked for Celeste Jones and died in a fall from Weavers Needle. John Bacon's daughter, Alice, married Floyd Stone and they were owners of Reavis Ranch from 1955 to 1966. The Stones later ran cattle from the IV Ranch just east of Fish Creek.[157]

Tortilla Creek cuts northwest across the Wilderness some 16 miles, starting from Tortilla Pass in the south, draining to the north into Canyon Lake near Tortilla Flat. Barry Storm and Estee Conatser considered the possibility that Tortilla Creek could be the Canon Fresco marked on the Gonzales treasure map. Both authors refer to placer gold being found in Tortilla Creek—above and below the waterfalls by early prospectors, and in an unnamed section of the creek during the mid-1960s. Russel Perkins, an early postmaster of Tortilla Flat, described the remains of a large encampment near the falls on Tortilla Creek which were still visible in the 1940s. In that same area, Carl Clark reported finding the remains of a Spanish hexagon drill bit.[158]

Alignments of mountain peaks, cacti and canyons have all been proposed as clues leading to the Lost Dutchman Mine. Estee Conatser reported that

Fish Creek Hill in the early 1900s. Photograph by Walter Lubken. Courtesy Salt River Project History Services.

seven giant saguaros were growing in a straight line southeast of Tortilla Mountain.[159] We have not seen this group of seven cacti, but a similar alignment was photographed and reported in the newspapers. George "Brownie" Holmes, in his 1944 manuscript *Story of the Lost Dutchman*, wrote an account of another clue involving the alignment of Weavers Needle with Four Peaks when Four Peaks is viewed as one peak. The unnamed location of this alignment was through a saddle to a low ridge, with Fours Peaks to the north, and a high needle rising in the south. The Dutchman's camp was reputed to be in the canyon below the ridge.[160] While these clues are rather vague and probably not that useful for the serious mine seeker, they pique the imagination of many hikers and give ample reason to scan the landscape for these and other fascinating features.

Fish Creek Loop

Although Fish Creek is easily accessible from State Route 88, the narrow boulder-choked canyon deters many casual hikers. You will enjoy the solitude, seasonal pools of water and the dense canopy of trees.

ITINERARY: Park vehicle at the intersection of FS213 (Tortilla Road) and State Route 88, near milepost 221. Walk east on dirt State Route 88, down to the bottom of Fish Creek Hill. Hike up (south) Fish Creek, then head over to the old Tortilla Ranch site and follow dirt FS213 back to Apache Trail.

DIFFICULTY: Difficult day hike. Moderate overnight trip. Extensive boulder hopping required. Cross-country hiking required between Fish Creek and Tortilla Headquarters. Not recommended for horses. Elevation change is ±1045 feet.

LENGTH and TIME: 10.1 miles, 9 hours round trip.

MAPS: Horse Mesa Dam, Arizona USGS topo map.
Weavers Needle, Arizona USGS topo map.
Superstition Wilderness Tonto National Forest map.

FINDING THE TRAIL: The hike starts at a parking area on the south side of Apache Trail near milepost 221 **[17-E, 0]**.

THE HIKE: *Use Map 17.* It is possible to park a vehicle at the Fish Creek bridge but there isn't much room along the side of the road so the parking area **[17-E, 0]** near milepost 221 is a better choice. If you just want to take a short, easy hike up Fish Creek **[17-N, 0.5]** and return the same way, then it is more convenient to park at the Fish Creek Bridge **[17-F]**.

The trip starts from the parking area **[17-E, 0]**. Walk east on the Apache Trail, State Route 88, 2.2 miles to the Fish Creek Bridge **[17-F, 2.2]** at the bottom of Fish Creek Hill. There is no trail in Fish Creek Canyon so you begin from the bridge and drop down into the creek bed and head south. The hiking is pleasant in the canopy of Arizona sycamores and Fremont cottonwoods. There are many boulders and obstacles to negotiate so you should estimate your hiking speed at 0.5 miles per hour. At a ravine entering from the east **[17-G, 4.5]**, author Jack Carlson made a loop trip over Fish Creek Mountain and down Mud Spring Canyon. He was really surprised when he found a black bear in the thicket at Mud Spring.

Eventually Fish Creek Canyon opens up **[17-H, 5.0]** making the walking easier, but the shade and seasonal water disappear. If you continue up Fish Creek another half-mile, the seasonal water may be flowing on the surface again. The cross-country route from Fish Creek Canyon over to the Tortilla Ranch site is a matter of preference, but we usually head up Lost Dutch Canyon, then go east **[17-I, 5.5]** before reaching Lost Dutch Spring (often dry). Once you get up on the low ridge **[17-J]**, you can see the dirt roads below in the Tortilla Ranch valley (and possibly the Tortilla Well windmill **[17-B]** or Tortilla Ranch windmill **[17-K]** towers). The windmills are not in operation, and there is no water here. Adjust your course to intersect FS213 **[17-E, 6.9]** and return on FS213 north to State Route 88 **[17-A, 10.1]** where the trip description ends.

HISTORY AND LEGENDS. Hacksaw Tom was a notorious roadman along the Apache Trail from 1905 to 1910. He is known for robbing wagons and stagecoaches at the bottom of Fish Creek Hill with a sawed-off shotgun and then disappearing up Fish Creek Canyon. Hacksaw Tom's last robbery may have been in 1910 when the only automobile robbery on the Apache Trail occurred. A 1978 discovery of items in a carpetbag was identified with Hacksaw Tom. The carpetbag containing locks, a flour-sack mask with eye-holes and a twelve-gauge double-barreled shotgun was unearthed in a cave near Apache Gap. After seeing the shotgun Larry Hedrick, Director of the Superstition Mountain Museum, concluded Hacksaw Tom acquired his name from the appearance of his weapon—a shotgun a with sawed-off barrel and stock. Previously it was assumed he was named for hacksawing the locks from the strong boxes. All of Hacksaw Tom's memorabilia is on display at the Superstition Mountain Museum in Apache Junction.[161]

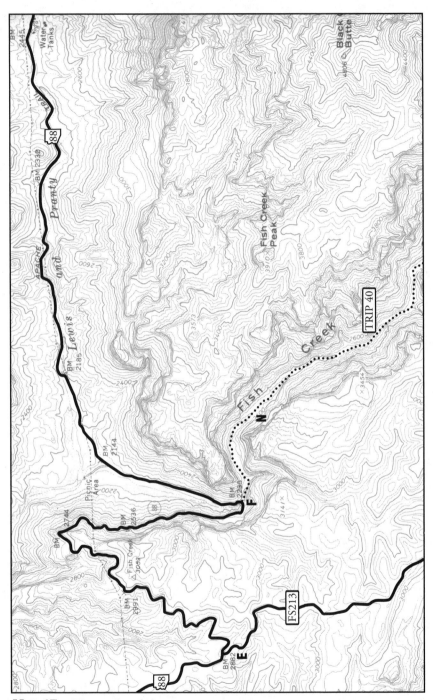

Map 17 - *Trips 36 and 40.*

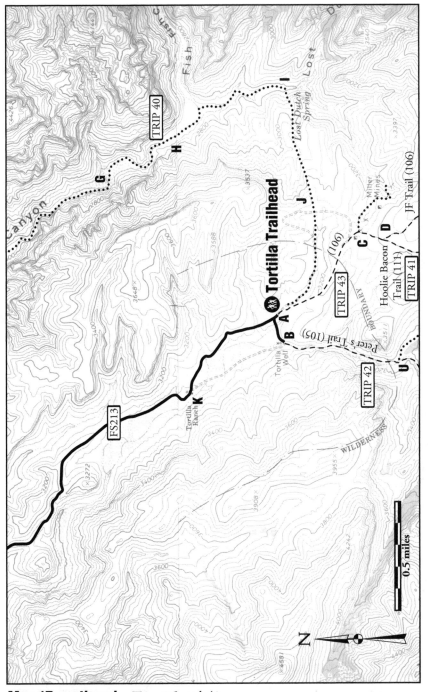

Map 17 continued - *Trips 36 and 40.*

Hoolie Bacon—Peters Trail Loop

This enjoyable hike crosses a lesser-traveled region of the Wilderness. Miller mines near the Tortilla Trailhead are easy to find (although not much remains there). The Hoolie Bacon Trail takes you down to Tortilla Creek where you can make a short loop back to Tortilla Well or continue through Cedar Basin and over the ridge to Horse Camp Basin. The cross-country route north to the Peters Trail is difficult (lots of catclaw), but the view of Music Mountain to the west and Tortilla Mountain to the north is especially nice. Peters Trail takes you past Kane Spring and back to the trailhead via Tortilla Well.

ITINERARY: From Tortilla Trailhead at the end of FS213 follow the JF Trail (106) to the junction with the Hoolie Bacon Trail (111). Take the Hoolie Bacon Trail across Tortilla Creek and over Horse Ridge to Horse Camp Basin. Follow a cross-country course northwest to Peters Trail (105). Go north on Peters Trail to the trailhead at Tortilla Well.

DIFFICULTY: Difficult. Some rugged off-trail hiking. Elevation change is ±1520 feet.

LENGTH and TIME: 8.2 miles, 8 hours round trip.

MAPS: Horse Mesa Dam, Arizona USGS topo map.
Weavers Needle, Arizona USGS topo map.
Superstition Wilderness Tonto National Forest map.

FINDING THE TRAIL Start on the JF Trail at the end of FS213 (one-tenth mile east of the Tortilla Well windmill). There are no trailhead signs.

THE HIKE: *Use Map 18.* The hike starts at the end of FS213 **[18-A, 0]** where the JF Trail begins on the south side of the road barricade. The JF Trail follows the wide track up the hill to an open gate with posts made of railroad ties **[18-C, 0.7]**. If you want to make the side trip, this is the junction with the Miller Mines Trail. The Miller Mines Trail goes straight (southeast) along a very faint path and soon disappears in the grass. Down in the ravine are the remains of an old metal stove and wash tub. There is evidence of mining in the area, but there isn't much to see here. We didn't see any water at the Miller Tunnel Spring when everything else in the area was dry.

Continuing your trip from the gate **[18-C]**, head south up the ridge to the top of the hill **[18-D, 0.8]** where the JF Trail meets the Hoolie Bacon Trail (111). The JF Trail branches off to the left (southeast), but our trip follows the Hoolie Bacon Trail which continues straight (southwest). The vegetation is sparse on the hillside; prickly pear, honey mesquite and catclaw acacia are scattered across the grassy landscape.

The trail soon drops down to the north side of Tortilla Creek where one-seed juniper, netleaf hackberry, redberry buckthorn and mesquite grow along the bench of the creek. Along here the catclaw mimosa invades the trail.

The trail crosses to the south side of Tortilla Creek **[18-X, 1.5]** where you have the option of going down the canyon (northwest) and returning to the trailhead via Tortilla Well **[18-B]**. This is a really nice section of Tortilla Creek and this part of the trip is only considered moderately difficult. The total trip mileage for this shorter loop is 3.4 and should take about 3 hours.

After the trail crosses Tortilla Creek **[18-X]**, it continues south, passing a group of netleaf hackberry trees, before it crosses back to the north side again where it leads through a short section of catclaw mimosa. The last creek crossing **[18-Y, 1.9]** takes you to a small flat area where there are some camp-sites. From the pictures in her book, we think this was Estee Conatser's camp when she explored the Lost Dutchman Mine, Jr. on the rocky peak **[18-F]** to the east.[162] See History and Legends in Trip 43 for the story of the Lost Dutchman Mine, Jr. From this flat camp area, the Hoolie Bacon Trail leaves Tortilla Creek, takes a right turn to the southwest, and crosses a major wash coming down from Cedar Basin Canyon. It is easy to follow the well-defined horse trail since there are large rock cairns marking the way.

The trail heads up to Horse Ridge passing through an area with abundant one-seed juniper trees. The trail is well marked to the top of the hill with large cairns. Cedar Basin Canyon to the east is appropriately named. Many people refer to these juniper trees as cedar because the aroma and appearance of the cut wood are similar to cedar. Standing juniper should not be cut, nor should dead-looking branches be removed because of the way the trees grow. They may look dead, but the trees will often grow foliage the following season. The trail reaches a low saddle **[18-Z, 2.6]**, where a lone Arizona rosewood tree grows, then continues higher through manzanita, sugar sumac, and redberry buckthorn. At the top of Horse Ridge **[18-BB, 2.9]**, the pass is marked by a lone mesquite tree.

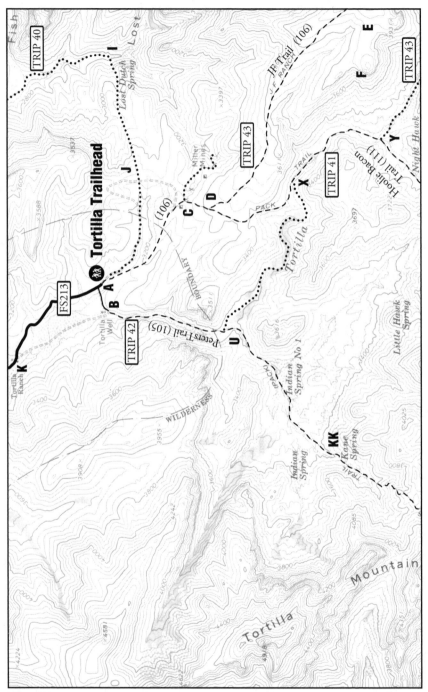

Map 18 - *Trips 41, 42 and 43.*

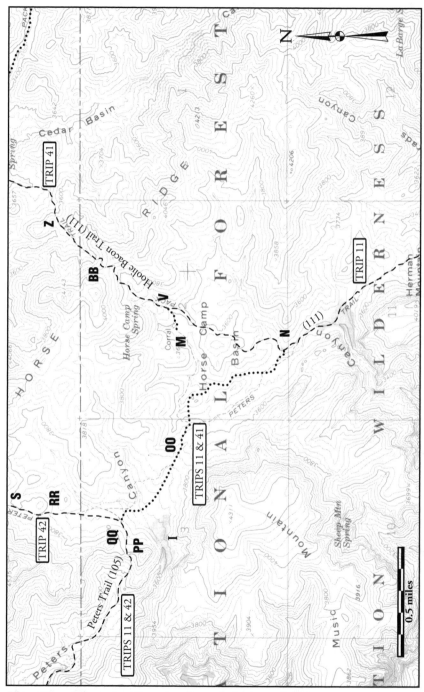

Map 18 continued - *Trips 41, 42 and 43.*

The trail drops down into Horse Camp Basin where the landscape is much dryer. Here you are more likely to encounter thickets of catclaw mimosa. A spur trail **[18-V, 3.4]** heads off to the right (west) for 0.1 miles to the abandoned Horse Camp Corral **[18-M]**, but the trail becomes faint and difficult to follow just south of the corral. Back on the Hoolie Bacon Trail **[18-V, 3.4]**, the trip continues over a low hill and drops down to a ravine coming in from the left (east). This is the point **[18-N, 4.1]** where this trip leaves the Hoolie Bacon Trail and goes cross-country to the northeast.

If you want to continue on the Hoolie Bacon Trail to La Barge Canyon, it is another 1.4 miles to the end of the Hoolie Bacon Trail. The catclaw mimosa has invaded the trail in many places so the walking is a bit slow.

From the ravine **[18-N]**, the trip becomes much more difficult. The route follows the old alignment of the Peters Trail northwest toward Tortilla Mountain. We have attempted this trek using several strategies and have concluded there is no easy way to get from here **[18-N]** to there **[18-OO]**. One time we bushwhacked through the catclaw mimosa by following the abandoned Peters Trail—that should be your last choice. More recently, we walked up the open wash which heads directly north; then we cut across to the top of the ridge above Peters Canyon. Except for a few places, the wash is free of vegetation and the footing is as good as many trails. Follow the wash as far as possible since the catclaw mimosa covers most of the landscape here. After leaving the wash, head for the ridge line for easier walking where you can sometimes find good game trails. There are a few Arizona rosewood trees growing on this grassy hillside. From the ridge **[18-OO, 5.0]** overlooking Peters Canyon, you can see the soldier camp and cut timber area to the west **[18-I]** and the cliffs of Tortilla Mountain straight ahead to the north. Peters Trail (105) heading to Charlebois Spring goes west over the large knob on the horizon **[18-PP]**, but our trip heads east toward Tortilla Well. From the ridge **[18-OO]**, pick the easiest route down the slope, cross the wash of Peters Canyon, and head up the bench until you intersect a well-traveled horse trail—Peters Trail **[18-QQ, 5.5]**. Some Lost Dutchman Mine authors refer to this section of the Peters Trail as the Spanish Trail. After the bushwhacking episode, Peters Trail will seem like a superhighway.

Follow Peters Trail north up to a low pass **[18-RR, 5.9]**, then down and up to the high pass **[18-S, 6.1]**. The steep rocky trail descends the spine of a ridge with steep drop-offs on either side. Watch your footing here on the loose rocks. From the trail, the view into the valley below is superb. Kane Spring **[18-KK, 6.5]** is to the east of the trail and is identified by the large corpus of trees; sugar sumac, juniper, honey mesquite, netleaf hackberry, and Fremont cottonwood. Kane Spring may have water but check with the

Peters Trail sign at Tortilla Well.

Forest Service before you go. At one time, there was a metal and wooden cover over the spring opening, but that is in disrepair and the spring is full of leaves. The water is clear when you clean the leaves out and seems okay, but is not great tasting. Always purify your drinking water. A few feet down from the spring is an abandoned, cement water trough with a float that was used to control the water flow. The water trough is filled with dirt.

From Kane Spring **[18-KK]**, the trip continues southeast, downhill, and the trail surface changes from rock to soft dirt. The last time we traveled this trail, in November 1993, it showed signs of recent work where new water diversion channels were dug in the soft dirt. After crossing the open flat valley, the trail crosses a major wash, passes between two small hills and then intersects Tortilla Creek **[18-U, 7.4]**. The creek crossing is well marked by large rock cairns. From here **[18-U]**, the trail goes north following either bank of the creek and sometimes down the center of the creek bed. The walking is easy when there is little water or the bed is dry, but this section of trail would be impassable when Tortilla Creek is at flood stage.

This stretch of Tortilla Creek is very scenic with a thick growth of netleaf hackberry, mountain mahogany, lemonade berry, one-seed juniper, and scrub oak, but the narrow canyon is dominated by the canopy of large Arizona Sycamore trees. The pale red cliffs are covered with green lichen. Even when Tortilla Creek is dry, this is a pretty area. When the steep cliff to the east recedes, the end of Peters Trail is approaching. The trail ends on the east side of Tortilla Creek at the Tortilla Well windmill **[18-B, 8.1]**. It is a short walk up the road to the end of FS213 where the hike started **[18-A, 8.2]** and this trail description ends.

HISTORY AND LEGENDS. For Sims Ely's stories about the soldier and Mexican camps, cut timber for the mines, and the Spanish Trails, see Trip 42. For the Estee Conatser story about the Lost Dutchman Mine, Jr. along Tortilla Creek, see Trip 43.

Peters Trail to Charlebois Spring

This is one of the shortest routes to Charlebois Spring through a lesser traveled region of the Wilderness. The trip takes you past Kane Spring which may have water. Historic Peters Mesa offers a place to relive the accounts of many Lost Dutchman stories. Short excursions are possible from centrally-located Charlebois Spring, including Peters Mesa, Music Canyon and La Barge Canyon.

ITINERARY: From Tortilla Trailhead follow Peters Trail (105) into Peters Canyon, up to Peters Mesa and down to La Barge Canyon. A short distance on the Dutchman's Trail (104) brings you to Charlebois Spring.

DIFFICULTY: Difficult day hike due to length and elevation change. Moderate overnight. All trail hiking. Elevation change is ±3000 feet.

LENGTH and TIME: 14.8 miles, 7.5 hours round trip.

MAPS: Weavers Needle, Arizona USGS topo map.
Horse Mesa Dam, Arizona USGS topo map.
Superstition Wilderness Tonto National Forest map.

FINDING THE TRAIL: The trail starts at the Tortilla Well windmill **[18-B]** at a wooden trail-sign and heads south along Tortilla Creek.

THE HIKE: *Use Maps 16 and 18.* The trip to Charlebois Spring can be a long day hike or the first leg of a longer overnight trip. From Tortilla Well windmill **[18-B, 0]**, Peters Trail (105) follows Tortilla Creek and makes many crossings that are well marked by rock cairns. Tortilla Creek is very scenic with a thick growth of netleaf hackberry, mountain mahogany, juniper, and scrub oak, but the narrow canyon is dominated by the canopy of large Arizona sycamore trees. In the Fall, the golden leaves of the sycamore trees and the pale red cliffs covered with green lichen add a splash of color to this narrow canyon. Hikers taking an easy day hike can turn around when the large wash enters on the right (south) **[18-U, 0.7]**. The trail leaves Tortilla Creek **[18-U]** and heads southwest on the south side of a large wash. Much of the trail through here is across soft dirt which is uncharacteristic of the typically rocky trails in the Wilderness. The trail continues across a wide valley and goes uphill toward Kane Spring. Kane Spring **[18-KK, 1.6]** may have water but check with the Forest Service before you go. The spring is in disrepair, but the water seems to be drinkable if purified. The wooden cover has rotted so the water is full of leaves from the nearby sugar sumac, netleaf hackberry and Fremont cottonwood trees.

From Kane Spring **[18-KK]**, Peters Trail continues up a very steep hill to a pass **[18-S, 2.0]**. The trail drops through a small ravine, continues over a lower pass **[18-RR, 2.2]** and descends into the Peters Canyon drainage. The impressive cliffs of Tortilla Mountain rise in the west while the rolling hills of the Horse Country open to the southeast. At the bottom of the descent **[18-QQ, 2.6]** a trail marked by a cairn leads to the left (southeast).

Our trip continues on the Peters Trail (southwest) but it is worth mentioning some details about the old trail heading southeast. This unmaintained trail **[18-QQ]** leads to Horse Camp Basin connecting with the Hoolie Bacon Trail (111). Near the start of this trail on the northwest side of Peters Canyon wash there is an old mesquite tree with a very large rock in the fork of the branches. Lost Dutchman Mine hunters are always looking for "signs" such as this! This unnamed trail is the former alignment of the Peters Trail and is difficult to follow because it is overgrown with catclaw mimosa (also called wait-a-minute or, locally called, cougar claw). Sometimes the dry washes and ridge lines are easier to follow than the overgrown trail. If you try this route, the intersection with the Hoolie Bacon Trail **[18-N]** may be difficult to find. Despite the catclaw, however, day hikers who are persistent may enjoy returning to Tortilla Trailhead over this slightly longer trek (see Trips 11 and 41).

From the trail intersection **[18-QQ]**, Peters Trail goes up to a saddle **[18-PP, 2.9]** just north of a big knob on the horizon and then the trail drops to the bed of Peters Canyon. The detailed description for the rest of the trip is given in Trip 11. Here are a few of the important mileage reference points. At a signed junction **[16-O 4.5]** in Peters Canyon, Peters Trail heads west up a ravine to historic Peters Mesa **[16-T, 5.0]**. Peters Trail drops into La Barge Canyon where it intersects the Dutchman's Trail (104) **[16-M, 7.0]**. Following the Dutchman's Trail west takes you into Charlebois Canyon where a spur trail leads north to the spring **[16-BB, 7.4]** where this trip description ends. Trip 9 describes the Charlebois Spring area. Return the same way to Tortilla Well **[18-B, 14.8]** or plan an extended trip from this central location in the Wilderness.

The remains of the windmill and tank at Tortilla Well in 1993.

In the early 1900s Tortilla Mountain was renamed Kit Carson Mountain, but the Tortilla name was soon restored when historians learned Kit Carson never explored this region.[163]

Sims Ely in his 1953 book, *The Lost Dutchman Mine*, describes the horse country and the possibility that a soldier camp, on the western end of horse country, was the site of a Mexican camp. The horse country that Ely recounts is the area shown on the Weavers Needle topographic map in Sections 2 and 3 where the landmarks are named Horse Ridge, Horse Camp Spring, and Horse Camp Basin. Rancher Jim Bark and Ely considered this area important because the camp was the site of cut wood (covering about 40 acres) which they believed was used as timber in the Mexican mines. We looked around one possible area where there might be cut timber **[18-I]** but only found one cut stump and two larger stumps that may have rotted. West of here was a dense thicket that was impossible to penetrate but it did look as if it once contained large mesquite trees. Ely reasoned that they could determine the direction of the Mexican mines by tracing the route that the timber was carried. He speculated that it could have been taken over two routes. The first was the old alignment of the Peters Trail that went south past Trap Canyon, connecting with the Hoolie Bacon Trail and over to the mouth of La Barge Canyon at Upper La Barge Box. Trip 41 uses this cross-country route that is now mostly overgrown with catclaw. In 1910, Ely said he saw sections of this trail that were three feet wide and cut into the rock. The other possible route went northwest on the Peters Trail past Kane Spring down toward Tortilla Creek. Many authors refer to this section of the Peters Trail, along the base of Tortilla Mountain, as the Spanish Trail.[164]

JF Trail to Woodbury Trailhead

This enjoyable hike crosses a lesser traveled-region of the Wilderness. Miller mines near the Tortilla Trailhead are easy to find (although not much remains there). The Lost Dutchman Mine, Jr. will take some extra effort to locate. A side trip to the cliff dwellings in Rogers Canyon is worthwhile if you have time. JF Headquarters near the Woodbury Trailhead is an interesting place to visit and photograph.

ITINERARY: From Tortilla Trailhead follow JF Trail (106) over Tortilla Pass to Woodbury Trailhead.

DIFFICULTY: Moderate. Elevation change is +2120 and -1720 feet.

LENGTH and TIME: 9.4 miles, 5.5 hours one-way. One-way vehicle shuttle distance is 58 miles.

MAPS: Horse Mesa Dam, Arizona USGS topo map.
Weavers Needle, Arizona USGS topo map.
Iron Mountain, Arizona USGS topo map.
Superstition Wilderness Tonto National Forest map.

FINDING THE TRAIL: JF Trail begins at the end of FS213 (0.1 miles east of Tortilla Well windmill). There are no trailhead signs.

THE HIKE: *Use Maps 18, 19 and 23.* This hike can be done as a 9.4 mile trans-wilderness trek requiring a 58-mile vehicle shuttle, or a round-trip 12.6 mile day hike to Tortilla Pass and back. Some hardy day hikers may prefer to return by boulder hopping down Tortilla Creek to the Tortilla Trailhead.

The hike starts at the end of FS213 **[18-A, 0]** where the JF Trail begins on the south side of the road barricade. The JF Trail follows the wide track uphill to an open gate with posts made of railroad ties **[19-C, 0.7]**. If you want to make the side trip, this is the junction with the Miller Mines Trail. The Miller Mines Trail goes straight (southeast) along a very faint trail and soon disappears in the grass. Down in the ravine are the remains of a stove and wash tub. There is evidence of mining in the area but there isn't much to

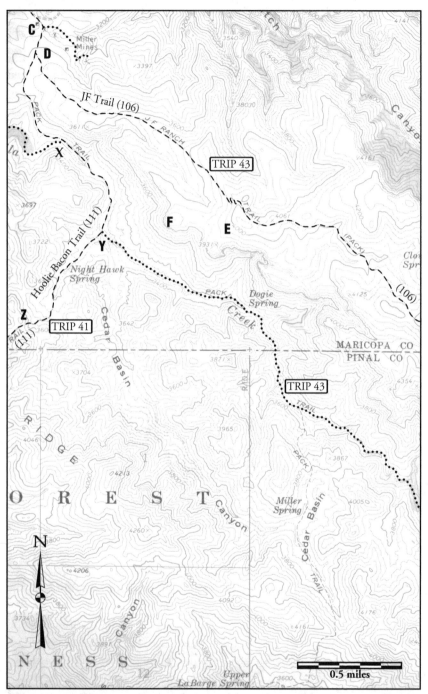

Map 19 - *Trip 43.*

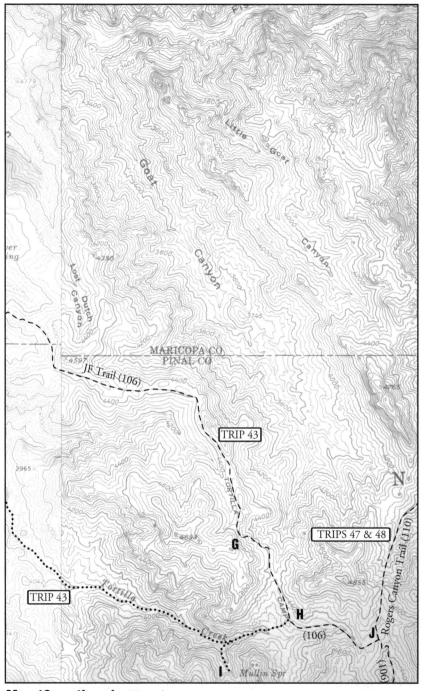

Map 19 continued - *Trip 43.*

see here. We didn't see any water at the Miller Tunnel Spring when everything else in the area was dry.

Continuing your trip from the open gate **[19-C]**, head south up the ridge to the top of the hill **[19-D, 0.8]** where the JF Trail meets the Hoolie Bacon Trail (111). The vegetation is very sparse here with prickly pear, mesquite, and catclaw growing among the grasses. The Hoolie Bacon Trail continues straight while the JF Trail branches off to the left (southeast). The JF Trail begins a gentle climb along the crest of some small hills.

The trail begins to climb some short switchbacks where the mesquite trees grow next to the path. At the ridge **[19-E, 2.0]**, you can take a side trip to the cliff where author Estee Conatser found an old mine **[19-F]** which she named the Lost Dutchman Mine, Jr. See History and Legends for the story of the mine. The view from the cliff near the mine into Tortilla Creek and Cedar Basin is spectacular, and these areas would make a good destination for a day hike or overnight trip using the Hoolie Bacon Trail. See Trip 41.

As the JF Trail continues to climb, the vegetation is more abundant and varied—mountain mahogany, juniper, mesquite, manzanita, catclaw acacia and mimosa, Arizona rosewood, shrub oak, sugar sumac and yucca. The horizon is broken with the towering stalks of the century plant and sotol and the rocks are covered with green lichen. Long sections of the trail pass over rock imbedded with crystals and geodes. The JF Trail follows a hogback ridge, crossing many saddles until it finally turns east on a saddle **[19-G]** and makes a quick descent through a switchback into the upper drainage of Goat Canyon. The trail then crosses a low saddle into the Tortilla Creek drainage and meets the trail junction **[19-H, 5.5]** to Mullin Spring **[19-I]**. The trail to Mullin Spring, marked by a rock cairn, heads down the hill to the west. There are several partially-dead juniper trees in the area, one of which marks this junction. It is about a half mile to Mullin Spring which often has water. Verify the water conditions with the Forest Service before you go.

The trail is thick with shrub oak, tomatillo, manzanita, juniper and Arizona rosewood, but pushing through the vegetation is fairly effortless. From the trail junction **[19-H, 5.5]**, it is a short distance up to Tortilla Pass **[19-J, 6.3]** where the Rogers Canyon Trail (110) comes in from the north. La Barge Mountain is the high mountain to the west, rising to 5077 feet— twenty feet higher than Superstition Mountain. On a hike to Tortilla Pass in November 1993, we were greeted with snow that covered all the trees and bushes.

You have several trip choices from Tortilla Pass **[19-J]**. First, continuing south on the JF Trail takes you to the Woodbury Trailhead for the completion of this hike. Second, a side trip to the cliff dwellings in Rogers Canyon

Jack Carlson in a November 1993 snow storm that covered the juniper trees and cactus at Tortilla Pass.

is 1.8 miles down the Rogers Canyon Trail. There are good camping places in the grassy flat in Angel Basin **[23-F]** where Trail 110 enters Rogers Canyon (Trip 47). And finally, day hikers can return to Tortilla Trailhead via the same way (JF Trail 106) or take the slower, boulder hopping route through Tortilla Creek which ends at Tortilla Well **[18-B]**. On the map we drew the dotted line over the old trail along Tortilla Creek, but the last time we hiked here in the early 1980s we found it easier to walk down the dry bed of the creek.

Continuing toward the Woodbury destination, the JF Trail ascends south from Tortilla Pass into Randolph Canyon. After the trail passes though some green thickets of mountain mahogany, juniper, tomatillo, sugar sumac and shrub oak, you have good views across the valley to the south and west. About halfway down this slope you start to see evidence of cattle which continues to the closed gate at the Woodbury Trailhead. The trail crosses Randolph Canyon **[23-N, 8.1]**, which may have potholes of water (often fouled by cattle), then goes up a hill and follows the west bank of Randolph Canyon. After dropping to creek bed level, the trail crosses the wash twice before passing the Wilderness Boundary sign **[23-D, 8.7]**. About 30 feet south of the Wilderness Boundary sign is the trail spur heading west to the JF Headquarters. This trail is the old alignment for the JF Trail and connects with Woodbury Trail (114) and Coffee Flat Trail (108) to the southwest.

Proceed south on the JF Trail toward the Woodbury windmill **[23-C, 8.9]**. In November, 1993, the windmill seemed to be in operation but no water was coming out of the pipes. The trail near the Woodbury windmill is very faint but becomes more distinct as you proceed south to the signed junction **[23-B, 8.9]** with Woodbury Trail (114). Woodbury is cow country and you will likely see numerous cows lazing under the mesquite trees. The JF Trail follows a dirt road over a small hill to the Woodbury Trailhead parking lot where the trip ends **[23-A, 9.4]**. If you want to take a walk over to the JF Headquarters see Trip 49 for the directions.

HISTORY AND LEGENDS. George Miller and two partners, Earnest Martin and John Hluper, had mining claims near the Tortilla Well area in the 1920s and 1930s. Miller died of a heart attack at his mine in 1936 when he was showing the area to some friends. Following his wishes, he was buried near the mines; a grave was blasted out of solid rock. Martin died in 1927 and is also buried on a hill near the diggings. Several of the local landmarks are named for Miller: Miller Mines, Miller Tunnel Spring, and Miller Spring.[165]

Estee Conatser, author of *The Sterling Legend*, searched the Superstition Mountains for the Lost Dutchman Mine (LDM) and found a mine that at first seemed to fit the description of the LDM. She named the mine Lost

The windmill near the site of the Woodbury cabin in 1993. The junction of the JF Trail and Rogers Canyon Trail at Tortilla Pass is hidden between the highest peaks on the horizon.

Fallen cottonwood trees silhouette the sky along Fraser wash near JF Ranch, 1993.

Dutchman Mine, Jr. The mine **[19-F]** is located on a rocky cliff 0.3 miles northwest of Hill 3931 and is not very hard to find if you are persistent and follow the hike description here. Only seasoned hikers with climbing experience should attempt this side trip. We had to walk down below the cliffs to see the round, black hole of the cave and the shape of the rock fin that points the way down to the mine and cave. Then, back on top of the cliffs where the highest point looks like a stack of broken rocks, we headed north and followed the ravine until we saw the hole in the mine ceiling. It is a sheer drop off the Tortilla Creek side of the cliff, so be careful. From the ceiling hole, it is a steep scramble in the ravine to the mine entrance which faces northwest. To us, the mine looked like a natural opening in the rock, although there are some cuts on the walls that could be pick marks. We will let you decide. The approach to the cave below looked too steep, so we did not attempt it. You will enjoy reading the complete description, with pictures and story, in Estee Conatser's 1972 book, *The Sterling Legend.*[166]

Reavis Trailhead

The Reavis Trailhead is off State Route 88, between mileposts 227 and 228, about 30 miles northeast of Apache Junction. Turn south on FS212 and drive uphill 2.8 miles to the end of the road.

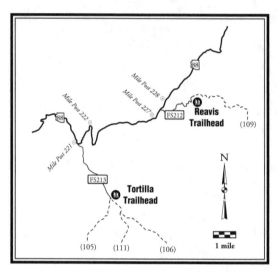

FINDING THE TRAILHEAD. Forest Service road FS212 is a one lane, dirt road with several eroded sections that require a high-clearance vehicle. There are only a few turnaround places on the road and it would be difficult to back down if you decided your vehicle was not going to make it across the rough eroded portion of the road. The 3700-foot trailhead elevation provides a panoramic view of the Salt River Canyon and Apache Lake to the northwest.

FACILITIES. There is a hitching post for horses at the trailhead but no other facilities. **Bring your own water.**

THE TRAIL. There is only one trail from this trailhead, the Reavis Ranch Trail (109). From the road barricade at the end of FS212, the trail follows the old eroded road to Reavis Ranch.

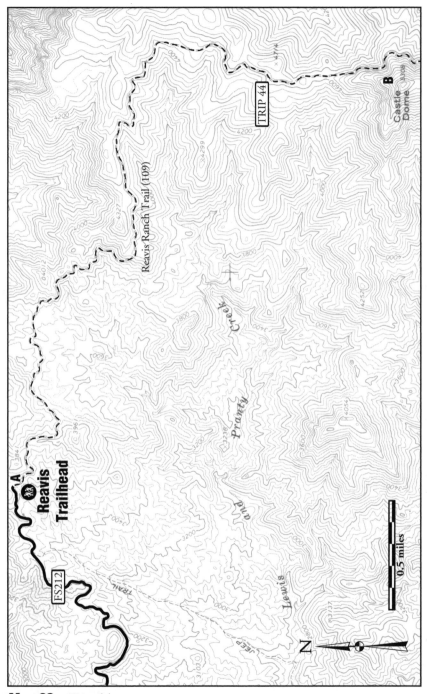

Map 20 - *Trip 44.*

Reavis Ranch

The Reavis Ranch hike makes a good two to three day trip to a beautiful and historic region in the Wilderness. The tall ponderosa pine, black walnut, sycamore, cottonwood and alligator juniper trees make this valley a pleasant destination. The Reavis Ranch house burned in November 1991, but the nearby orchard still produces apples each Fall. Several miles north of the ranch is the 196-foot Reavis Falls on Reavis Creek and to the south is Circlestone ruin next to Mound Mountain.

ITINERARY: From the Reavis Trailhead, follow the Reavis Ranch Trail (109) to Reavis Ranch. Return same way.

DIFFICULTY: Moderate 2 or 3 day trip. Elevation change is ±2160 feet.

LENGTH and TIME: 18.6 miles, 10 hours round trip.

MAPS: Pinyon Mountain, Arizona USGS topo map.
Iron Mountain, Arizona USGS topo map.
Horse Mesa Dam, Arizona USGS topo map.
Superstition Wilderness Tonto National Forest map.

FINDING THE TRAIL: The trail starts beyond the FS212 road barricade and follows the old Reavis Ranch Road.

THE HIKE: *Use Maps 20, 21 and 22.* From the Reavis Trailhead **[20-A, 0]**, Reavis Ranch Trail follows the abandoned dirt road as it ascends 1400 feet to its high point **[21-C, 5.8]** just before reaching Windy Pass. Maybe it is the road, or the panoramic vistas that change slowly, or just the uphill grade, but this hike always seems to be longer than it actually is. Before Castle Dome, there is a well worn unmaintained trail leading east toward Lime Mountain Spring and on to Reavis Falls **[21-R]**. Castle Dome **[21-B, 4.4]**, on the west side of the road, is the landmark signaling the upcoming Windy Pass and some up and downhill sections of road. Just past Windy Pass is Plow Saddle **[21-D, 6.5]** where it is possible to cut across to the Frog Tank Trail (112).

The signed Frog Tank Trail meets the Reavis Ranch Trail at a well-marked intersection **[21-E, 7.8]**.

Continuing on the Reavis Ranch Trail, the road turns south along a fence line and begins to parallel Reavis Creek. At the first opening in the fence, to the east, there is a very large group-camping area under a canopy of black walnut, ponderosa pine and sycamore trees **[22-F, 8.3]**. This is the first easy access to Reavis Creek where you can often find water. We didn't see the pipe that is called Reavis Spring, but Lowell Bailey, Bill Hall and Greg Hansen told us the pipe is on the west side of the creek, near water level, north of the old wagon. Check with the Forest Service for the latest water conditions before you go. Farther south on the Reavis Ranch Trail, the signed Reavis Gap Trail (117) enters from the east where a large tree blocks the old road **[22-G, 8.9]**. The apple orchard is on the east side of the Reavis Ranch Trail **[22-H, 9.0]** just before you reach the site of the Reavis Ranch house **[22-I, 9.3]** which is on a bench above and to the west of the trail. Only the cement floor of the ranch house remains today. South of the ranch house is another orchard to the east of the trail. The trail continues south, passes through a forest of southwestern locust trees, crosses Reavis Creek and intersects the signed Fire Line Trail (118) on the east bank **[22-J, 9.6]**.

Reavis Ranch House in the summer of 1939. Left to right, Woman's name unknown, Eli Drakulich (kneeling), Johnny McDaniels, Jim Hughes, Ellis Toney, Lenora Martin, William H. Martin, Neta Grey, Jack Grey, Billy Martin, Jr. PHOTO BY MARION BURKE. COURTESY OF THE MARTIN RANCH AND WILLIAM MARTIN FAMILY AND OF GREGORY DAVIS, SUPERSTITION MOUNTAIN HISTORICAL SOCIETY, CLEMANS CATTLE COMPANY FILE.

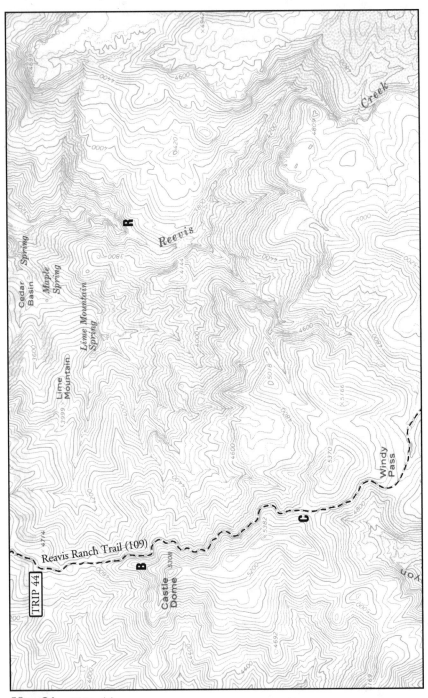

Map 21 - *Trip 44.*

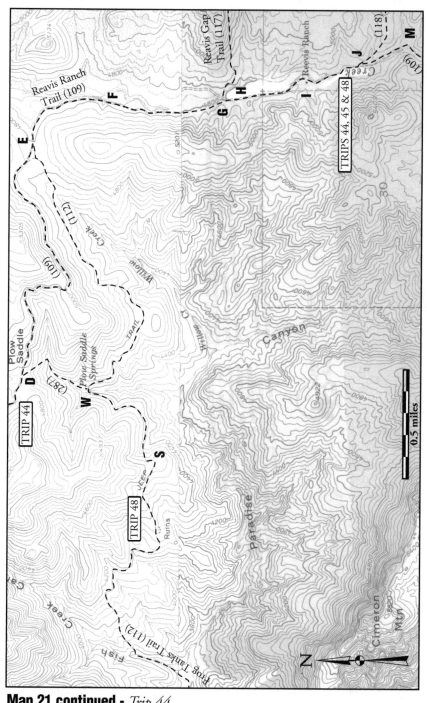

Map 21 continued - *Trip 44.*

Since Reavis Ranch is a popular destination you might find others here, but there is plenty of room for camping along the two-mile corridor by Reavis Creek. Fewer people camp south of the Fire Line Trail so you can find some solitude there among the towering ponderosa pine trees. Reavis Creek usually has some water, but verify the water conditions with the Forest Service before going.

Circlestone ruin, about 2.7 miles from the Reavis Ranch house site, is on a lower knoll just to the northeast of Mound Mountain **[22-O, 6010]**. It is a 1160 foot elevation change to the ruin but the trip is worth the effort. Kollenborn and Swanson describe two routes to Circlestone ruin. At the trail intersection **[22-J, 0]**, take the Fire Line Trail (118) east to the pass **[22-K]**, continue down trail for three-tenths mile and look for an unsigned trail **[22-L, 1.6]** heading south up the hill—the Allen Blackman Trail. The Allen Blackman Trail goes uphill steeply at first, then contours along the east side of the ridge before striking out across the ridge line to Circlestone **[22-O, 2.4, 6010]**. This is the easiest trail for both horses and hikers. A more direct but steeper route, the unsigned 1.3-mile Slope Trail, starts near **[22-N]**. The Slope Trail leaves the Reavis Ranch Trail before the Reavis Ranch Trail crosses Reavis Creek for the second time. We haven't hiked the Slope Trail, but others have told us it is probably just a cross-country route since they couldn't find a definite trail. Circlestone ruin is on the top of a knoll partially hidden among a growth of manzanita and large alligator junipers. Please don't camp or build fires in or around the ruin.

The trip description ends here, but you should consult Trips 45 and 48 for more ideas. Return by the same route.

HISTORY AND LEGENDS. Tom Kollenborn and James Swanson have written extensively on the Superstition Mountains. Their 1986 work titled *Circlestone: A Superstition Mountain Mystery*, is an excellent book to read before visiting the Reavis area and small enough to take with you for reading around the campfire. It is helpful to refer to their description and drawings of Circlestone ruin when you visit the site. We've selected a few facts from their book to entice you read the complete story.

Elisha Reavis first came to the Superstitions around 1874 and established his farm. He was well known for his vegetables which he sold in Phoenix, Tempe, Mesa and Florence. Reavis died in April 1896 near his grave site along the Reavis Trail not far from Rogers Canyon. His original house burned. Another wooden house was built by Jack Fraser which burned in the mid 1930s. That house was replaced by a sandstone and adobe structure constructed by two cowboys employed by Twain Clemans. Over the years,

Reavis Ranch House, November 1993. The building was destroyed by fire in November 1991.

the house was modified to accommodate the needs of its many owners. Only the cement floor and stone walls of the building remained after it burned in a November 1991 fire.[167] The stone walls were taken down in January 1994.

Reavis Ranch was a prime location for ranching, farming and tourists because it had good spring water and a cool summer climate. After Reavis died, Jack Fraser acquired the property and developed it as a tourist pack-trip destination named Bloomerville. In 1899, the *Arizona Daily Gazette* reported four hardy Phoenicians venturing into the Superstitions on a hunting trip. Their snowy January horse ride took them to the Rogers Canyon cliff dwellings and to Reavis Ranch for a visit with Mr. Fraser.[168]

In 1910, the Clemans Cattle Company purchased the ranch and tried to promote the area as a summer resort called Mountain Air. In the 1930s, the area was promoted as a resort named Pineair. Twain Clemans is credited with planting six hundred apple trees here. In 1938, the ranch was sold to John Bacon and Charlie Upton. "Hoolie" was John Bacon's nickname and Forest Service Trail (111) bears his name today—the Hoolie Bacon Trail. Construction on the Reavis Ranch Road, begun in 1910, was finally finished in 1947 by Bacon and Upton. Alice Bacon married Floyd "Stoney" Stone and, with a partner, purchased the ranch in 1955. They are credited with planting more apple trees during their ownership. Reavis Ranch was sold in

Apple drying in the field north of Reavis Ranch, circa 1930. COURTESY OF THE MARTIN RANCH AND WILLIAM MARTIN FAMILY AND OF THE TONTO NATIONAL FOREST, REAVIS RANCH FILE.

1966 to the Tonto National Forest and, a year later, was incorporated into the Superstition Wilderness.[169]

The November 1993 issue of *Arizona Highways* has a feature article on Reavis Falls by Stan Smith and photographs by David Elms, Jr. The photographs and article are worth reviewing if you attempt this trek. In 1998 we hiked to the falls on a route suggested by David. The route follows a good trail which leaves the Reavis Ranch Trail (109) north of Castle Dome and heads southeast up to a ridge. From the ridge the trail descends into the valley, crosses the hogback ridge of Lime Mountain, passes Maple Spring and continues northeast over a low ridge before dropping into Reavis Creek. Once in the creek bed, the route goes upstream (south) to the falls **[21-R]**.[170]

Elisha Reavis was probably the first settler to see the falls, but author and historian Tom Kollenborn is credited with measuring the 196 foot falls and describing its location. On the USGS Pinyon Mountain map, Reavis Falls **[21-R]** is located in Reavis Creek about one half mile southeast of Maple Spring, where four contour lines are closely spaced.[171]

Five miles, as the crow flies, northeast of Reavis Ranch Peter "Bigfoot" Busnack is reliving some of the same adventures Elisha Reavis experienced over 100 years ago. With his partner, Peter grows fruit, herbs and vegetables on a farm at the edge of the Wilderness on Campaign Creek. They take their produce and herbal remedies to market in Tempe and are becoming well-known for their classes on botanical medicine. The farm is located at the Reevis Mountain School of Self-Reliance which teaches what you might expect—herbal medicine, self-healing, wilderness survival and many other skills. We learned our plant identification skills from Peter over the years and hope we do justice to his patient instruction. The school which was founded in 1979 is located at the Upper Horrell Trailhead (Campaign Trailhead), one of the trailheads closer to Reavis Ranch (seven miles by trail).

Circlestone ruin makes an excellent side trip when visiting the Reavis area. In *Circlestone: A Superstition Mountain Mystery*, Swanson and Kollenborn describe Circlestone ruin in complete detail while analyzing it with experts from many scientific disciplines. Located on a small knoll, at 6010 feet to the northeast of Mound Mountain, Circlestone is best approached from the west on the ridge-line trail blazed by Allen Blackman. The ruin is constructed of a three-foot wide sandstone wall. The diameter of the not-quite-circular ruin is about 133 feet with the outline of a 17 foot by 17 foot building in the center.[172] Circlestone dates to A.D. 1250 – A.D. 1300.[173] Some experts believe Circlestone to be celestially oriented.

Tales of the Lost Dutchman might seem out of place in the eastern Superstition Wilderness, but there is a story Barry Storm told about Jacob Waltz traveling though the region. Waltz was reported to have stayed at Blevins' cabin which was near the present town site of Roosevelt. When Blevins returned from a trip, his son told him of their overnight guest who had just departed. Blevins followed Waltz and tracked him to a little flat just south of the junction of Reavis and Pine Creeks (4 miles north of Reavis Ranch). At that point, the tracks disappeared and Waltz's destination was never determined, although he shortly arrived in Tucson with $1,600 in gold ore.[174] On another occasion, when Elisha Reavis was packing his produce to market, he met Waltz in Fraser Canyon and had a conversation with him.[175] These chance encounters with the Dutchman never produced enough clues to reveal the location of his mine.

Tule Trailhead

From Apache Junction, on U.S. Route 60 drive east 49 miles to State Route 88, just east of Globe. Turn north on State Route 88 for 21 miles to FS449 (Cross P Ranch Road) between mileposts 252 and 251. Drive west on FS449 for 2 miles to its junction with FS449A. Stay right on FS449 for 1.2 miles to the end of the road. Tule is locally pronounced "Two-lee."

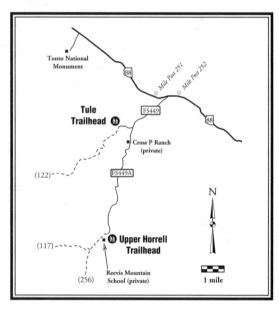

FINDING THE TRAILHEAD. The FS449 road is well marked and easy to follow. The road ends at a turnaround and small parking area.

FACILITIES. There are no facilities at the Tule Trailhead except for a small parking area. **Bring your own water.**

THE TRAILS. Tule Canyon Trail (122) begins from the parking area and is marked with wooden trail signs. From the trailhead you have a clear view toward Two Bar Mountain across the open desert. In this edition of the *Hiker's Guide to the Superstition Wilderness*, we haven't described any trips from this trailhead, but we plan to field check this interesting area for a future edition.

Tonto National Monument is only a few miles northwest of the Tule Trailhead on Route 88. Visitors are permitted to tour the interior of the cliff dwelling at Tonto National Monument.

Upper Horrell Trailhead

From Apache Junction, on U.S. Route 60 drive east 49 miles to State Route 88, just east of Globe. Turn north on State Route 88 for 21 miles to FS449 (Cross P Ranch Road) between mileposts 252 and 251. Drive west on FS449 for 2 miles to its junction with FS449A. Take FS449A left for 6 miles to Reevis Mountain School (Upper Horrell Place).

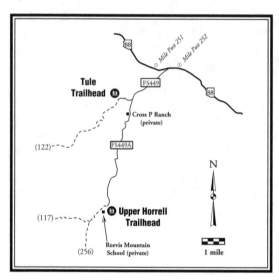

FINDING THE TRAILHEAD. FS449 road is well marked to the junction with FS449A. FS449A is a four-wheel drive road that follows the bed of Campaign Creek. This road may be impassable during periods of heavy rain. During the dry season we drove FS449A in a high-clearance vehicle and had no problems except for getting stuck in the deep sand.

FACILITIES. There are no facilities at the Upper Horrell Trailhead except for a small parking area. **Bring your own water.**

THE TRAILS. Campaign Trail (256) begins from the parking area and is marked with wooden trail signs. In the Spring of 1994, the Campaign Trail was realigned so that it goes around the west side of Reevis Mountain School on the west side of Campaign Creek. Do not use the old trail that passes through the Reevis Mountain School (private property). Reavis Gap Trail (117) branches off to the west at a signed trail intersection about a half mile up the Campaign Trail from the trailhead. In this edition of the *Hiker's*

Guide to the Superstition Wilderness, we haven't described any trips from this trailhead, but we have plans to field check this area for a future edition.

Stewart Aitchison and Bruce Grubbs in their book, *The Hiker's Guide to Arizona,* describe the Campaign Creek—Pine Creek loop hike that passes by Reavis Ranch. They rate this a 3 or 4 day, moderate trip on lesser-traveled trails.

HISTORY AND LEGENDS. Upper Horrell still retains its name on many of the maps, but the former Horrell ranch has been the Reevis Mountain School of Self-Reliance since 1979. The non-profit school and farm is a division of the Pateman-Akin-Kachina Foundation. Peter "Bigfoot" Busnack and John Goodson are the founders of the school. See History and Legends in Trip 44 for information on Peter and this quiet farm sanctuary.

The last time we visited with Peter he told us about the flooding during January of 1993. High water in Campaign Creek closed FS449A to all vehicle traffic. Their only contact with the outside world was a long hike out to the main road. In the spring of 1993, Peter used his stone masonry skills to repair major damage to several creek crossings using rocks to create an underground drainage for the water.

Even when FS449A is dry, the deep sand can be a problem. Peter told us that his technique for getting out of the soft sand is to lower the air pressure in the rear tires until they are flat enough to float through the sand. After visiting with Peter, we drove down FS449A and were okay until we got stuck in the deep sand near Cross P Ranch. We drove down the dry wash without a problem after lowering the rear tire pressure to 35 psi. Our tires normally hold 80 psi.

If you get stuck on FS449A, remember that the local ranchers and farmers are not waiting for your call of distress. They are busy people and will have to take time from their business to lend you a hand. Be friendly and non-demanding and expect to incur delays of hours or even a day. The best plan would be to come prepared with the right equipment so you can rescue your own vehicle.

Campaign Creek along the Campaign Trail south of the Upper Horrell Trailhead.

Miles Ranch Trailhead

From Apache Junction, on U.S. Route 60, drive 32 miles to Superior. Continue east toward Miami and Globe on U.S. Route 60 for 12 more miles. One mile east of the Pinto Creek highway bridge, turn left (north) on FS287 (Pinto Valley Mine Road) between mileposts 239 and 240. Follow FS287 and FS287A to the trailhead.

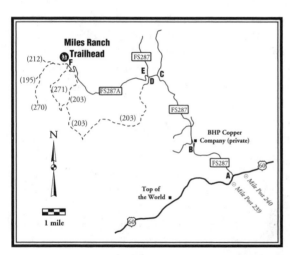

FINDING THE TRAILHEAD. The approach to the trailhead follows a confusing road, FS287, across the facilities of the BHP Copper Company. The road takes you along several large, mine-tailing ponds. Forest Service road FS287 is not the most-traveled road in the area and the FS287 intersections with the BHP Mine roads are not always well marked. Follow the signs indicating public access and do not drive on any roads marked Active Mining Area. The route of the public access road may change to accommodate mine operations, so you need to pay close attention to the road signs and speed limit.

From U.S. Route 60 **[A, 0]** drive north on paved FS287 for 2.8 miles to the BHP Mine entrance **[B, 2.8]** and bear left as FS287 turns into a dirt road. Continue on dirt FS287 through the BHP Mine property following the public access road signs. Turn left (east) at the signed major intersection and cattle guard **[C, 7.5]**. Continue east on FS287 and cross the iron bridge at Pinto Creek **[D, 7.9]**. At the signed intersection with FS287A **[E, 8.0]**, take FS287A west for 5.5 miles to the end of FS287A **[F, 13.5]**. A medium-clearance vehicle is required.

Allow extra driving time for getting lost on the first section of the road **[B, 2.8 to C, 7.5]**. Following the old Anderson Ranch and Bohme Ranch signs will help you stay on FS287. At the intersection of FS287 and FS287A, there is a large sycamore tree and plenty of room for car camping. Pinto Creek in this area is pretty and there is usually some water flowing in the creek. Don't drink the creek water. Bring your own drinking water.

If you look beyond the immediate mining operation, you can see a good cover of vegetation and a few cows grazing. A revegetation program uses the cows to prepare and seed the mine tailings. On a return trip at night, we saw three small deer on the road at the main mine entrance and a skunk running across the road at the FS287A junction. At the beginning of the West Pinto Trail (212) and all throughout the Miles Ranch Trailhead area, we often see fresh bear scat full of manzanita berries.

FACILITIES. There are no facilities at the Miles Ranch Trailhead except for some corrals and a barn. **Bring your own water**.

THE TRAILS. The sign for the Miles Ranch Trailhead parking lot is on the south side of FS287A at the end of FS287A. The West Pinto Trail (212) is next to the small parking lot and is well marked with a trail sign and large rock cairn. Some people still start their hikes here, but you can now drive into the former ranch property which is part of the Tonto National Forest and start your hike from there.

The Tonto National Forest purchased the western portion of the ranch property in 1986 which now has a Wilderness designation. The eastern end of the ranch was purchased by the Tonto National Forest in 1997 and is now used as the trailhead area. There is plenty of room here for parking cars and horse trailers. The large sycamore and Emory oak trees make this a nice place to car camp and prepare for day trips. The West Pinto Trail (212) and Rock Creek Trail (195) provide easy hiking and horse riding along the seasonal creeks. Many other trails in the area provide superb hiking and riding possibilities.

The Haunted Canyon Trail (203) going over to Haunted Canyon and Tony Ranch (private) is 1.7 miles on FS287A, from the Miles Ranch Trailhead, and is also well marked. The east end of the Haunted Canyon Trail terminates near the iron bridge on Pinto Creek.

In this edition of the *Hiker's Guide to the Superstition Wilderness*, we haven't described any trips from the Miles Ranch Trailhead, but we have plans to write about this area in a future edition.

Rogers Trough Trailhead

From Apache Junction, go east 16 miles on U.S. Route 60 to Florence Junction. Two miles east of Florence Junction on U.S. Route 60, between mileposts 214 and 215, turn north on Queen Creek Road for 1.6 miles to FS357 (Hewitt Station Road), go right 3 miles to FS172, go left 10 miles to junction of 172A and go right 3 miles on 4WD road to end of road. A high-clearance vehicle is required on FS172 and 4WD on FS172A.

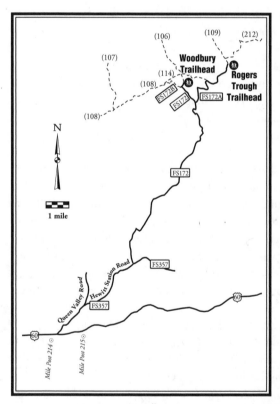

FINDING THE TRAILHEAD.
Hewitt Station Road makes several unbridged crossings of Queen Creek. After heavy rains there may be high water in Queen Creek which will make this route impassable. FS172 is a scenic dirt road through Hewitt Canyon which makes unbridged crossings of the wash. Jagged mountains surround FS172 for the first few miles, then the country opens up into a wider valley. There are numerous places to car camp along this road. Ten miles on FS172 brings you to the junction of FS172A (4WD road) where you go right (east) for 3 miles to Rogers Trough Trailhead. If you can't make it up the 4WD FS172A road, you can use the Woodbury Trailhead as an alternate parking

The large flat parking area at Rogers Trough Trailhead is a pleasant sight after traveling on the steep and rugged four-wheel drive road.

area, but you will have to walk 3.7 miles to the Rogers Trough Trailhead. Sections of 172A are steep and narrow where it is impossible to turn around or back down. Most people consider 4WD a requirement for FS172A.

FACILITIES. There are no facilities at the Rogers Trough Trailhead parking lot except for a hitching post. **Bring your own water.**

THE TRAILS. Reavis Ranch Trail (109) goes northwest from the Rogers Trough parking lot. A short distance from the Rogers Trough parking lot the Pinto Peak Trail (212) branches off to the northeast. Expect to see some cows in the area.

HISTORY AND LEGENDS. About 300 yards down the Reavis Ranch Trail from the Rogers Trough Trailhead there is a small hill to the right (east). The top of this hill is the site of the old Rogers Mill. The concrete foundation is still there. The old boiler was still there in the 1950s but it is now gone.[176] Rogers Spring is to the east up a small drainage.

When complete, the 750-mile Arizona Trail will extend from the Mexican border north to Utah. The Arizona Trail makes use of existing trails within the Superstition Wilderness. From the south, the Arizona Trail enters the Superstition Wilderness at Rogers Trough Trailhead and follows the Reavis Ranch Trail (109) to Reavis Ranch. It then follows the Reavis Gap Trail (117) and Two Bar Ridge Trail (119) to the northern boundary of the wilderness a few miles south of Roosevelt. For information on other sections of the Arizona Trail, contact the Arizona Trail Association which is listed under Useful Addresses.

Rogers Trough to Reavis Ranch

The trip to Reavis Ranch is a popular hike and trail ride for many apple lovers each Fall. Reavis Ranch has more to offer than the apple orchards. Reavis Valley usually has some water, and the large stands of Arizona walnut, Arizona sycamore, alligator juniper, and ponderosa pine make this area a special destination. Worthwhile side trips to Circlestone Ruin and Reavis Grave make this an outstanding trip.

ITINERARY: From Rogers Trough Trailhead follow Reavis Ranch Trail (109) to Reavis Ranch. A side trip to Circlestone ruin uses the Fire Line Trail (118) and the Allen Blackman Trail. Return the same way.

DIFFICULTY: Moderate 2 or 3 day backpack trip. Elevation change is ±1920 feet.

LENGTH and TIME: 12.2 miles, 9 hours round trip.

MAPS: Iron Mountain, Arizona USGS topo map.
Pinyon Mountain, Arizona USGS topo map.
Superstition Wilderness Tonto National Forest map.

FINDING THE TRAIL: Reavis Trail (109) starts at the northeast side of the Rogers Trough parking area at the end of FS172A.

THE HIKE: *Use Map 22 and 23.* The trip starts on Reavis Trail (109) at the Rogers Trough Trailhead **[23-U, 0]** and immediately crosses the upper arm of Rogers Creek. There are a few cows in this area. West Pinto Creek Trail (212) enters from the east **[23-T, 0.1]** and heads 7.8 miles over to the Miles Ranch Trailhead. The Reavis Ranch Trail continues down Rogers Canyon making many stream crossings. There is seasonal water here, and the water course is dotted with netleaf hackberry, Arizona sycamore, and juniper trees. At the signed junction with Rogers Canyon Trail (110) **[23-S, 1.6]**, the Reavis Ranch Trail heads northeast toward Reavis Ranch. Just north of the junction **[23-S]** the trail passes through an open gate and follows the Grave Canyon drainage through some large stands of manzanita. Sycamore trees dot the ravine. The trail wanders back and forth across the water course until it passes the unsigned spur trail to Reavis Grave **[23-R, 2.3]**. The last time we were there, in October of 2000, a tall rock cairn marked the spur trail up the hill to the west. It is only a few yards up to the small flat grassy area where the grave site is marked by a rectangular mound of rocks. A good way to find the spur trail is to note that the Reavis Ranch Trail leaves the rocky wash and goes up a set of switchbacks about 200 feet north of the Reavis Grave spur trail.

After visiting the grave site, continue on Reavis Ranch Trail which follows the switchbacks up the west side of the ravine. After an elevation gain of 700 feet the trail tops out at Reavis Saddle **[23-Q, 3.0]**, and you get your first glimpse of the inviting forest on the north side of the ridge. There are some flat, grassy campsites at the pass. From Reavis Saddle, it is an easy and enjoyable downhill walk all the way to Reavis Ranch. There may be water at Honeycutt Spring **[22-P, 3.9]** which is up a wide ravine to the west. Check with the Forest Service for current water conditions. There are many nice campsites along Reavis Ranch Trail, and the forest of emory oak, alligator juniper and ponderosa pine make this stretch of the trip one of the most pleasant experiences of the hike. The trail makes many crossings of Reavis Creek and then favors the west bank for most of the remainder of the trek.

Reavis Ranch House and pond, circa 1940s. COURTESY OF THE MARTIN RANCH AND WILLIAM MARTIN FAMILY AND OF GREGORY DAVIS, SUPERSTITION MOUNTAIN HISTORICAL SOCIETY, CLEMANS CATTLE COMPANY FILE.

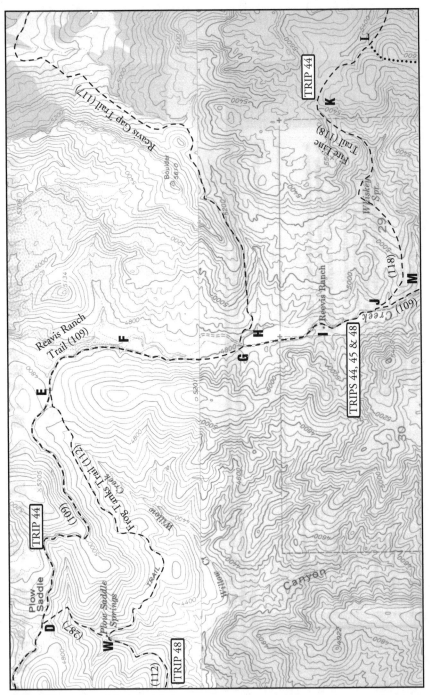

Map 22 - *Trips 44, 45 and 48.*

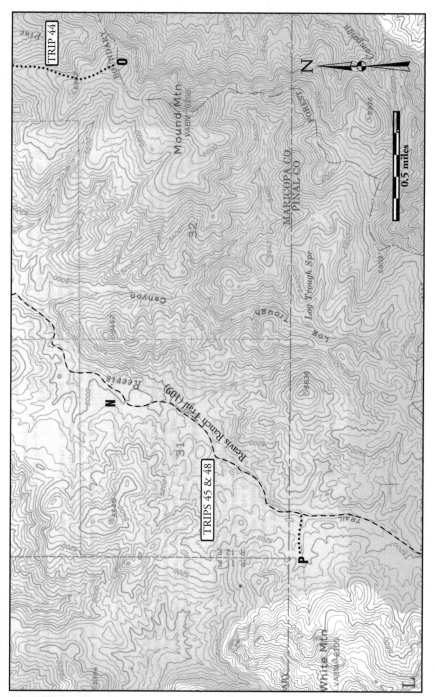

Map 22 continued - *Trips 44, 45 and 48.*

Evidence of the May 1966 Iron Mountain Burn is still present but detracts little from the beauty of the area. Greg Hansen of the Forest Service said the tall lovegrass was planted to stop erosion after the fire, but the non-native lovegrass stifled the indigenous grasses and shrubs.[177] The forest here has a feeling of openness with the grassy undercover being broken only by scattered ponderosa pine trees. Nearby, a large alligator juniper tree **[22-N, 5.2]** along the trail is often measured by hikers to determine its circumference. It takes about five people holding hands to span the girth of this ancient tree.

The trail continues north and soon drops down near the water course of Reavis Creek. There may be intermittent water here. At this point, the trail crosses to the east side of the creek and closely follows the water course, then returns to the west bank. About fifteen minutes downstream, the trail crosses again to the east bank which should alert you to watch for the junction with the Fire Line Trail (118) **[22-J, 5.9]**. The Fire Line Trail is the beginning of the 2.4-mile side trip to Circlestone ruin. See Trip 44 for the Circlestone trail description. Reavis Ranch Trail continues north as it crosses to the west bank and cuts through the ranch area. There is a small orchard to the east just

before you reach the site of the ranch house. The Reavis Ranch house site **[22-I, 6.1]** is on the west side of the trail. The ranch house burned in November 1991 and only the cement floor remains now. A few feet to the south, you can still see the depression in the earth where the pond was located. Trip 44

The horse corral at Reavis Ranch, circa 1920-30. COURTESY OF THE MARTIN RANCH AND WILLIAM MARTIN FAMILY AND OF TONTO NATIONAL FOREST.

explains more about the Reavis Valley including the north apple orchard, Reavis Gap Trail and Reavis Falls. Trip 48 also covers this area and will give you another perspective.

The hike description ends here. Return the same way to the Rogers Trough Trailhead **[23-U, 12.2]**.

HISTORY AND LEGENDS. See Trip 44 for the history and legends.

Rogers Canyon Cliff Dwellings

This hike leads you through beautiful Rogers Canyon along the shortest trail to the cliff dwellings near Angel Basin. You will enjoy the wide variety of trees and the seasonal pools of water in this scenic canyon. Angel Basin offers excellent camping.

ITINERARY: From Rogers Trough parking lot follow Reavis Ranch Trail (109) northeast to the junction with Rogers Canyon Trail (110). Follow Rogers Canyon Trail to the cliff dwellings. Return the same way or return to the Woodbury Trailhead via Tortilla Pass on JF Trail (106).

DIFFICULTY: Moderate. Elevation change is ±1000 feet.

LENGTH and TIME: 8.2 miles, 4 hours round trip.

MAPS: Iron Mountain, Arizona USGS topo map.
Superstition Wilderness Tonto National Forest map.

FINDING THE TRAIL: Reavis Ranch Trail (109) starts at the northeast side of the Rogers Trough parking lot at the end of FS172A.

THE HIKE: *Use Map 23.* The trip starts on Reavis Ranch Trail (109) at the Rogers Trough Trailhead **[23-U, 0]**. The trail crosses Rogers Creek a few yards from the parking lot. Although there may be water here the cows make the water unpotable. Within a tenth mile, West Pinto Creek Trail (212) comes in from the east **[23-T, 0.1]**. It is 7.8 miles to the Miles Ranch Trailhead on Trail (212). The Reavis Ranch Trail continues down Rogers Canyon making many stream crossings. This part of Rogers Canyon has seasonal water, and the canyon supports netleaf hackberry, Arizona sycamore and juniper trees. At the signed junction with Rogers Canyon Trail (110) **[23-S, 1.6]** the Reavis Ranch Trail is heading northeast toward Reavis Ranch. This hike goes left (west) on the Rogers Canyon Trail and continues down Rogers Canyon toward the cliff dwellings. Rogers Canyon has seasonal water although it may be intermittent. The trail now follows the bed of the water course more closely and continues to make many crossings. Arizona sycamore, emory oak,

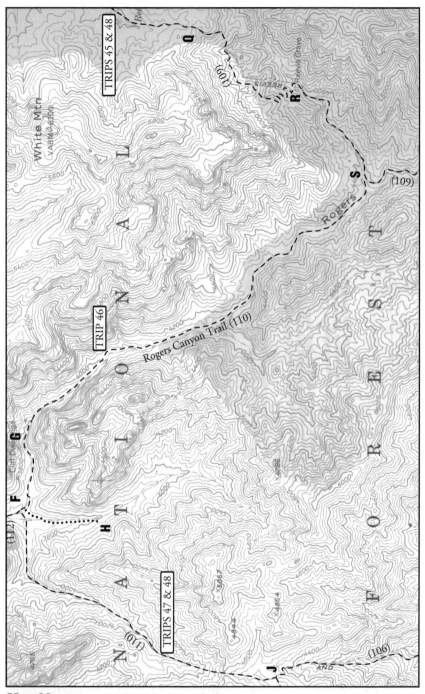

Map 23 - *Trips 43, 45, 46, 47 and 48.*

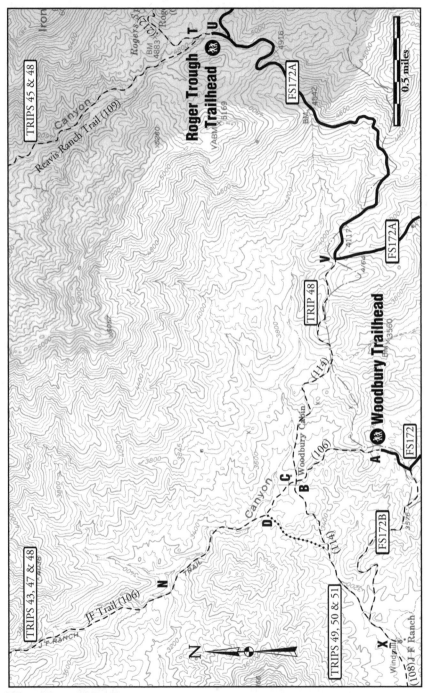

Map 23 continued - *Trips 43, 45, 46, 47 and 48.*

netleaf hackberry, Arizona walnut and Fremont cottonwoods make this a pleasant change from the desert terrain at the start of the trail.

The cliff dwellings **[23-G, 4.1]** are located on the north side of Rogers Canyon just after the canyon makes a gradual bend to the west. Located in a cave about 100 feet above the canyon floor, the cliff dwellings are easy to see from the trail. At the ruins, the trail is on the south side of the canyon. From below the ruins, walk up a rough, steep trail to the lower ruin. A Forest Service sign, a few feet from the lower cliff dwelling, provides some important information for visitors. These ruins were occupied by the Salado around A.D. 1300. Don't take anything. Don't camp here. Don't do anything to degrade the ruins. Climbing on the walls and roof can cause them to crumble and building a fire may cause a hidden roof structure to burn.

The hike description ends at the cliff dwellings. Return the same way to Rogers Trough Trailhead **[23-U, 8.2]**, or if you came here to camp, there are large campsites down the canyon near Angel Basin **[23-F]**. See Trip 47 for more area information and the details for a loop hike ending at Woodbury Trailhead.

HISTORY AND LEGENDS. The Rogers Canyon cliff dwellings were built and occupied by the Salado around A.D. 1300. Archaeologists have two theories about the Salado. Harold Gladwin, noted archaeologist from the 1920s through the 1940s, proposed that the Salado migrated from the north near the Little Colorado and were mingling with the Hohokam about A.D. 1300. At that time, the Hohokam were located in the Salt River and Gila River basins and contact with the Salado seemed to be a friendly and peaceful cultural exchange. More recent theories suggest that the Salado evolved from within the Hohokam culture by adopting cultural traits from the surrounding communities.[178]

The thick-wall, multi-story architecture of the Salado is evident in Hohokam construction. The Hohokam, before the Salado influence, built single-story, thin-wall houses. Some of the other well-known structures built or influenced by the Salado are the Great House at Casa Grande National Monument, Besh-Ba-Gowah Pueblo at Globe and the cliff dwellings at Tonto National Monument. By A.D. 1450 both the Hohokam and Salado people left this area. Some historians speculate that they left because of drought and the resulting shortage of food. This may have led to hostility between communities.[179]

Since some of the Rogers Canyon buildings were constructed in a cave, they have survived the elements rather well. The wood and mud roof is still in good shape on part of one structure. The area is devoid of the usual

View of the lower ruin at Rogers Canyon cliff dwellings looking west toward Angel Basin.

graffiti seen at many other prehistoric sites. We hope everyone continues to preserve these unique structures.

Rogers Canyon cliff dwellings have been the destination of many hikers and trail riders since the late 1890s. Four men from Phoenix reportedly made the ride to the ruins in January 1899. After a stop at the Bark and Criswell Ranch (now the Quarter Circle U Ranch) they proceeded to the ruins. The newspaper article did not give the complete itinerary of their hunting trip but they rode over to Reavis Ranch, after leaving the ruins, to visit with rancher Jack Fraser.[180]

Down the canyon from the ruins about three-tenths mile is a large, flat grassy area locally called Angel Basin. This is where the Rogers Canyon Trail meets the Frog Tank Trail. The tall trees, netleaf hackberry, Arizona sycamore and Arizona Walnut in Angel Basin are silhouetted against the surrounding sheer, buff-colored cliffs. Some older maps show a spring (Angel Springs) in the wash 0.1 mile to the south of the grassy area. We couldn't find Angel Springs and have read Forest Service reports that the spring is in disrepair. Newer maps do not show the Angel Springs notation. We like the names Angel Basin and Angel Springs and hope everyone continues to use them.

Southwestern artist Ettore "Ted" DeGrazia is well known for his paintings of the land and people he loved. DeGrazia made many treks into the Superstition Mountains and several of his trail rides were well publicized. In protest of Federal estate taxes on artwork to be left to his heirs, DeGrazia burned a collection of his paintings valued at over a million dollars in Angel Basin on January 27, 1976.[181] The March 1983 issue of *Arizona Highways* shows a photograph of his paintings engulfed in the bonfire on the grassy flat at Angel Basin.[182] Ted DeGrazia died in Tucson at the age of 73 on September 17, 1982.

Woodbury Trailhead

From Apache Junction, go east 16 miles on U.S. Route 60 to Florence Junction. Two miles east of Florence Junction on U.S. Route 60, between mileposts 214 and 215, turn north on Queen Creek Road for 1.6 miles to FS357 (Hewitt Station Road), go right 3 miles to FS172, go left 11.2 miles to end of road. A high-clearance vehicle is required.

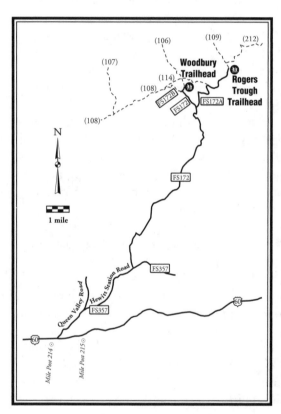

FINDING THE TRAILHEAD.
Hewitt Station Road makes several unbridged crossings of Queen Creek. After heavy rains, there may be high water in Queen Creek which will make this route impassable. FS172 is a scenic dirt road through Hewitt Canyon making many unbridged crossings of the wash. Jagged mountains surround FS172 for the first few miles, then the country opens up into a wider valley. There are numerous places to car camp along this road. Ten miles on FS172 brings you to the junction of FS172A (4WD road) which takes you to Rogers Trough Trailhead in another 3 miles. Continue straight on FS172 for another mile where FS172 turns right and continue 0.2 miles east to the Woodbury Trailhead parking

lot. FS172B to JF Ranch Headquarters is blocked by a locked gate 1.2 miles south of JF Ranch Headquarters.

FACILITIES. There are no facilities at the Woodbury Trailhead parking lot except for a hitching post. **Bring your own water.**

THE TRAILS. At the parking lot, the old dirt road to the Woodbury Cabin site is blocked to vehicles. Heading north, a half mile up the dirt road from the parking lot brings you to a signed trail junction where the JF Trail goes straight ahead (north) toward the windmill. The Woodbury Trail (114) goes east from here 1.3 miles to FS172A and west one mile to the JF Ranch Headquarters and the Coffee Flat Trail (108). The Coffee Flat Trail starts on the north side of the large corral. This is still cattle country so you will likely find cows around the water holes.

HISTORY AND LEGENDS. JF Ranch, named for pioneer cattleman Jack Fraser, has been in existence since the 1890s when Fraser ran cattle here and in the Reavis area until 1910. JF Headquarters is still an active working ranch. Bill Martin of Queen Creek holds the grazing allotment.

The old barn and windmill at JF Ranch in 1993.

The JF Ranch buildings are government owned improvements located just outside the Wilderness boundary. Bill Martin uses these buildings in conjunction with the cattle operation under a permit with the Forest Service. The main building is a modern cinder-block structure and there is a wood and metal barn with historic shoeing equipment outback. The windmill pumps water into a cement cistern in front of the ranch house, but the windmill might not always be operating. On the north side of Fraser Canyon wash is a large corral area made of vertical logs. Huge cottonwood trees grow here and some have fallen due to the eroding soil.

Robert Garman, in his book, *Mystery Gold of the Superstitions*, tells a story about James Whetlach and his discovery of silver in the Randolph area. Sometime between 1890 and 1893, Whetlach found a vein of ore and was packing ore out of the mountains down Randolph Canyon. When Whetlach left the area, Jesse Mullins made a search for the silver vein in 1893 but was not successful. Using information from an interview with Mullins, Robert Garman continued the search in 1950. He, too, failed to find the Whetlach vein, but did find a promising outcrop of silver in Millsite Canyon about three miles north of Quail Spring.[183]

The famous Peralta stone maps were found by Travis Tumlinson and his uncle, Robert Tumlinson, northwest of Queen Valley. The stone maps were found along Queen Creek a little east of Black Point Ridge about 1951. The discovery was made public about 1965 and replicas of the stone carvings are on display at the Superstition Mountain Museum.[184]

The corral at JF Ranch in 1993. The Coffee Flat Trail skirts the north side of the corral.

Rogers Canyon Cliff Dwellings

This trip takes you to the prehistoric cliff dwellings in Rogers Canyon. Rogers Canyon at Angel Basin, just down canyon from the ruins, is an ideal place to camp. Tall Arizona black walnut, Arizona sycamore and netleaf hackberry trees surround a large, flat grassy area here. Along the canyon floor are shaded camping places under the emory oaks. This is a great destination for an overnight trip.

ITINERARY: From Woodbury Trailhead follow JF Trail (106) to Tortilla Pass. Continue on Rogers Canyon Trail (110) to Rogers Canyon and the cliff dwellings. Return the same way. An optional return follows Rogers Canyon to Reavis Ranch Trail (109) and Rogers Trough Trailhead. From Rogers Trough, follow 4WD FS172A to Woodbury Trail (114) and JF Trail (106) to Woodbury Trailhead.

DIFFICULTY: Difficult day hike or Moderate two day trip. Elevation change is ±2960 feet.

LENGTH and TIME: 10.6 miles, 10 hours round trip.

MAPS: Iron Mountain, Arizona USGS topo map.
Pinyon Mountain, Arizona USGS topo map.
Superstition Wilderness Tonto National Forest map.

FINDING THE TRAIL: JF Trail (106) starts at the barricade on the north side of the Woodbury Trailhead parking lot.

THE HIKE: *Use Map 23.* From the Woodbury Trailhead parking lot **[23-A, 0]**, walk around the road barricade, proceed along the JF Trail (106) north, up the dirt road, to a small saddle, then descend to a signed trail junction with Woodbury Trail (114) **[23-B, 0.5]**. At this junction we continue north on the JF Trail, walk to the left (west) of the Woodbury windmill **[23-C]** and pass a severely-weathered green sign and metal post that reads *TRAIL*. Although there are many flat places to camp along the trail near the windmill, the cows have made claim to the area. The trail becomes more defined as it passes the

Wilderness boundary sign **[23-D, 0.8]**. The old alignment of the JF Trail (from JF Headquarters) comes in from the west about 30 feet south of the Wilderness boundary sign. After crossing Randolph Canyon Wash twice, the JF Trail follows the west bank of Randolph Canyon and passes along a hill-side dotted with honey mesquite, sugar sumac, single-leaf pinyon, redberry buckthorn and mountain mahogany. Potholes of water in Randolph Canyon are not potable due to the cattle in the area. After crossing the bed of Randolph Canyon **[23-N, 1.4]**, the trail heads uphill across the ridge through prickly pear, ocotillo, jojoba, saguaro and mesquite. Farther up the hill, the trail is surrounded by a dense growth of mountain mahogany, sugar sumac, juniper and shrub oak. At the signed junction on Tortilla Pass **[23-J, 3.2]**, we leave the JF Trail as it turns west through a closed gate. This trip follows the Rogers Canyon Trail (110) which begins at Tortilla Pass.

From Tortilla Pass proceed north up to a higher pass on Rogers Canyon Trail (110), then descend a short, steep section of eroded trail. After the trail crosses a small drainage, the trail conditions improve and you may find some water here after a rain. Farther down this wash there may be a few seasonal potholes of water. The trail continues down to the canyon floor, passing through a patch of catclaw acacia, before meeting the seasonal stream bed of Rogers Canyon. Across Rogers Canyon drainage, you can see a large inviting grassy area **[23-F, 5.0]** where a wooden sign marks the junction with Frog

Forest Service sign at Rogers Canyon cliff dwelling gives good advice.
"Enjoy, but do not destroy your cultural heritage."

Tanks Trail (112). This is Angel Basin. Large Arizona black walnut, netleaf hackberry and Arizona sycamore trees shade this ideal camping area. The Rogers Canyon cliff dwellings are about 0.3 miles east in Rogers Canyon **[23-G, 5.3]**. From the grassy area follow the Rogers Canyon Trail east as it crosses the drainage several times. There are more ideal camping places along here under the large emory oaks. When the trail starts to go uphill, look across the canyon to the north and you will see the cliff dwellings in a cave. The cliff dwellings are located on the north side of the

The ruins inside the cave at Rogers Canyon cliff dwelling have been protected from the weather.

canyon about 100 feet up from the bottom of the wash. A rough trail goes steeply up the slope to a Forest Service sign that provides some useful information. See History and Legends in Trip 46 for the story of the Salado who occupied these dwellings around A.D. 1300. Don't take anything. Don't camp here. Don't do anything to degrade the ruins. Climbing on the walls can cause them to crumble and building a fire may cause a hidden roof structure to burn.

Seasonal water may be found in Rogers Canyon. The wash may be dry near the grassy area, but there may be water up canyon near the cliff dwellings or even farther east. We couldn't find Angel Springs, but there is a trail leading southwest from the south side of the grassy area that ends at an old corral with some abandoned cement water troughs. There wasn't any water here, but we followed the pipes south to a seep that had some water in shallow pools in the dirt **[23-H]**. There is a lot of bear scat around the area so be sure to make some noise to let the bear know you are visiting.

This is the end of the hike description. Return the same way to Woodbury Trailhead **[23-A, 10.6]**. You can also make a loop hike up Rogers Canyon to Rogers Trough, then follow FS172A back to Woodbury Trailhead. See Trips 46 and 48 for all the details.

HISTORY AND LEGENDS. See Trip 46 for the history and legends.

Woodbury Trailhead

Reavis Ranch Loop

From the desert terrain at Woodbury, this trip takes you to the high country where a ponderosa pine and alligator juniper forest, near Reavis Ranch, provides a setting for ideal camping and relaxation. The weather is usually cooler here, and in the winter months of December and January you might see snow. This trek takes you to the Rogers Canyon cliff dwellings, upper Fish Creek, Reavis Ranch, Reavis apple orchards, Circlestone ruin and Reavis Grave. This is a popular November destination for many apple lovers.

ITINERARY: From Woodbury Trailhead, follow JF Trail (106) to Tortilla Pass. Continue on Rogers Canyon Trail (110), Frog Tanks Trail (112), and Reavis Ranch Trail (109) to Reavis Ranch. Return on Reavis Ranch Trail (109) to Rogers Trough Trailhead and follow 4WD FS172A, Woodbury Trail (114), and JF Trail (106) to Woodbury Trailhead.

DIFFICULTY: Moderate 3 to 5 day backpack trip. Not recommended for horses. Elevation change is ±4520 feet.

LENGTH and TIME: 22.9 miles, 26 hours round trip.

MAPS: Iron Mountain, Arizona USGS topo map.
Pinyon Mountain, Arizona USGS topo map.
Superstition Wilderness Tonto National Forest map.

FINDING THE TRAIL: JF Trail (106) starts at the barricade on the north side of the Woodbury Trailhead parking lot.

THE HIKE: *Use Maps 22, 23 and 24.* For the first leg of this trip, follow Trip 47 (Rogers Canyon Cliff Dwellings) from Woodbury Trailhead **[23-A, 0]** to Angel Basin **[23-F, 5.0]** in Rogers Canyon.

After viewing the Rogers Canyon cliff dwellings, retrace your steps back to the Angel Basin area **[24-F, 5.0]** and head north, down Rogers Canyon on the Frog Tanks Trail (112). Frog Tanks Trail is difficult to follow when it drops in and out of the bed of Rogers Canyon. The first part of the trail is overgrown with catclaw mimosa (cougar claw), and you may find walking in the bed of the canyon easier. Good sections of trail exist on either side of the water course, but the many crossings, and sometimes lack of any trail, can make the Frog Tank Trail a tiring trek. For hike planning, use an estimated 0.5 miles per hour hiking speed—it is slow going. A nice canopy of sycamore and oak trees shades the canyon, and nearby **[24-I, 6.0]** you may find water where some reeds grow in the bed of the canyon. The Superstition Wilderness Forest Service map shows Hole Spring 0.2 miles up canyon (south) from where we found water in the stream bed. Intermittent seasonal water may be found from Hole Spring **[24-I]** down to the junction with Fish Creek. Verify the water conditions with the Forest Service before you go. Near Fish Creek, the trail on the east side of Rogers Canyon crosses an unnamed ravine **[24-K]** entering from the east. This ravine is spanned by a barbed wire fence that seems to hang in the air and makes a good landmark signaling the entrance of Fish Creek only five minutes downstream.

Rogers Canyon ends when the small drainage of Fish Creek enters from the east **[24-J, 6.6]**. It is easy to miss this junction. Fish Creek is a very pretty area, and you may find seasonal running water north of here. The Frog Tanks Trail (112) goes to Frog Spring, but finding the trail at the Rogers Canyon and Fish Creek junction is difficult. Look for some rock cairns on the north side of Fish Creek, 100 yards or less from where Fish Creek enters from the east. Follow any sign of a trail and be persistent until you break through the bushes onto a well-defined horse trail. The trail parallels a fence that runs north, so you might see the fence first. The trail is on the west side of the fence. It is a steep uphill climb to Frog Spring which may be dry even when there is water in Fish Creek. To the east, there are good views of Cimeron Mountain and Rough Canyon before the trail drops back into Fish Creek. As the trail heads east, it passes the cement cow troughs at Frog Tank where the catclaw mimosa (cougar claw) grows in nearby patches. Catclaw mimosa (*mimosa biuncifera*) is also called "wait-a-minute bush" but some local people appropriately refer to it as cougar claw. After seasonal rains there may be water along this section of Fish Creek.

At a sharp bend in the creek **[24-L, 8.3]**, the trail leaves Fish Creek, passes an abandoned corral, and heads uphill on a well-defined path. The terrain changes to open, grassy areas with clumps of sugar sumac, mesquite, prickly pear, and juniper. At the saddle **[24-S, 9.5]** there is a prehistoric ruin just a few yards to the right (south) of the trail. Only the outline of the rock structure remains. As the trail continues east, it crosses a ravine **[22-W, 10.1]** which may have seasonal water flowing from the direction of Plow Saddle. Some tall Fremont cottonwood and Arizona sycamore trees grow in the ravine, and thick grass covers the banks. Two former Reavis Ranch owners carved their

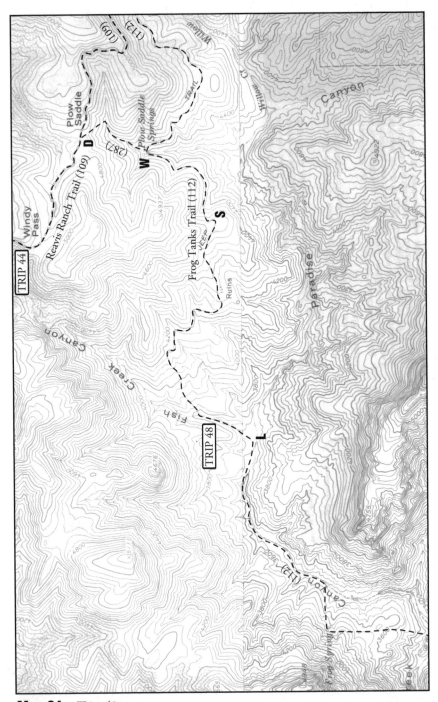

Map 24 - *Trip 48*

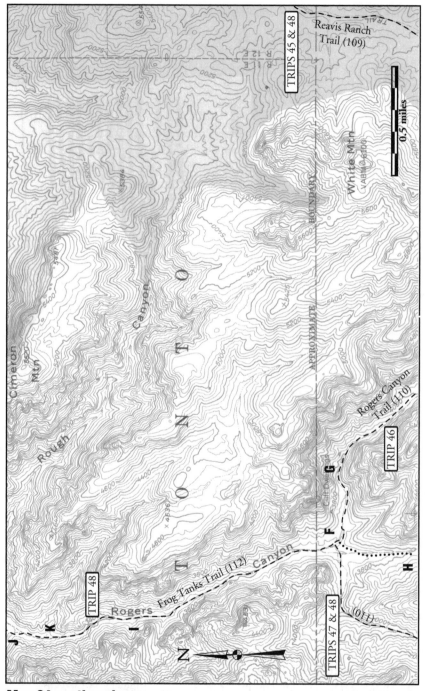

Map 24 continued - *Trip 48.*

names in the cement cow tank here—*Bacon & Upton 12-2-48*. If you want to check out Plow Saddle Springs, which may contain seasonal water, take Trail 287 to the north for about 0.3 miles. This hike continues east on Frog Tanks Trail where the trail ends at a junction **[22-E, 11.6]** with Reavis Ranch Trail (109). Bear right (east) onto the Reavis Ranch Trail. Within 0.2 miles the trail turns south as it enters Reavis Valley.

We briefly describe Reavis Ranch and Circlestone in this section, but we suggest you read Trip 44 for a full description of the Reavis Valley. The Reavis Ranch Trail follows a fence line south as it passes a large group camping area **[22-F]**, Reavis Gap Trail **[22-G]**, an apple orchard **[22-H]** and Reavis Ranch **[22-I, 13.1]**. Only the cement floor of Reavis Ranch remains now. The debris from the November 1991 fire was removed in 1993 and the ranch house walls were taken down in January 1994. Reavis Creek usually has some water and there are plenty of good campsites in Reavis Valley. Check with the Forest Service for current water conditions before you go.

From Reavis Ranch, continue south on Reavis Ranch Trail past another apple orchard. The trail crosses the creek to the east side near the signed junction **[22-J, 13.3]** with the Fire Line Trail (118). For a 4.8 mile (round trip) side trip to Circlestone ruin **[22-O]**, take the Fire Line Trail east, up and over the pass **[22-K]**, then connect with the unsigned Allen Blackman Trail **[22-L]** that heads south across the ridge line. Circlestone **[22-O, 6010]** is on the small knoll (elevation 6010 feet) just northeast of Mound Mountain. It is an 1160 foot elevation gain to the ruin, so allow at least three hours for the round trip to Circlestone.

From the junction with the Fire Line Trail **[22-J]**, the hike continues on the east side of Reavis Creek for a short distance before crossing to the west side. Then the trail is diverted through the creek bed for a short stretch. In the dry season, the creek water becomes intermittent and this is often the last place to find water as you go upstream (south) along Reavis Creek. The trail resumes on the west side and goes up on a high bench where there is a nice stand of ponderosa pine and alligator juniper trees. Some signs of the May 1966 Iron Mountain Burn are visible, but do not detract from the beauty of the forest. We enjoy this section of the trail because the trail is well defined, the forest is pleasant, and the uphill grade is very gradual all the way to Reavis Saddle. An old alligator juniper tree **[22-N 14.0]** stands alone in a field of lovegrass. The large tree, near ground level, is about 7 feet in diameter. The tall lovegrass that covers the ground was planted after the forest fire to prevent erosion. The grass is so dense in some areas that it covers the trail. Here you have to follow the trail by feeling the worn track with your feet. Depending on the season, you might see some wildflowers. Honeycutt

The alligator juniper trees at Circlestone ruin have invaded the stone structure.

Spring **[22-P, 15.3]** is in a wide drainage to the west of the trail and has seasonal water. Reavis Creek might have a few small puddles of water here, but the terrain is much dryer, and the wash begins to resemble a seasonal water course. At Reavis Saddle **[23-Q, 16.2]**, there are some flat camping places and several shade trees. A few yards down from Reavis Saddle, the terrain quickly changes to a dry desert where you see redberry buckthorn, catclaw mimosa (cougar claw), sugar sumac, manzanita and shrub oak. Iron Mountain is directly to the south. The trail is steep, hot and dry along here compared to the cool pine forest on the north side of Reavis Saddle.

At the bottom of the switchbacks, the trail enters and heads down a wash. Look for the spur trail to Reavis Grave **[23-R, 17.0]** about 200 feet south of where the trail enters the rocky wash. The spur trail, marked by a tall cairn, goes up the bank (west) for a few yards to the Reavis Grave. Reavis Grave is on a small, flat grassy bench above the wash. The gravestone is not there anymore, but a rectangular mound of rocks marks the grave site. Elisha Reavis was buried here in April of 1896. The trail continues down the wash and soon parallels a large ravine, named Grave Canyon, which is lined with sycamore trees. The trail makes several ravine crossings and passes through a closed gate before it arrives at the signed junction **[23-S, 17.6]** with the Rogers Canyon Trail (110). If you have time, a short trip down Rogers Canyon, which has seasonal water, is enjoyable. The Reavis Ranch trail turns south at the trail junction **[23-S]** and heads toward Rogers Trough. This section of Rogers Canyon has seasonal pools of water and is dotted with netleaf hackberry, sycamore and walnut trees. The trail makes numerous creek crossings and tends to go up and down more than most hikers prefer. Soon after the trail passes through an open gate, the terrain becomes open and flat. The West Pinto Trail (212) **[23-T, 19.1]** comes in from the east, and the parking lot can be seen a few hundred yards to the south. There are still a few cows in the Rogers Trough area. The Reavis Ranch Trail ends at the Rogers Trough Trailhead parking lot **[23-U, 19.2]**. If you have a four-wheel drive vehicle, you could leave it at Rogers Trough parking lot. If you don't, it is an easy, but long, 3.7 mile walk back to Woodbury Trailhead. Walk down the 4WD dirt road (FS172A) to the junction with Woodbury Trail (114) **[23-V, 21.2]**. It is easy to spot this junction because FS172A turns south through a closed gate in the barbed wire fence. Woodbury Trail goes west on an old road along the north side of the hill, then drops down to the JF Trail junction **[23-B, 22.4]**. From here **[23-B]**, head south on the JF Trail to the Woodbury Trailhead parking lot **[23-A, 22.9]** where the hike ends.

HISTORY AND LEGENDS. See Trips 44, and 46 for the narratives on Angel Basin, Ted DeGrazia, Rogers Canyon cliff dwellings, Reavis Falls, Reavis Ranch and Circlestone.

The Ponderosa forest along the Reavis Trail about one mile south of Reavis Ranch.

Dripping Spring

Once you leave the JF Ranch area, Fraser Canyon begins to narrow and the rounded hilltops turn to jagged cliffs. Seasonal water in Fraser Canyon supports small groves of Fremont cottonwood, Arizona sycamore and willow trees. The junction of Fraser and Randolph Canyons is very pretty with smooth, reddish bedrock and shallow pools of seasonal water. Dripping Spring seeps from the ledges above the canyon floor. A small cave is nearby.

ITINERARY: From the Woodbury Trailhead, walk down FS172B to the JF corral, north of JF Headquarters. Follow the Coffee Flat Trail (108) down Fraser Canyon to Dripping Spring.

DIFFICULTY: Moderate. Elevation change is ±1260 feet.

LENGTH and TIME: 8.8 miles, 6.5 hours round trip.

MAPS: Iron Mountain Arizona USGS topo map.
Weavers Needle, Arizona USGS topo map.
Superstition Wilderness Tonto National Forest map.

FINDING THE TRAIL: From the west side of Woodbury Trailhead parking lot **[25-A, 0]**, walk west on FS172.

THE HIKE: *Use Map 25.* From the west side of Woodbury Trailhead parking lot **[25-A, 0]** follow FS172 to the top of the hill where FS172B is blocked by a locked gate **[25-L, 0.2]**. Climb over the gate and continue down FS172B to the wash in Fraser Canyon and on to the JF Ranch Headquarters corral **[25-X, 1.3]**. To avoid the locked gate **[25-L, 0.2]**, horse riders need to take the JF Trail and Woodbury Trail to the corral at JF Ranch Headquarters **[25-X, 1.3]**. The Coffee Flat Trail (108) heads around the north side of the corral, but if you have time you can take a side trip across the sandy wash to the JF Ranch buildings.

At JF Ranch, the enormous Fremont cottonwood trees along the sandy creek bed provide a pleasant canopy of shade, although a few trees have lost their footing in the eroding soil. If the windmill is in operation, there may be

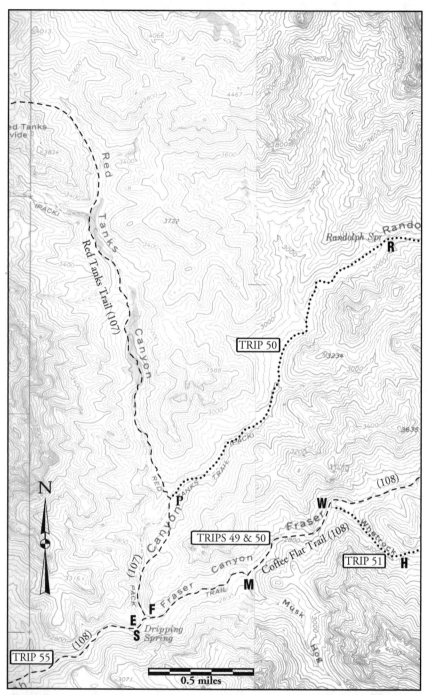

Map 25 - *Trips 49, 50 and 51.*

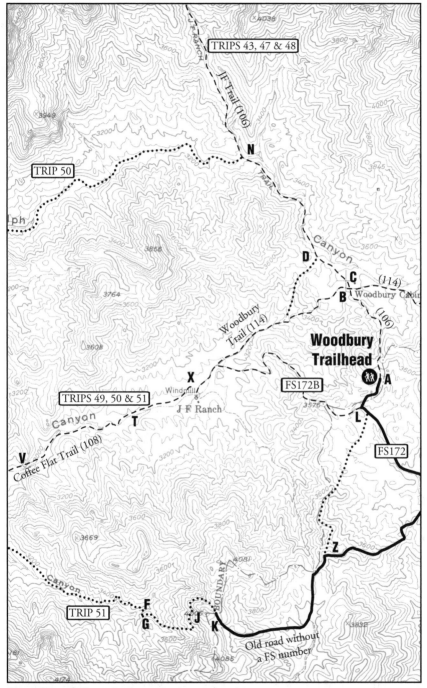

Map 25 continued - *Trips 49, 50 and 51.*

water here, but don't count on it. The old barn and outdoor blacksmith shop are interesting to examine and photograph. JF Ranch is still a working cattle ranch. Please respect the private property.

The signed Coffee Flat Trail (108) starts at the north side of the big corral. The trail goes through a closed gate **[25-X, 1.3]**, then follows the corral fence west on the north side of Fraser Canyon. At the corner of the fence line, the trail heads toward Fraser Canyon. You can enter the wash here or continue on the trail that stays on the north bank. The big Fremont cottonwood tree that hikers and horse riders use as a landmark is in the bed of the wash just to the south of here **[25-T, 1.7]**. Fraser Canyon usually has seasonal water after a rain.

The trail crosses Fraser Canyon many times but the crossings are well marked by large rock cairns. On the map, in several places, we drew the dashed line down the center of the wash since it is almost impossible to keep track of the many crossings. Horse riders have kept the vegetation from invading the trail, and the walking is fairly easy. Hikers can elect to walk down the bed of the wash or follow the trail. The horse trail bypasses some smooth rock sections that are worthwhile to explore. You can see the remains of the old freight road along one section of trail **[25-V, 2.3]**.

The trail is on the north side of Fraser Canyon when it passes the mouth of Whetrock Canyon **[25-W, 3.1]**, so you will miss this drainage if you are not looking for it. Trip 51 describes a difficult trek up Whetrock Canyon. About 15 minutes west of Whetrock Canyon, the trail enters the creek bed where twelve willow trees grow in a line down the wash. The Tonto National Forest map is the only map that shows a spring here—Whetstone Spring. Don't count on Whetstone Spring for water. The trail then follows the south bank and crosses the drainage at Musk Hog Canyon **[25-M, 3.7]**. Musk Hog Canyon may have seasonal water. Small groves of sugar sumac, Arizona sycamore, and mesquite dot the canyon floor as the trail continues west. Overnight trekkers will find several flat places to camp between Musk Hog Canyon and Dripping Springs.

A hundred feet or so west of a large Fremont cottonwood tree blocking the north channel of the wash in Fraser Canyon, you will pass the Coffee Flat Trail sign. The Red Tanks Trail (107) sign is another fifty feet to the west. The trail intersection **[25-F, 4.3]** and signs, on the northeast bank, are easy to find. The junction of Fraser and Randolph Canyons is very pretty. The smooth, reddish bedrock, shallow pools of seasonal water and openness of the canyon make this a special place. Dripping Spring is a short distance southwest in Randolph Canyon. Dripping Spring **[25-S, 4.4]** is on the south wall of the canyon where water drips from the ledges into the wash. From

The Coffee Flat Trail crosses the creek bed near Dripping Spring at the junction of Randolph Canyon and Fraser Canyon.

the spring, looking north across Randolph Canyon, there is a small cave **[25-E]** in the low cliff. The cave, with a low ceiling, extends back 40 to 50 feet. The flat bench along the creek below the cave offers flat camping and a shady place for lunch. Return the same way to the Woodbury parking lot **[25-A, 8.8]** where the trip ends. See Trips 50 and 51 for more ideas.

HISTORY AND LEGENDS. John Dahlmann in his 1979 book, *A Tiny Bit of God's Creation*, describes the old freight road through Fraser Canyon. Unless you see the road for yourself, it is hard to believe freight wagons traveled this canyon. You can see the retaining wall and roadbed along the north side of the canyon where it cuts through a cliff to bypass the smooth bedrock canyon **[25-V]**. Dahlmann said this was only a freight wagon road since it was too rough for stage coaches.[185]

Gertrude Barkley, Tex Barkley's wife, described the route of the old freight road to John Dahlmann. From Mesa, it ran along the southern slopes of Superstition Mountain, past Barkley's Quarter Circle U Ranch, up Whitlow Canyon and into Fraser Canyon. It continued past the JF Ranch and Woodbury Mill before reaching Superior.[186]

The front cover of the July 1982 *Superstition Mountain Journal* shows a picture of a cave photographed by Nyle Leatham. We looked for the cave on our hikes in the Fraser Canyon area, but didn't recognize it from the photograph when we explored the cave in December of 1993. The cave **[25-E]** is on the north side of Randolph Canyon across the creek from Dripping Spring. Greg Davis from the Superstition Mountain Historical Society checked his files and verified the Dutchman's Cave to be the one at the junction of Fraser and Randolph Canyons. The growth of vegetation on the sandy flat below the cave makes it more difficult to identify the cave in the photograph. Greg Davis said there are several caves with this name, and there is no evidence that the Dutchman (Jacob Waltz) was ever at this one.[187]

Val Paris (Bob Ward), in a 1984 *Superstition Mountain Journal* article, describes the mines he located in the late 1950s using the Polka maps. J. J. Polka was an Apache who gave three maps to Bob Ward when they met in the Armed Services. Polka Map #2 makes reference to Fraser Canyon and Red Tanks Canyon. We haven't tried to find these mines, but it seems the area described is on the steep, rugged northern slope of Fraser Canyon near the junction with Randolph Canyon. Copies of the maps are on display at the Superstition Mountain Museum and are also reprinted in the 1984 *Superstition Mountain Journal.*[188]

See Trip 15 (Whiskey Spring Trail) for the Wagoner lost gold mine story and Barry Storm's map of the the area.

Alan Blackman on the old haul road (now part of the Coffee Flat Trail) in Fraser Canyon. PHOTOGRAPH BY NYLE LEATHAM, 1977. COURTESY SUPERSTITION MOUNTAIN HISTORICAL SOCIETY, TOM KOLLENBORN COLLECTION.

Randolph Canyon

This loop trip takes you through a seldom-traveled section of Randolph Canyon. There is ample opportunity for viewing wildlife here.

ITINERARY: From the Woodbury Trailhead, walk down FS172B to the corral north of JF Headquarters. Follow the Coffee Flat Trail (108) down Fraser Canyon to Dripping Spring. Follow Red Tanks Trail (107) to Randolph Canyon, then hike up the bed of Randolph Canyon to JF Trail (109). Follow JF Trail south to the Woodbury Trailhead.

DIFFICULTY: Moderate. Route finding ability required. Mostly boulder hopping in the creek bed. Not recommended for horses. Elevation change is ±1280 feet.

LENGTH and TIME: 9.7 miles, 9 hours round trip.

MAPS: Iron Mountain, Arizona USGS topo map.
Weavers Needle, Arizona USGS topo map.
Superstition Wilderness Tonto National Forest map.

FINDING THE TRAIL: From the west side of Woodbury Trailhead parking lot **[26-A, 0]**, walk west on FS172.

THE HIKE: *Use Map 25.* Follow Trip 49 (Dripping Spring) to Dripping Spring for the first part of the hike. From the trail sign **[25-F, 4.3]** at the junction of Coffee Flat Trail and Red Tanks Trail, head north on the Red Tanks Trail (107). The trail begins on the east side of Randolph Canyon and soon enters the bed of the wash. Someone has spray-painted a blue arrow on the white rock in the center of the wash. Please don't paint the rocks. The trail goes on the west bank—another blue arrow. Back in the creek bed, the trail passes a blue arrow near some seasonal pools of water before heading up a steep slope on the east side of the canyon. The trail climbs high above the canyon floor and then turns northeast as it follows Randolph Canyon. Some hikers may enjoy walking along the smooth rock canyon floor rather than taking the trail over the hill.

Woodbury Trailhead   **289**

Sign on the gate to the JF Ranch in 1993.

The trail drops down to creek bed level on the first flat bench after Randolph Canyon turns northeast. Several trails of use are here, so make your best guess and cross to the north side of Randolph Canyon where you pick up the trail at the wooden trail sign **[25-P, 4.9]**. This is one of the few trail signs that still show trail mileages—*Fraser Canyon 0.5*, and *La Barge Canyon 3.5*. The Red Tanks Trail heads uphill (north) to Red Tanks Canyon. Our trip leaves the trail and follows the bed of Randolph Canyon. No continuous trails go up Randolph Canyon, so the best plan is to walk up the creek bed and make use of the old cow trails on the bench.

Randolph Spring **[25-R, 6.7]** which has seasonal flow is easy to find if you are following the creek bed. A cement dam, back-filled with rock, spans the wash at Randolph Spring. Several large willows grow here. The wash goes through a narrow, smooth rock section, so we walked up the south slope where we found an old trail that took us a good distance up Randolph Canyon. This may have been the unimproved trail shown on the USFS Superstition Wilderness map. After crossing a ravine, we lost the trail which may have turned south toward JF Ranch. Continuing on the south bank of Randolph Canyon, we soon crossed a closed gate in a broken fence before dropping into the creek bed.

JF Trail (106) crosses Randolph Canyon **[25-N, 8.4]** where a large wash enters from the north. There are no signs here, but you can see the eroded trail heading up the red dirt bank to the south. From here **[25-N]** it is smooth walking. The trail goes up the hill, crosses the wash twice, then passes the wooden Tonto National Forest Superstition Wilderness sign **[25-D, 9.0]**. About 30 feet south of the Wilderness Boundary sign is a trail heading west to the JF Headquarters. This trail is the old alignment for the JF Trail and connects with Woodbury Trail (114) and Coffee Flat Trail (108) to the southwest. Proceed south on the JF Trail toward the Woodbury Windmill **[25-C, 9.2]**. In December of 1993 the windmill seemed to be in operation, but no water was coming out of the pipes. The trail near the windmill is very faint, but becomes more distinct as you proceed south to the signed junction **[25-B, 9.2]** with Woodbury Trail (114). The JF Trail follows the dirt road over a small hill to the parking lot at Woodbury Trailhead where the hike ends **[25-A, 9.7]**.

HISTORY AND LEGENDS. On our December 1993 hike in Randolph Canyon, we saw some wildlife and tracks that we normally don't see. About a half mile west of Randolph Spring, we saw a full-grown javelina dart up the slope. The hooves striking the ground made a powerful sound. A few seconds later, two more large javelina ran up the slope after the first. These animals were a lot larger than the javelina we often see in La Barge Canyon. After the hike while driving down FS172 in the dark, we saw four more javelina cross the road. There were two adults and two of the smallest javelina we've ever seen. The two juveniles couldn't make it over the dirt embankment along the road, and one of the adults came back to give them directions. The family scurried into the darkness.

About a half mile east of Randolph Spring, we spotted a large woodpecker (Common Flicker) preening itself in a dead tree. The characteristic black crescent on the throat and the red-orange under-feathers were identifiable through our binoculars. After flying to the ground, it looked like a big, overstuffed bird as it searched for insects on the desert slopes. Farther east in the canyon we saw tracks in the wet sand. We think they were the tracks of a kit fox.

Whetrock Canyon Loop

This loop hike takes you up Whetrock Canyon to several abandoned mines.

ITINERARY: From the Woodbury Trailhead, walk down FS172B to the corral north of JF Headquarters. Follow the Coffee Flat Trail (108) down Fraser Canyon to Whetrock Canyon. Hike up Whetrock Canyon to the mines, then follow an old road back to Woodbury Trailhead.

DIFFICULTY: Difficult. No trail in Whetrock Canyon. Not recommended for horses. Elevation change is ±1440 feet.

LENGTH and TIME: 6.4 miles, 6.5 hours round trip. Add 2.6 miles and 3 hours if you go to Dripping Spring.

MAPS: Iron Mountain, Arizona USGS topo map.
Weavers Needle, Arizona USGS topo map.
Superstition Wilderness Tonto National Forest map.

FINDING THE TRAIL: From the west side of Woodbury Trailhead parking lot **[25-A, 0]**, walk west on FS172.

THE HIKE: *Use Map 25.* Follow Trip 49 (Dripping Spring) to Whetrock Canyon for the first part of the hike. Whetrock Canyon **[25-W, 3.1]** is difficult to locate since the horse trail bypasses the smooth rock at the canyon entrance. One helpful landmark across from Whetrock Canyon is the prominent cliff that dominates the horizon on the north side of Fraser Canyon. Whetrock Canyon is south of the cliff that juts out into Fraser Canyon. If you walk down Fraser Canyon too far and cross Musk Hog Canyon **[25-M]**, you will need to retrace your steps by hiking up Fraser Canyon for 20 minutes. When hiking up Fraser Canyon, look to the south for the telltale narrow cut through the bedrock at the mouth of Whetrock Canyon.

Enter Whetrock Canyon and walk along the canyon floor until you see an easy place to go up on the east bench. Walking on the east bench is sometimes easier than walking in the bottom of the canyon. Follow one of the many old cow paths that head south into the canyon. The remains of an old stone wall cross the creek bed where the channel makes a sharp bend **[25-H, 3.6]**. The stone wall was probably an extension of the collapsed barbed wire fence on the hill. There are some flat camping places on the terraces where the creek bed makes a slight bend before and after the stone wall.

As you continue on the east side of Whetrock Canyon, the mine tailings on the hill at the far end of the canyon come into view. Look for a game trail that contours around the ravines, staying high, until you are directly across from the mines. Below, in the ravine, you will see the remains of a rusty, white panel truck **[25-F]**. Walk down to the truck, then up to the lower mine with the gray-white tailings.

The entrance to the lower mine **[25-G, 4.5]** has been covered with dirt but you can look inside through a small hole. Don't enter the unsafe mine. Continue up the steep hill on the eroded road to the other two mines. The mine above, with the gray-white tailings **[25-J, 4.9]**, has an open mine shaft that could be dangerous. Don't enter the mine. Rocks have crushed the entrance timbers. The wide, timbered shaft goes down at a steep incline toward the west. There is another mine farther up on the west side of the same hill.

From the mine **[25-J]**, follow the dirt road north as it curves around the peak of the hill heading southeast. The road crosses the Wilderness

Falling rocks have collapsed the timbers to the shaft entrance at this mine on Frazier Mountain.

Saguaro cactus cover the hillside along Fraser Canyon.

boundary. From the Wilderness boundary, the walk back to the Woodbury Trailhead is easy. Go through the closed barbed wire gate **[25-K, 5.1]**. A few hundred yards down the road there is an ore loading chute made of timber. Continue down the road to the earth stock tank and head north to another closed, barbed wire gate. About 0.1 mile north of the gate, an old road **[25-Z, 5.9]** heads north, while the newer road turns east. Take the old road north. This old, abandoned road eventually follows the fence line and brings you to FS172 one hundred yards south of the locked gate on FS172B **[25-L, 6.2]**. From here, it is a short walk east on FS172 to the Woodbury Trailhead parking lot where the trip ends **[25-A, 6.4]**.

HISTORY AND LEGENDS. John Dahlmann in his 1979 book, *A Tiny Bit of God's Creation,* describes a horse ride he and others made from Millsite Canyon to the mines at the end of Whetrock Canyon. From the mines, he continued down Whetrock Canyon to Fraser Canyon. We hiked the same route and wondered how he negotiated that rough canyon on a horse. Although there is a lot of smooth bedrock here, it seems that he followed the canyon floor beyond the stone wall **[25-H]** to a slick, rock passage where he dismounted and walked up the east slope about one hundred feet. Here he found a cave that contained a skeleton, some prospector tools, and supplies.

He could not see Fraser Canyon from the cave. We looked for the cave but couldn't find it. This trip is not recommended for horses.[189]

The rusty carcass of a panel truck in the ravine below the Whetrock Canyon mines is only a shell. The engine and all mechanical parts are missing. The faded paint on the white rear doors reads, *MODERN DAIRY, GLOBE, ARIZONA.*

Robert Garman in his 1975 book, *Mystery Gold of the Superstitions*, writes about his experiences in the south-central part of the Superstition Mountains. He shows one picture of the ore chute on the mountain with the Whetrock Canyon mines. Garman refers to this mountain as Frazier Mountain, but that name does not appear on the USGS Iron Mountain topographic map. One of Garman's treasure maps shows a trail that goes north through Millsite Canyon and seems to end at the Whetrock Canyon mines. Garman makes reference to silver mining in this area. He also refers to Whetlach Canyon which may be the Whetrock Canyon shown on the map.[190]

Tom Kollenborn helped us sort out the confusion among the old-timers names. John "Jack" J. Fraser was the rancher and miner who owned the JF Ranch and later the Reavis Ranch. Fraser was born in Nova Scotia in 1855 and worked at Comstock in Nevada and the Silver King in Arizona. Jack Frasier was the owner of a store in the town of Roosevelt, Arizona. Frazier may be another spelling variation of Frasier's name. James Whetlach was a rancher and miner in the Fraser Canyon area in the 1890s where he prospected for silver. We haven't been able to determine if there is a connection between James Whetlach's name and Whetrock Canyon but Kollenborn suggests that Whetrock is derived from Whetlach.[191] Garman uses the name Whetlach Canyon, but the maps show Whetrock Canyon.

Trans-Wilderness Trips

There are many long hikes (and horse rides) that can be made from one trailhead to another. We selected eight trips to get you started. There are more possibilities. All trips can be traveled in either direction. You can enhance the quality of the treks by including your choice of off-trail routes and side trips. Shuttle distance is rounded to the nearest mile. Roads are okay for passenger cars except as noted.

Trip 52. Peralta Trailhead to First Water Trailhead. Follow Peralta Trail (102) to Fremont Saddle and East Boulder Canyon, connect with Dutchman's Trail (104) in East Boulder Canyon, go over Parker Pass to First Water Trailhead. See Trips 1, 6 and 30. Trail distance is 11.2 miles. Vehicle shuttle distance is 23 miles.

Trip 53. Peralta Trailhead to Canyon Lake Trailhead. Follow Peralta Trail (102) to Fremont Saddle and East Boulder Canyon, connect with Dutchman's Trail (104) in East Boulder Canyon, go down Boulder Canyon on Boulder Canyon Trail (103) to Canyon Lake Trailhead. See Trips 1, 6, 30 and 34. Trail distance is 14.0 miles. Vehicle shuttle distance is 30 miles.

Trip 54. Peralta Trailhead to Tortilla Trailhead. Follow the Dutchman's Trail (104) to Bluff Spring, La Barge Spring and Charlebois Spring. Take Peters Trail (105) to Tortilla Trailhead. See Trips 5, 9 and 42. Trail distance is 14.6 miles. Vehicle shuttle distance is 42 miles. Four-wheel drive required for Tortilla Trailhead or add 3.2 miles to trail distance.

Trip 55. Peralta Trailhead to Reavis Trailhead. Follow the Dutchman's Trail (104) connecting with the Coffee Flat Trail (108) to JF Ranch. Follow JF Trail (106) connecting with Rogers Canyon Trail (110) to Reavis Trail (109). Follow Reavis Trail (109) to Reavis Ranch, then continue to Reavis Trailhead. See Trips 4, 49, 47, 46 and 45. Trail distance is 31.7 miles. Vehicle shuttle distance is 48 miles.

Trip 56. First Water Trailhead to Canyon Lake Trailhead. Follow Second Water Trail (236) to Boulder Canyon connecting with Boulder Canyon Trail (103) to Canyon Lake Trailhead. See Trips 27, 29 and 34. Trail distance is 7.6 miles. Vehicle shuttle distance is 12 miles.

Trip 57. First Water Trailhead to Reavis Trailhead. This is Tom Kollenborn's well-known *Ride Through Time* trail ride. Follow the Dutchman's Trail (104) over Black Top Mesa Pass, up La Barge Canyon to Charlebois Spring. Take Peters Trail (105) to Tortilla Ranch connecting with JF Trail (106), Rogers Canyon Trail (110), and Reavis Trail (109) to Reavis Ranch. Follow Reavis Trail (109) to Reavis Trailhead. See Trips 30, 31, 42, 43, 46, 45 and 44. Trail distance is 42.8 miles. Vehicle shuttle distance is 29 miles.

Trip 58. Carney Springs Trailhead to Lost Dutchman State Park Trailhead. See Trip 19 for the full description. Trail distance (mostly cross-country) is 10.5 miles. Vehicle shuttle distance is 20 miles. Not recommended for horses.

Trip 59. Tortilla Trailhead to Woodbury Trailhead. See Trip 43 for the complete description. Trail distance is 8.9 miles. Vehicle shuttle distance is 58 miles. Four-wheel drive required for Tortilla Trailhead or add 3.2 miles to trail distance.

Trip 60. Woodbury Trailhead to Rogers Trough Trailhead. Follow JF Trail (106) to Tortilla Pass. Follow Rogers Canyon Trail (110) to Reavis Trail (109) continuing to Rogers Trough Trailhead. See Trips 47, 46 and 48. Trail distance is 9.4 miles. Vehicle shuttle distance is 4 miles. Four-wheel drive required for Rogers Trough Trailhead or add 3.7 miles to the trail distance.

Reference Notes

1. James Swanson and Tom Kollenborn, *Superstition Mountain, A Ride Through Time* (Phoenix, Arizona: Arrowhead Press, 1981), pp. 27-37.
2. Robert Blair, *Tales of the Superstitions, the Origins of the Lost Dutchman Legend* (Tempe, Arizona: Arizona Historical Foundation, 1975).
3. Robert Sikorsky, *Quest for the Dutchman's Gold, the 100-year Mystery* (Phoenix, Arizona: Golden West Publishers, 1983-1993), pp. 73-75.
4. Clay Worst, speaker at the Superstition Mountain Historical Society annual meeting (Apache Junction, Arizona: Superstition Mountain Museum, February 15, 1994).
5. John Wilburn, *Dutchman's Lost Ledge of Gold, and the Superstition Gold Mining District* (Mesa, Arizona: Publications Press, 1990, 1993).
6. Jay Fraser, *Lost Dutchman Mine Discoveries* (Tempe, Arizona: Affiliated Writers of America, 1988).
7. Blair, pp. 104-111.
8. Swanson, *Superstition Mountain*, p 176.
9. Helen Corbin, *The Curse of the Dutchman's Gold* (Phoenix, Arizona: Foxwest Publishing, 1990), p. 87. Swanson, p. 43.
10. Sims Ely, *The Lost Dutchman Mine* (New York, New York: William Morrow, 1953), p. 17.
11. Corbin, *The Curse*, pp. 231-234.
12. Clay Worst, communication on April 11, 1994.
13. Swanson, *Superstition Mountain*, p. 182. Ely, pp. 134-145.
14. Wilburn, p. 12.
15. Thomas Kollenborn, *Superstition Mountain Journal*, v11, 1992, p. 38.
16. Thomas Kollenborn, *Superstition Mountain Journal*, v11, 1992, p. 37.
17. Swanson, *Superstition Mountain*, p. 112.
18. Swanson, *Superstition Mountain*, p. 188.
19. Corbin, *The Curse*, Tom Kollenborn centerfold map.
20. Superstition Mountain Museum, display map.
21. Milton Rose, *Superstition Mountain Journal*, 2:3, July 1982, p. 7.
22. James Swanson and Thomas Kollenborn, *In the Shadow of the Superstitions; The History of Apache Junction* (Apache Junction, Arizona: Goldfield Press, 1990), p. 9.
23. Jim Byrkit and Bruce Hooper, *The Story of Pauline Weaver; Arizona's Foremost Mountain Man, Trapper, Gold-Seeker, Scout, Pioneer,* (Sierra Azul Productions, 1993), pp. 1-62. Edwin Corle, *The Gila River of the Southwest* (Lincoln, Nebraska: University of Nebraska Press, 1951), pp. 33, 34, 145. Estee Conatser, *The Sterling Legend, The Facts Behind the Lost Dutchman Mine* (Pico Rivera, California: Gem Guides Book Co., 1972), p. 42.
24. Jim Waugh, *Phoenix Rock, a Guide to Central Arizona Crags* (Glendale, Arizona: Polar Designs Publications, 1987), p. 318.
25. Swanson, *Superstition Mountain*, pp. 84-91.
26. Gregory Davis, Edwin Green, Fred Guirey, Art Weber, *Superstition Mountain Journal*, 2:4, October 1982, pp. 7-23.
27. Davis, ibid. Gregory Davis, *Superstition Mountain Journal*, 2:3, July 1982, pp. 21-23. Greg Davis, communication on April 12, 1994.
28. Davis, ibid.
29. Conatser, p. 36.
30. Conatser, p. 36.
31. Ely, pp. 51-73.
32. Ely, pp. 128-129.
33. John Dahlmann, *A Tiny Bit of God's Creation: Our Majestic Superstitions* (Tempe, Arizona: Reliable Reproductions, 1979), pp. 97-99.
34. Thomas Kollenborn, *Superstition Mountain Journal,* 1:4, October 1981, pp. 15-16.
35. Corbin, *The Curse*, Tom Kollenborn centerfold map.
36. Kollenborn, ibid., pp. 15-16.
37. Kollenborn, ibid., p. 14.
38. Harry Black, *The Lost Dutchman Mine, A Short Story of a Tall Tale* (Boston: Branden Press, 1975), p. 117. Tonto National Forest Trail Survey Report, Mesa District Office, November 3, 1970.
39. Dahlmann, pp. 66-67.
40. Erle Stanley Gardner, *Hunting Lost Mines by Helicopter* (New York, William Morrow, 1965), p. 54.
41. Swanson, *Superstition Mountain*, p. 83.
42. Robert Sikorsky, *Quest for the Dutchman's Gold* (Phoenix, Arizona: Golden West Publishers, 1983, 1991, 1993), pp. 66-67.
43. Sikorsky, pp. 7, 119.
44. Arizona Daily Star, August 13, 1962.

45. Black, p. 65.
46. Barry Storm, *Thunder God's Gold* (Apache Junction, Arizona: Schoose Publishing, 1986), pp. 40-41.
47. Corbin, *The Curse*, Tom Kollenborn centerfold map.
48. Swanson, *Superstition Mountain*, pp. 187, 192.
49. Louis Ruiz, conversation on December 7, 1993.
50. Albert Morrow, *Famous Lost Gold Mines of Arizona's Superstition Mountains* (Apache Junction, Arizona: Superstition Mountain Historical Society, 1990, original manuscript 1957), p. vi.
51. Corbin, *The Curse*, Tom Kollenborn centerfold map.
52. Waugh, pp. 296-327.
53. Bill Sewery, conversation on April 15, 1993. Story first told to us by Jan Holdeman in early 1993.
54. Sewery, conversation on April 15, 1993.
55. Storm, p. 19. Thomas Kollenborn, *Superstition Mountain Journal*, v11, 1992, pp. 35-39.
56. Black, p. 64. Conatser, pp. 66-68.
57. Ely, pp. 123-128.
58. Walter Gassler, *The Lost Peralta-Dutchman Mine* (Apache Junction, Arizona: Superstition Mountain Historical Society, 1990, original manuscript 1983), p. 46.
59. Curt Gentry, *The Killer Mountains, A Search for the Legendary Lost Dutchman Mine* (New York: The New American Library, 1968), p. 164. Swanson, *Superstition Mountain*, p. 191.
60. Gentry, p. 174.
61. Corbin, *The Curse*, p. 227.
62. Gentry, pp. 146-147.
63. Gentry, pp. 162-169, 182-184, 193.
64. Corbin, *The Curse*, Tom Kollenborn centerfold map.
65. Ely, p. 124.
66. Ely, pp. 123-128.
67. Gentry, centerfold Map D.
68. Gentry, pp. 135, 136, 167, 169, 186, 193.
69. Corbin, *The Curse*, p. 145.
70. Storm, p. 19. Thomas Kollenborn, *Superstition Mountain Journal*, v11, 1992, pp. 35-39.
71. Michael Sheridan and Jan Sheridan, *Recreational Guide to the Superstition Mountains and the Salt River Lakes* (Phoenix, Arizona: Impression Makers, 1984), p. 7.
72. Ray Ruiz, Louis Ruiz, conversation on July 4, 1994.
73. Thomas Kollenborn, *Superstition Mountain Journal*, 2:3, July 1982, pp. 10-11, and 1:1, January 1981, p. 17.
74. Conatser, p. 87. Barry Storm, *Thunder God's Gold* (Quincy, Illinois: Storm-Mollet Publishing, 1953), pp. 70-72 and map p. 87. Barry Storm, *Bonanza of the Lost Dutchman* by B. Storm, a collection of *Desert Magazine* articles reprinted by Allied Services, Orange, CA., no date, pp. 3-5. Wagoner Map, *Superstition Mountain Journal*,

2:1, January 1982, pp. 20-21.
75. Greg Davis, communication on April 12, 1994.
76. Thomas Kollenborn, *Superstition Mountain Journal*, v11, 1992, pp. 35-39.
77. Greg Davis, conversation on February 18, 1994.
78. Thomas Kollenborn, *Superstition Mountain Journal*, v11, 1992, pp. 35-39.
79. Martin Prinz, *Guide to Rocks and Minerals* (New York: Simon and Schuster 1978), pp. 302, 597, 599.
80. Greg Davis, communication on April 12, 1994.
81. Thomas Kollenborn, *Al Senner's Lost Gold of Superstition Mountain* (Apache Junction, Arizona: Superstition Mountain Historical Society, 1990, original manuscript date 1982).
82. *Arizona Daily Herald*, October 5, 1899, p. 1, col. 4, reprinted in *Superstition Mountain Journal*, 2:3, July 1982, p. 20. Thomas Kollenborn, *Superstition Mountain Journal*, v11, 1992, p. 38.
83. John Annerino, *Outdoors in Arizona, A Guide to Hiking and Backpacking* (Phoenix, Arizona: Arizona Highways, 1989), pp. 57-61.
84. Rosemary Shearer, communication on July 26, 1994.
85. Thomas Kollenborn, *Superstition Mountain Journal*, v11, 1992, pp. 35-39. Dahlmann, p. 37.
86. Communication with Rosemary Shearer and information from Boma Johnson, June 28, 1994.
87. Wilburn, p. 20.
88. Wilburn, pp. 12-31.
89. John Wilburn, conversation on December 7, 1993.
90. Thomas Kollenborn, *Superstition Mountain Journal*, 1:1, pp. 14-15. Wilburn, p. 26. Swanson, *Superstition Mountain*, pp. 93-97.
91. Waugh, p. 307.
92. Waugh, p. 296.
93. Storm, Schoose reprint, p. 3.
94. Ely, pp. 134-145. Corle, pp. 155-156.
95. Ely, pp. 144-145.
96. Ely, p. 135.
97. Swanson, *Superstition Mountain*, pp. 181. Conatser, p. 54.
98. Swanson, *Superstition Mountain*, pp. 182.
99. Ely, p. 135.
100. Swanson, *Superstition Mountain*, pp. 183.
101. Swanson, *Superstition Mountain*, pp. 184. Corbin, *The Curse*, p. 169. *Superstition Mountain Journal* 1:4, October 1981, p. 9.
102. Robert Garman, *Mystery Gold of the Superstitions* (Mesa, Arizona: Lane Printing, 1975, 1980), pp. 7-16.
103. Corbin, The Curse, pp. 192, 200-206. Swanson, Superstition Mountain, pp. 47-64. James Kearney, *Death in the Superstitions: The Fate of Adolph Ruth, The Journal of Arizona History*, 33:2, Summer 1992, pp. 117-152.
104. Greg Davis, communication on April 12, 1994.

105. Dahlmann, p. 35.

106. George (Brownie) Holmes, *Story of the Lost Dutchman* (Apache Junction, Arizona: Superstition Mountain Historical Society, 1990, original manuscript 1944, Phoenix, Arizona), p. 31. *Arizona Daily Gazette*, August 16, 1893, p. 2, col. 1, reprinted in *Superstition Mountain Journal*, 2:2, April 1982, p.19.

107. Superstition Mountain Museum, Apache Junction, Arizona, map display.

108. Dick Nelson and Sharon Nelson, *Hiker's Guide to the Superstition Mountains* (Glenwood, New Mexico: Tecolote Press, 1978), p. 65.

109. Thomas Kollenborn, *Superstition Mountain Journal*, 1:3, July 1981, p. 7 and 2:3, July 1982, p. 21.

110. Joan Baeza, *Arizona Highways*, November 1981, pp. 33-34.

111. Clay Worst, *Superstition Mountain Journal*, vol. 11, 1992, p. 40.

112. Swanson, *History of Apache Junction*, p. 20.

113. Swanson, *Superstition Mountain*, pp. 123-126, 186.

114. Holmes, p. 40.

115. Superstition Mountain Museum, museum display and description, Apache Junction, Arizona. Clay Worst communication on May 18, 1994.

116. Barry Storm, *Thunder God's Gold* (Phoenix, Arizona: Southwest Publishing, 1946), pp. 22, 115.

117. Storm, Schoose reprint, p. 50. Corbin, *The Curse*, Tom Kollenborn centerfold map. Don Van Driel conversation on July 22, 1993.

118. Don Van Driel conversation on July 22, 1993. Tom Kollenborn conversation on October 28, 1993.

119. Swanson, *Superstition Mountain*, p. 185.

120. Corbin, *The Curse*, Tom Kollenborn centerfold map.

121. Storm, Schoose reprint, p. 50. Corbin, *The Curse*, Tom Kollenborn centerfold map. Don Van Driel conversation on July 22, 1993.

122. *Phoenix Gazette*, six part series March 17 to 22, 1986, reprinted in *Superstition Mountain Journal*, vol. 5, 1986, pp. 31-41.

123. Don Van Driel, conversation on July 22, 1993.

124. Clay Worst, *Superstition Mountain Journal*, 1985, vol. 4, pp. 27-35. Clay Worst communication on May 18, 1994.

125. Larry Hedrick, conversation on August 27, 1993. *Arizona Republic*, February 22, 1989, B3, and February 7, 1989, B1. Thomas Kollenborn, *Superstition Mountain Journal*, 1988, vol. 7, pp. 5-6.

126. Corbin, *The Curse*, pp. 103, 176. Swanson, *Superstition Mountain*, p. 57.

127. Nelson, pp. 53-54.

128. Greg Davis, conversation on February 18, 1994.

129. Greg Davis, communication on April 12, 1994.

130. Storm, Schoose reprint, p. 9.

131. Nelson, pp. 53-54.

132. Corbin, *The Curse*, p. 157.

133. Greg Davis communication on April 12, 1994.

134. Storm, Schoose reprint, p. 50-53.

135. L. L. Lombardi, *Tortilla Flat, Then and Now* (Tortilla Flat, Arizona: Sunshower Corporation, to be published in 1994).

136. Storm, Schoose reprint, pp. 32-35.

137. Superstition Mountain Museum, Apache Junction, Arizona, map display.

138. Milton Rose, *Superstition Mountain Journal*, July 1982, 2:3, pp. 6-7. Conatser, p. 56. Swanson, *Superstition Mountain*, p. 43.

139. Ely, pp. 115-116.

140. Wilburn, p. 8.

141. Rose, p. 7.

142. Conatser, pp. 45-46.

143. Gassler, pp. 1-3. Corbin, *The Curse*, p. 212.

144. Gassler, p. 17.

145. Gassler, pp. 1-3.

146. Ely, pp. 137-145. Our book editor, Gerry Benninger, noted an inconsistency in Sims Ely's account of Scholey's story. The symptoms of arsenic and strychnine poisoning are very different. Serita Deborah Stevens, *Deadly Doses, A Writer's Guide to Poisons*, (Cincinnati, Ohio, Writer's Digest Books, 1990), pg. 10-20.

147. Gassler, pp. 1-16.

148. Gassler, p. 16.

149. Corbin, *The Curse*, pp. 226-229.

150. Tom Kollenborn, conversation on March 8, 1994.

151. Gassler, Part II p. 5.

152. Clay Worst, conversation on February 15, 1994.

153. Gassler, pp. 10-11, Part II p. 5.

154. Tom Kollenborn, conversations on March 8 and March 28, 1994.

155. Holmes, p. 30.

156. Conatser, pp. 89-91.

157. Swanson, *Superstition Mountain*, pp. 26, 111.

158. Conatser, pp. 87, 39, 40. Storm, Schoose reprint, p. 35.

159. Conatser, p. 74.

160. Holmes, pp. 15, 34.

161. Larry Hedrick, Superstition Mountain Museum, unpublished manuscript. Jim Files, *Superstition Mountain Journal*, 1989, vol. 8, pp. 5-6. James Colton, *Superstition Mountain Journal*, 2:2, p. 21. Hank Brown, *Superstition Mountain Journal*, 1989 vol. 8, pp. 27-28. Swanson, *Superstition Mountain*, pp. 148-149.

162. Conatser, photographs, no page number.

163. Thomas Kollenborn, *Superstition Mountain Journal*, vol. 11, 1992, pp. 35-39.

164. Ely, pp. 129-133.

165. Thomas Kollenborn, *Superstition Mountain Journal*, 1:4, October 1981, p. 19.

166. Conatser, pp. 82-84.

167. James Swanson, Thomas Kollenborn, *Circlestone, A Superstition Mountain Mystery* (Apache Junction, Arizona: Goldfield Press, 1986). Thomas Kollenborn, *Superstition Mountain Journal*, vol. 8, 1989, pp. 8-12.

168. *Arizona Daily Gazette*, January 26, 1899, p. 5, col. 2, reprinted in Gregory Davis, *Early Newspaper Articles of The Superstition Mountains and The Lost Dutchman Gold Mine* (Apache Junction, Arizona: Superstition Mountain Historical Society 1992), pp. 44-45.

169. Swanson, *Circlestone*, pp. 21-29. Swanson, *Superstition Mountain*, p. 26. Thomas Kollenborn, *Superstition Mountain Journal*, vol. 8, 1989, pp. 8-12. Thomas Kollenborn, conversation on October 28, 1993.

170. Stan Smith, *Arizona Highways*, November 1993, pp. 38-44.

171. Ibid.

172. Swanson, *Circlestone*, pp. 67-77.

173. Michael Sullivan, communication on 4-7-94.

174. Storm, Schoose reprint, p. 28.

175. Swanson, *Superstition Mountain*, p. 22.

176. Greg Davis, communication on April 12, 1994.

177. *Phoenix Gazette*, April 1, 1988, Sec. A, p. 1.

178. Scott Wood, Martin McAllister, Michael Sullivan, *11,000 Years on Tonto National Forest* (Albuquerque, New Mexico: Southwest Natural and Cultural Heritage Association) pp. 12-30. H. Wormington, *Prehistoric Indians of the Southwest* (Denver, Colorado, The Denver Museum of Natural History, 1947-1968), pp. 118-147. Ernest Snyder, *Prehistoric Arizona*, (Phoenix, Arizona, Golden West Publishers, 1987), pp. 75-83. Robert Bigando, *Besh-Ba-Gowah Archaeological Park Interpretive Guide*, (Globe, Arizona, City of Globe, 1987), pp. 1-40.

179. Ibid.

180. *Arizona Daily Gazette*, January 26, 1899, p. 5, col. 2, reprinted in Gregory Davis, *Early Newspaper Articles of The Superstition Mountains and The Lost Dutchman Gold Mine* (Apache Junction, Arizona: Superstition Mountain Historical Society 1992), pp. 44-45. Corbin, *The Curse*, p. 93.

181. Dahlmann, p. 144. Swanson, *Superstition Mountain*, p. 193.

182. Maggie Wilson, *Arizona Highways*, March 1983, p. 6.

183. Garman, pp. 41-44.

184. Garman, p. 74. Robert Garman, *Superstition Mountain Journal*, vol. 3, 1984, p. 41. Travis Marlowe, *Superstition Treasures* (Phoenix, Arizona: Tyler Printing Co., 1965), pp. 23-51. Richard Robinson, *The Superstition Tablets, Window to Lost Treasures* (Mission Viejo, California: R. Robinson, 1987, 1993).

185. Dahlmann, p. 122.

186. Dahlmann, p. 39.

187. Nyle Leatham, cover photograph, *Superstition*

Mountain Journal, 2:3, July 1982. Gregory Davis, conversation on February 18, 1994.

188. Bob Ward (Val Paris), *Superstition Mountain Journal*, vol. 3, 1984, pp. 35-38.

189. Dahlmann, pp. 122-126.

190. Garman, pp. 74-84.

191. Thomas Kollenborn, conversations on October 28, 1993 and March 8, 1994.

Bibliography

Aitchison, Stewart, and Bruce Grubbs. *The Hiker's Guide to Arizona*. Helena, Montana: Falcon Press, 1987.

Allen, Robert J. *The Story of Superstition Mountain and the Lost Dutchman Gold Mine*. New York: Pocket Books, 1971.

Annerino, John. Outdoors in Arizona, *A Guide to Hiking and Backpacking*. Phoenix, Arizona: Arizona Highways, 1989.

Arizona State Parks. *Lost Dutchman State Park Information*. Phoenix, Arizona.

Arnold, Oren. *Ghost Gold*. San Antonio, Texas: The Naylor Company, 1954.

Bigando, Robert. *Besh-Ba-Gowah Archaeological Park Interpretive Guide*. Globe, Arizona: City of Globe, 1987.

Blair, Robert. *Tales of the Superstitions, The Origins of the Lost Dutchman Legend*. Tempe, Arizona: Arizona Historical Foundation, 1975.

Brock, Robert M. *History of Tortilla Flat*. Apache Junction, Arizona: Orion Publishing, 1985, 1992.

Brock, Robert M. *The Apache Trail Guidebook and Lost Dutchman Legend*. Tortilla Flat, Arizona: Robert M. Brock, 1986, 1991.

Byrkit, Jim and Bruce Hooper. *The Story of Pauline Weaver; Arizona's Foremost Mountain Man, Trapper, Gold-seeker, Scout, Pioneer*. Sierra Azul Productions, 1993.

Conatser, Estee. *The Sterling Legend, The Facts Behind the Lost Dutchman Mine*. Pico Rivera, California: GEM Guides Book Co., 1972-1987.

Corbin, Helen. *Senner's Gold*. Phoenix, Arizona: Foxwest Publishing, 1993.

Corbin, Helen. *The Curse of the Dutchman's Gold*. Phoenix, Arizona: Foxwest Publishing, 1990.

Corle, Edwin. *The Gila River of the Southwest*. Lincoln, Nebraska: University of Nebraska Press, 1951-1971.

Dahlmann, John L. *A Tiny Bit of God's Creation: Our Majestic Superstitions*. Tempe, Arizona: Reliable Reproductions, 1979.

Davis, Gregory, E. *Early Newspaper Articles of the Superstition Mountains and the Lost Dutchman Gold Mine*. Apache Junction, Arizona: Superstition Mountain Historical Society, 1992.

Elmore, Francis. *Shrubs and Trees of the Southwest Uplands*. Tucson, Arizona: Southwest Parks and Monuments Association, 1976.

Ely, Sims. *The Lost Dutchman Mine*. New York: William Morrow and Co., 1953.

Farish, Thomas. *History of Arizona*. Phoenix, Arizona: Second Legislature of the State of

Arizona, 1915. Volumes I and II.

Fraser, Jay. *Lost Dutchman Mine Discoveries and a History of Arizona Mining*. Tempe, Arizona: Affiliated Writers of America, 1988.

Freeman, Roger and Ethel Freeman. *Day Hikes and Trail Rides in and Around Phoenix*. Baldwin Park, California: Gem Guides Book Co., 1991.

Garman, Robert. L. *Mystery Gold of the Superstitions*. Mesa, Arizona: Lane Publishing, 1975.

Gassler, Walter. *The Lost Peralta-Dutchman Mine*. Apache Junction, Arizona: Superstition Mountain Historical Society Rare Book Reprint, 1990, (original manuscript dated 1983).

Gentry, Curt. *The Killer Mountains, A Search for the Legendary Lost Dutchman Mine*. New York: The New American Library, 1968.

Holder, Ralph. *Mistic Memories of the Superstition Mountains*. Apache Junction Arizona: Ralph Holder, (no date).

Holmes, George (Brownie). *Story of the Lost Dutchman*. Apache Junction, Arizona: Superstition Mountain Historical Society Rare Book Reprint, 1990, (original manuscript Phoenix, Arizona, dated 1944).

Jennings, Gary. *The Treasure of the Superstition Mountains*. New York: W. W. Norton and Co., 1973.

Kearney, James R. *A Death in the Superstitions: The Fate of Adolph Ruth*. The Journal of Arizona History, Tucson, Arizona: Arizona Historical Society, Vol. 33, No. 2, pp. 117-152, Summer 1992.

Kenworthy, Charles. *Spanish Monuments and Trail Markers to Treasure in the United States*. Encino, CA: Quest Publishing, 1993.

Kollenborn, Thomas. *Al Senner's Gold of Superstition Mountain*. Apache Junction, Arizona: Superstition Mountain Historical Society Rare Book Reprint, 1990, (original manuscript dated 1982).

Krause, Steve. *Streamside Trails: Day Hiking Central Arizona's Lakes, Rivers, and Creeks*. Tempe, Arizona: Pinyon Press, 1994.

Lamb, Samuel. *Woody Plants of the Southwest*. Santa Fe, New Mexico: Sunstone Press, 1989

Lee, Robert. *The Making of the Motion Picture, The Lost Dutchman Mine*. San Diego, California: Dick Martin Co. (no date).

Lombardi, L. *Tortilla Flat, Then and Now*. Tortilla Flat, Arizona: Sunshower Corporation, 1994.

Loughman, Michael. *Learning to Rock Climb*. San Francisco, CA: Sierra Club, 1981.

Lovelace, Leland. *Lost Mines and Hidden Treasure*. San Antonio, Texas: The Naylor Co., 1956.

Marlowe, Travis. *Superstition Treasures*. Phoenix, Arizona: Tyler Printing Company, 1965.

Mazel, David. *Arizona Trails, 100 Hikes in Canyon and Sierra*. Berkeley, California: Wilderness Press, 1981, 1993.

Mitchell, James. *50 Hikes in Arizona*. Baldwin Park, California: Gem Guides Book Co., 1973, 1991.

Mitchell, John. *Lost Mines and Buried Treasures.* Glorieta, New Mexico: Rio Grande
   Press, 1982.

Morrow, Albert E. *Famous Lost Gold Mines of Arizona's Superstition Mountains, Lost Dutchman,
   Lost Peralta Mines.* Apache Junction, Arizona: Superstition Mountain Historical
   Society Rare Book Reprint, 1990, (original manuscript dated 1957).

Nelson, Dick, and Sharon Nelson. *Hiker's Guide to the Superstition Mountains.* Glenwood,
   New Mexico: Tecolote Press, 1978.

Robinson, Richard A. *The Superstition Tablets, Window To Lost Treasures.* Mission Viejo,
   California: R. Robinson, 1987, 1993.

Robinson, Richard A. *Why Me? Conquest of the Lost Dutchman Mine.* Laguana Hills,
   California: Aegean Park Press, 1977.

Rose, Milton, F. *Rainbow's End.* Apache Junction, Arizona: Superstition Mountain Historical
   Society, (original manuscript dated 1940 with revisions in the 1970s and 1980s).

Sheridan, Michael F. and Jan B. Sheridan. *Recreational Guide to the Superstition Mountains
   and the Salt River Lakes.* Tempe, Arizona: Impression Makers, 1984.

Sheridan, Michael F. *Superstition Wilderness Guidebook.* Phoenix, Arizona: Courier Graphics,
   1971-1978.

Sikorsky, Robert. *Quest for the Dutchman's Gold.* Phoenix, Arizona: Golden West Publishers,
   1983-1993.

Snyder, Ernest. *Prehistoric Arizona.* Phoenix, Arizona: Golden West Publishers, 1987.

Squires, Mark. *The Dutchman, A Novel Based on the True Story of the Lost Dutchman Gold
   Mine.* Apache Junction, Arizona: Desert Candle Publishing, 1994.

Storm, Barry. *Bonanza of the Lost Dutchman.* Collection of Desert Magazine articles
   distributed by Allied Services, Orange, California, 92667.

Storm, Barry. *Thunder God's Gold.* Apache Junction, Arizona: Schoose Publishing, 1986.

Storm, Barry. *Thunder God's Gold.* Phoenix, Arizona: Southwest Publishing, 1946.

Storm, Barry. *Thunder God's Gold.* Quincy, Illinois: Storm-Mollet Publishing Associates, 1953.

Superstition Mountain Journal. Apache Junction, Arizona: Superstition Mountain Historical
   Society, 1981-1992.

Swanson, James, and Tom Kollenborn. *Circlestone, A Superstition Mountain Mystery.* Apache
   Junction, Arizona: Goldfield Press, 1986.

Swanson, James, and Tom Kollenborn. *Superstition Mountain, A Ride Through Time.* Phoenix,
   Arizona: Arrowhead Press, 1981.

Swanson, James, and Tom Kollenborn. *The History of Apache Junction, Arizona.* Apache
   Junction, Arizona: Goldfield Press, 1990.

U. S. Forest Service. *Superstition Wilderness, Tonto National Forest.* Phoenix, Arizona, 1991.

Walker, Henry and Don Bufkin. *Historical Atlas of Arizona.* University of Oklahoma Press,
   Norman and London, second edition 1989.

Ward, Bob. *True Story of Superstition Mountains, Ripples of Lost Echo's.* Apache Junction,
   Arizona: Tract Evangelistic Crusade, (no date).

Warren, Scott. *100 Hikes in Arizona*. Seattle, Washington: The Mountaineers, 1994.

Waterstrat, Elaine. *Commanders and Chiefs*. Fountain Hills, Arizona: Mount McDowell Press, 1993.

Wilburn, John D. *Dutchman's Lost Ledge of Gold and the Superstition Gold Mining District*. Mesa, Arizona: Publications Press, 1990, 1993.

Wood, Scott, Martin McAllister, and Michael Sullivan. *10,000 Years on Tonto National Forest*. Albuquerque, New Mexico: Southwest Natural and Cultural Heritage Association, no date.

Wormington, H. *Prehistoric Indians of the Southwest*. Denver, Colorado: The Denver Museum of Natural History, 1947-1968.

Useful Addresses

CAMPING EQUIPMENT — Phoenix Area

Arizona Hiking Shack, 11649 N. Cave Creek Road, Phoenix, AZ 85020,
(602) 944-7723, www.hikingshack.com

Popular Outdoor Outfitters, www.popularoutdooroutfitters.com

1036 E. Baseline Road, Tempe, AZ 85283, (480) 820-6362

4625 E. Ray Road, Phoenix, AZ 85044, (480) 705-9070

4025 N. 16th Street, Phoenix, AZ 85016, (602) 264-3535

15230 N. 32nd Street, Phoenix, AZ 85032, (602) 493-3223

2814 W. Bell Road, Phoenix, AZ 85023, (602) 863-2462

6750 W. Peoria Ave., Peoria, AZ 85345, (623) 979-5450

3536 W. Glendale Ave., Glendale, AZ 85051, (602) 841-2811

202 E. Southern Ave., Mesa, AZ 85210, (480) 844-1153

1845 S. Power Road, Mesa, AZ 85206, (480) 654-0755

7214 E. Thomas Road, Scottsdale, AZ 85251, (480) 423-5121

8734 E. Shea Blvd., Scottsdale, AZ 85260, (480) 948-2323

2050 N. Alma School Road, Chandler, AZ 85224, (480) 899-3662

5916 E. McKellips Road, Mesa, AZ 85215, (480) 325-3944

Recreational Equipment, Inc., www.rei.com, 1-800-426-4840

1405 W. Southern Ave., Tempe, AZ 85282, (480) 967-5494

12634 N. Paradise Village Parkway W., Paradise Valley, AZ 85032, (602) 996-5400

The Wilderness, 5130 N. 19th Ave., Suite 7, Phoenix, AZ 85015,
(602) 242-4945, 1-800-775-5650, www.thewilderness.com

CAMPING EQUIPMENT — Sedona Area

Canyon Outfitters, 2701 W. Highway 89A, Sedona, AZ 86336, (928) 282-5293

CAMPING EQUIPMENT — Flagstaff Area

Aspen Sports, 15 N. San Francisco Street, Flagstaff, AZ 86001,
(928) 779-1935, 1-800-771-1935

Babbitt's Backcountry, 12 E. Aspen Ave., Flagstaff, AZ 86001, (928) 774-4775

Mountain Sports, 1800 S. Milton Road, Suite 100, Flagstaff, AZ 86001,
(928) 779-5156, 1-800-286-5156, www.mountainsport.com

Peace Surplus, 14 W. Route 66, Flagstaff, AZ 86001, (928) 779-4521, www.peacesurplus.com

Popular Outdoor Outfitters, 901 S. Milton Road, Flagstaff, AZ 86001, (928) 774-0598

CAMPING EQUIPMENT — Show Low Area

Popular Outdoor Outfitters, 4201 S. White Mtn. Rd., Show Low, AZ 85901, (928) 537-0130

CAMPING EQUIPMENT — Prescott Area

Mountain Sports, 142 N. Cortez Street, Prescott, AZ 86303,
(928) 445-8310, www.mountainsport.com

Granite Mountain Outfitters, 320 W. Gurley Street, Prescott, AZ 86301, (928) 776-4949

Popular Outdoor Outfitters, 1841 E. Highway 69, Prescott, AZ 86301, (928) 445-2430

CAMPING EQUIPMENT — Tucson Area

Popular Outdoor Outfitters, www.popularoutdooroutfitters.com
6314 N. Oracle Road, Tucson, AZ 85704, (520) 575-1044
6315 E. Broadway Blvd., Tucson, AZ 85710, (520) 290-1644
2820 N. Campbell Ave., Tucson, AZ 85719, (520) 326-2520

The Summit Hut, www.summithut.com, 1-800-499-8696
5045 E. Speedway Blvd., Tucson, AZ 85712, (520) 325-1554
605 E. Wetmore, Tucson, AZ 85705, (520) 888-1000

MAPS

Tucson Map and Flag Center, 3239 N. 1st Ave., Tucson, AZ 85719, (520) 887-4234,
1-800-473-1204, www.mapsmithus.com

U.S. Geological Survey, P.O. Box 25286, Denver, Colorado 80225,
1-888-ASK-USGS, www.usgs.gov

USDA Forest Service, Southwestern Region, Public Affairs Office, 333 Broadway Blvd.,
Albuquerque, NM 87102, (505) 842-3292, www.fs.fed.us/

Wide World of Maps, 1-800-279-7654, www.maps4u.com
1444 W. Southern Ave., Mesa, AZ 85202, (480) 844-1134
2626 W. Indian School Road, Phoenix, AZ 85017, (602) 279-2323

Also see Camping, Mining Equipment, and Government Agencies listings

MINING EQUIPMENT

A & B Prospecting Supplies, Inc., 3929 E. Main Street, Mesa, AZ 85205, (480) 832-4524

Arizona Hiking Shack, 11649 N. Cave Creek Road, Phoenix, AZ 85020, (602) 944-7723
www.hikingshack.com

Desert Treasures Trading Co., 1801 S. Alvernon Way, #108, Tucson, AZ 85711,
(520) 747-0849

J.W.'s Prospecting Supplies, 6426 E. Hwy. 69, Prescott Valley, AZ 86314, (928) 772-4131
http://jwprospect.tripod.com/goldprospecting

Pro-Mack Mining Supplies South, Inc., 940 W. Apache Trail, Apache Junction, AZ 85220,
(480) 983-3484, 1-800-722-6463, www.promack.com

MUSEUMS AND COLLECTIONS

Blue Bird Mine Gift Shop, 5405 N. Apache Trail, Apache Junction, AZ 85219,
(480) 982-2653, 4.5 miles N. E. of Apache Junction on State Route 88.

Bob Jones Museum and Superior Historical Society, 300 Main Street, Superior, AZ 85273,
(520) 689-0200, www.superior-arizona.com

Buckboard Restaurant and Museum, 1111 W. Highway 60, Superior, AZ, 85273,
(520) 689-5800, www.worldssmallestmuseum.com

Gila County Historical Museum and Society, 1330 N. Broad Street, Globe, AZ 85501,
(928) 425-7385, www.globemiamichamber.com

Goldfield Ghost Town, 4650 N. Mammoth Mine Road, Apache Junction, AZ 85219,
(480) 983-0333, www.goldfieldghosttown.com. On Rte 88, north of Apache Junction.

Pinal County Historical Museum and Society, 715 S. Main St., Florence, AZ 85232,
(520) 868-4382. www.co.pinal.az.us/visitorcenter/

Superstition Mountain Museum and Society, P.O. Box 3845, Apache Junction, AZ 85217,
(480) 983-4888, www.superstitionmountainmuseum.org. In Goldfield Ghost Town.

Tortilla Flat Restaurant, One Main Street, Tortilla Flat, AZ 85290, (480) 984-1776,
www.tortillaflataz.com, 17 miles N. E. of Apache Junction on State Route 88.

RIDING STABLES

Apache Lake Ranch, P.O. Box 15623, Tortilla Flat, AZ 85290, (520) 467-2822, (602)
357-9326, 1-800-633-6063, 2 miles west of Apache Lake at milepost 227, Route 88.

Don Donnelly Stables, 6010 S. Kings Ranch Road, Gold Canyon, AZ 85218,
(480) 982-7822, 1-800-346-4403, www.dondonnelly.com

OK Corral Stables and RV Horse Campground, 2645 E. Whiteley, Apache Junction, AZ
85217, (480) 982-4040, www.okcorrals.com

GOVERNMENT AGENCIES

Arizona State Land Department, 1616 W. Adams St., Phoenix, AZ 85007,
(602) 364-2753 permits, (602) 542-4621 general information, www.land.state.az.us/

Forest Supervisors Office, Tonto National Forest, 2324 E. McDowell Road, Phoenix, AZ
85006, (602) 225-5200, www.fs.fed.us/r3/tonto

Globe Ranger District, Tonto National Forest, 7680 S. Six Shooter Canyon Road, Globe, AZ
85501, (928) 402-6200, www.fs.fed.us/r3/tonto

Mesa Ranger District, Tonto National Forest, 26 N. MacDonald Street, Mesa, AZ 85211,
(480) 610-3300, www.fs.fed.us/r3/tonto

Tonto Basin Ranger District, Tonto National Forest, HC02 Box 4800, Roosevelt, AZ 85545,
(928) 467-3200, located at Roosevelt Lake Visitors Center, www.fs.fed.us/r3/tonto

PARKS

Besh-Ba-Gowah Archaeological Park, c/o City of Globe, 150 N. Pine Street, Globe, AZ
85501, (928) 425-0320, www.globemiamichamber.com

Boyce Thompson Southwest Arboretum State Park, P.O. Box 5100, Superior, AZ 85273,
at milepost 223 on U.S. 60, (520) 689-2811, http://arboretum.ag.arizona.edu

Lost Dutchman State Park, 6109 N. Apache Trail, Apache Junction, AZ 85219,
on State Route 88 north of Apache Junction, (480) 982-4485, www.pr.state.az.us

Tonto National Monument, HC02 Box 4602, Roosevelt, AZ 85545, (928) 467-2241,
on State Route 88 across from Roosevelt Lake, www.nps.gov

ORGANIZATIONS

Apache Junction Chamber of Commerce, 567 W. Apache Trail., Apache Junction, AZ 85220,
(480) 982-3141, 1-800-252-3141, www.apachejunctioncoc.com

Arizona Mountaineering Club, P.O. Box 1695, Phoenix, AZ 85001,
(623) 878-2485, www.azmountaineeringclub.org

Arizona Trail Association, P.O. Box 36736, Phoenix, AZ 85067 (602) 252-4794,
www.aztrail.org

The Dons of Arizona, P.O. Box 44740, Phoenix, AZ 85064,
(602) 258-6016, www.donsofarizona.org

Reevis Mountain School and Sanctuary, HC02 Box 1534, Roosevelt, AZ 85545,
(928) 467-2675, www.reevismountain.org

Superstition Area Land Trust (SALT), P.O. Box 582, Apache Junction, AZ 85217,
(480) 983-2345, www.azsalt.org

Superstition Mountain Treasure Hunters, 940 W. Apache Trail, Apache Junction, AZ 85220,
(480) 983-3484, www.promack.com

Superstition Wilderness Rescue, P.O. Box 1123, Apache Junction, AZ 85217,
(480) 898-4265

EMERGENCY TELEPHONE NUMBERS

Dial 911 from any telephone for emergency help. For non-emergency problems see the
listings under "Government Agencies" and "Parks" and the comments below.

Pinal County Sheriffs Department has jurisdiction in the southern portion of the Superstition
Wilderness and the Apache Junction area. Contact them at 575 N. Idaho Road, Apache
Junction, AZ 85219, (480) 982-2241, 1-800-352-3796.

Maricopa County Sheriffs Department has jurisdiction in the northern portion of the
Superstition Wilderness. Contact them at 102 W. Madison St., Phoenix, AZ 85003,
(602) 256-1000, 1-800-352-4553. Crime Stop Number (602) 256-1011.

Index

Q

R

S

About the Authors

Jack Carlson has been hiking and exploring the Superstition Mountains since 1974. He is active in many outdoor activities such as cross-country skiing, canoeing, whitewater rafting, bicycling, hiking and backpacking. He enjoys traveling throughout the world and has extensive hiking experience in the US and Canada.

Jack is a native of Harrisburg, Pennsylvania and graduated from Pennsylvania State University with a BSEE degree in 1965. He moved to Flagstaff, Arizona in 1973 and attended Northern Arizona University, receiving an MBA degree in 1974.

Before moving to Arizona, he lived in Chicago where he was employed in the steel industry and worked with computer automated industrial equipment. More recently, he has worked as an electrical engineer in semiconductor manufacturing and has written professional papers on semiconductor yield-enhancement and processing technology. He has one patent pending in the area of semiconductor processing techniques.

He is a member of the Arizona Book Publishers Association, Arizona Authors Association, Superstition Mountain Historical Society and the Arizona Mountaineering Club. He currently resides in Tempe, Arizona.

Elizabeth Stewart has always loved the outdoors. As a child she traveled with her parents on many family vacations to the National Parks where she experienced the freedom of hiking and camping. Elizabeth's outdoor interests include cross-country skiing, canoeing, whitewater rafting, backpacking, hiking and scuba diving. She enjoys photography, theater, public speaking, adventure travel and family vacations.

Elizabeth was born in San Francisco, California and spent two of her high school years in London, England. She graduated from the University of California, Berkeley in 1966 with an A.B. degree and from the University of Arizona in 1969 with a J. D. degree. She worked for the Maricopa County Attorney in the Juvenile, Criminal and Civil Divisions and is now an Assistant Attorney General for the State of Arizona in the Civil Division.

Elizabeth is active in several professional organizations. She served as president of the Council on Licensure, Enforcement and Regulation and currently serves on the Council of State Governments Committee on Suggested State Legislation and on the Board of Directors of the National Association for Administrative Rule Review.

She is a member of the Superstition Mountain Historical Society Guild, Arizona Authors Association, Arizona Mountaineering Club (AMC) and the Central Arizona Paddlers Club. During the early 1980s, she was a member of the AMC Rescue Team and an instructor for the Basic Climbing School. Elizabeth and co-author Jack Carlson met when she was an instructor at the Basic School in which he was enrolled. She currently resides in Tempe, Arizona.

Order Form

The **Hiker's Guide to the Superstition Wilderness** is available in many of your favorite stores. If you prefer, you may order directly from Clear Creek Publishing.

	Quantity	$ Amount
Hiker's Guide to the Superstition Wilderness $14.95 for each book		
$2.50 for tax, shipping and handling	—	$2.50
Add $4.00 for foreign delivery	—	
	Total	

☐ Check here to have your copy autographed by the authors.

Quantity discounts are available for your group, club or organization. Write Clear Creek Publishing for details.

Mail to:
Clear Creek Publishing
P.O. Box 24666
Tempe, Arizona 85285

NAME _____

ADDRESS _____

CITY _____

STATE _____ ZIP CODE _____